ENCOUNTERS

WITH

PARAPSYCHOLOGY

Two Forthcoming Books
in the Same Series

by

R. A. McConnell

PARAPSYCHOLOGY
AND
SELF-DECEPTION IN SCIENCE

AN INTRODUCTION TO PARAPSYCHOLOGY
IN THE CONTEXT OF SCIENCE

ENCOUNTERS
WITH
PARAPSYCHOLOGY

EDITED AND
PUBLISHED
BY

R. A. McCONNELL

BIOLOGICAL SCIENCES DEPARTMENT
UNIVERSITY OF PITTSBURGH

REGRETFULLY,
AFTER REJECTION BY
29 TRADE PUBLISHERS AND
32 UNIVERSITY PRESSES

ACKNOWLEDGMENTS

The publication of copyrighted material appearing in chapters by the following authors is by permission given as listed.

Heywood, Rosalind:	Author and Chatto & Windus, Ltd.
Honorton, Charles:	Author
Hyman, Ray:	Author
Jahn, Robert G.:	Author
Margenau, Henry:	Author and the American Society for Psychical Research
McDougall, William:	The Society for Psychical Research
Murphy, Gardner:	Author and the Society for Psychical Research
Pratt, J. G.:	Author and the American Society for Psychical Research
Sinclair, Upton:	David Sinclair for the estate of Upton Sinclair

The front cover shows Galaxy M81 as photographed through the 200-inch Mt. Palomar telescope by Milton Humason in 1952 and published in *The Hubble Atlas of Galaxies*. This galaxy, located in Ursa Major, is distant 9 million light-years. The light that made this photograph had traveled most of the way toward Earth before conscious man came into being.

International Standard Book Number: 0-9610232-1-X
Library of Congress Catalog Card Number: 81-90032
© 1982 by R. A. McConnell. All rights reserved.
Manufactured in the United States of America.
Printed on alkaline-buffered archival paper.
Book design by R. A. McConnell.

CONTENTS

ENCOUNTERS
WITH
PARAPSYCHOLOGY

INTRODUCTION

It is generally agreed that we face serious problems in the economy of planet Earth and that their solution will depend upon our understanding of human nature.

In the social sciences each person is conceived to be a conscious entity with sensory inputs and motor outputs but otherwise isolated from the environment. This model of man has dominated scientific thinking for two centuries. It seems unlikely that scientists will be able to help solve our growing problems if the model they use in their planning is basically wrong.

That is what the parapsychological controversy is about. Does consciousness have additional unexpected access to information (extrasensory perception) and unacknowledged power over its environment (psychokinesis)? It is not unreasonable to suspect that a positive answer to this question could be of importance in the rebuilding of a civilization.

The present nontechnical book was prepared for educated laymen and busy scientists. In it there is very little direct evidence for the reality of ESP and PK—certainly none that would convince a sceptic. For that kind of evidence in a controversial field of science one must go to the professional journals and monographs. Rather, this book is offered as a guide for those who wish to grasp the scientific nature of parapsychology without examining the laboratory evidence. It should be especially welcomed by sceptics with neither time nor inclination for statistical analysis and tedious debate.

Whether we are sceptics or believers, we have difficulty grasping parapsychology. We nibble at it from the corners near to our own interests and tend to ignore the rest. We may puzzle over methodological questions about the psychological mechanisms of belief, the uncertain foundations of probability theory, the distinction between scientific and legal proof, or the demand for repeatability in a nonrepeating world. We find it hard to escape humanistic concern about the distinction between mind and brain, the possibility of disembodied consciousness, and the subjective aspects of interpersonal relations. It is not easy to focus upon the core question: Do the purported phenomena occur?

How can we reduce parapsychology to a manageable size without destroying its essential meaning—whatever that may be? How might an outsider to the field sample its literature without misleading himself? Perhaps the best initial approach is not to the phenomena directly but through people who have studied those phenomena. On that premise I have assembled a selection of perspectives from persons in the last hundred years who have thought at length about parapsychology and who, for one reason or another, have a claim to our attention. The result can be most simply described as a collection of personal encounters with parapsychology by outstanding people.

For ease of reading, I have shortened most of the writings and modified many titles. Before each selection I have inserted a brief explanatory comment. My chief contribution, however, has been in the choice of the perspectives of others that seem important to me on the basis of my belief as to the direction of the road ahead.

The selections in this anthology are arranged in roughly chronological order. Rather than start at the beginning, the casual reader may wish to skip along until he finds an author who communicates directly to him. For the layman, the best place to begin may be the autobiography of Rosalind Heywood, an educated English woman who enjoyed a long and successful life despite—or with the help of—her psychic ability. The behavioral scientist, the physicist, the philosopher, and perhaps the future statesman will each find one or more chapters touching upon his professional concerns. The reader who seeks a broad, nontechnical introduction to parapsychology may wish to read the entire work.

1

William Barrett

(1844–1925)

Sir William Barrett, professor of physics and, later, Fellow of the Royal (Scientific) Society of London, was instrumental in the founding of the Society for Psychical Research (1882) and of the short-lived, first American Society for Psychical Research (1885).

I have chosen excerpts from two documents that span almost fifty years of Sir William's life. The first is a paper that he read at a Glasgow meeting of the British Association for the Advancement of Science in 1876. The Association rejected it for publication and, as he later described the circumstances, "for weeks a great controversy ensued in the London Times, which . . . poured ridicule upon my daring to bring such a contemptible subject before the British Association." This paper is preserved in the Proceedings of the Society for Psychical Research (1, 238–244).

My second source of information is Barrett's reminiscences, published in a later Proceedings (34, 275–297) shortly before his death. From these I have selected a few paragraphs to show the temper of his final thoughts on psychic phenomena.

Like most of the founders of the London Society, Barrett had a strong interest in the scientific possibility of spiritual life after bodily death. Today, the situation has changed. I think I am correct in saying that parapsychologists, almost without exception, are unconvinced by the evidence for postmortem survival of individual human personality. As experimental investigators we are willing to speak of "mind" but not of "soul." Rightly or wrongly, in our cosmology we have abandoned anthropocentrism as incongruous with the universe as revealed by science. At the same time, our sense of awe has deepened. The suspicion has slowly grown that, in the words of J. B. S. Haldane, "the universe is not only queerer than we suppose, but queerer than we **can** suppose."[1]

---

1. J. B. S. Haldane, Possible Worlds. New York: Harper & Brothers, 1928, p. 298.

ON SOME PHENOMENA ASSOCIATED WITH ABNORMAL CONDITIONS OF MIND
(1876)

REMINISCENT EXCERPTS
(1924)

by WILLIAM BARRETT

There are certain conditions of the mind, either temporarily induced or habitual, which appear to be associated with many remarkable phenomena that have hitherto received but partial attention from scientific men. On various occasions during the last ten years I have had the opportunity of observing some of these singular states, and in the hope of eliciting further information or of stimulating inquiry by those more competent than myself, I venture to bring the following facts under the notice of the British Association. . . .

The experiments of the late Dr. Braid have led physiologists to recognise the existence of the fact that an extraordinary condition of the mind can be induced in certain susceptible or sensitive individuals by merely fixing the attention rigidly for several minutes upon any bright object. Whilst staying with a friend in Westmeath, now some years ago, I had the opportunity of frequently witnessing the production of this morbid condition, and, further, of observing some phenomena that are usually denied by eminent physiologists of the present day.

Selecting some of the village children and placing them in a quiet room, giving each some small object to look at steadily, it was found that one amongst the number readily passed into a state of reverie, resembling that dreamy condition between sleeping and waking. In this state the subject could readily be made to believe the most extravagant statements, such as that the table was a mountain; a chair, a pony; a mark on the floor, an insuperable obstacle. . . .

The fact that one mind can thus readily be thrown into a state of passive obedience to another mind is undoubtedly a fact of much importance. It is important, not only as exhibiting a state into which certain minds are liable to be exposed, but also as probably affording a clue to some of the extraordinary assertions that have been made by credible witnesses as to the elongation and levitation of the human body, the

4

handling of fire and the like. These facts are testified to by eminent men whose word one cannot for a moment question. Either the narrators *saw* the things they describe or they *thought* they saw them. The following considerations seem to render it highly probable that the latter affords a provisional explanation. . . .

It is highly probable that [their] vivid stream of consciousness . . . having been reduced by quietness and twilight, the minds of those who testify to the feats referred to would readily yield themselves to any emphatic suggestion on the part of the operator. However, to put this matter to the test of experiment, I selected (in the manner already described) a young lad, who in the course of fifteen minutes was hypnotised, as Mr. Braid would say. The lad now readily believed any assertion I made, with evident relish going through the farce of eating and drinking because I suggested the act, though the only materials I gave were a book and an empty vase. When subsequently he partly awoke, he was under the conviction that he had had his tea, yet could not understand how it was, as he associated the actual books with the forced idea of bread and butter, and the struggle of reason and memory was curious to witness. On another occasion, when the lad was hypnotised, I placed my shoes on the table and forcibly drew his attention to them. I then suggested that I was standing in them, and after he had given his assent, I said, "Now I am going to rise up and float round the room." So saying I raised my hand, and directing his sight upwards, pointed out the successive stages in my imaginary flight, and on my slowly depressing my hand, and asserting I was once more on the ground, he drew a sigh of relief. On awakening he held to the belief that I had in some indistinct way floated round the room and pointed to the course I had taken. I had not the slightest doubt that after a few trials, this extravagant idea might have been fixed in the lad's mind with the greatest ease. . . .

In his *Mental Physiology*, Dr. Carpenter states that he has seen abundant evidence that the sensibility of a hypnotised subject may be exalted to an extraordinary degree in regard to some particular class of impressions, this being due to the concentration of the whole attention upon the objects which excited them. Thus, he has known a youth in the hypnotised state to find out, by the sense of smell, the owner of a glove which was placed in his hand, from amongst a party of more than sixty persons, scenting at each of them one after the other, until he came to the right individual. In another case, the owner of a ring was unhesitatingly found out from amongst a company of twelve, the ring having been withdrawn from the finger before the somnambule was introduced.

He has seen other cases, again, in which the sense of temperature was extraordinarily exalted, very slight differences, inappreciable to ordinary touch, being at once detected.

Without denying the possibility of such an extraordinary sensibility, other facts I witnessed pointed in the direction of a *community of sensation* between the mesmeriser and the subject, for I noticed that if the operator tasted, smelt, or touched anything, or experienced any sudden sensation of warmth or cold, a corresponding effect was instantly produced on the subject, though nothing was said, nor could the subject have seen what had taken place upon the operator. To be assured of this, I bandaged the girl's eyes with great care, and the operator having gone behind the girl to the other end of the room, I watched him and the girl, and repeatedly assured myself of this fact. If he placed his hand over the lighted lamp, the girl instantly withdrew hers, as if in pain; if he tasted salt or sugar, corresponding expressions of dislike and approval were indicated by the girl. If, however, anyone else in the room other that the operator tried the experiment, I could perceive no indications on the part of the subject. Certainly, so far as my observations extended, there did seem to be a vast difference between the influence exerted on the subject by the operator, and that which could be exerted by anyone else. Dr. Carpenter believes, however, that there is no foundation for the "*rapport*" which is so often asserted to exist between a mesmerised subject and the operator. On this point he remarks: "If the subject be 'possessed' with the previous conviction that a particular individual is destined to exert a special influence over him, the suggestions of that individual are obviously received with greater readiness, and are responded to with greater certainty, than are those of any bystander. This is the whole mystery of the relationship between the 'biologiser' and his 'subject.'"

For my own part, I do not think that the whole mystery of this so-called "*rapport*" can be disposed of quite so easily. Not only do the facts I have just given negative Dr. Carpenter's easy solution, but the following still more remarkable experiments shew, at any rate, that the question is one deserving of more extended inquiry.

When the subject was in the state of trance or profound hypnotism, I noticed that not only sensations but also ideas or emotions occurring in the operator appeared to be reproduced in the subject without the intervention of any sign, or visible or audible communication. Having mesmerised the girl myself, I took a card at random from a pack that was in a drawer in another room. Glancing at the card to see what it was, I placed it within a book, and in this state brought it to the girl. Giving her the closed book, I asked her to tell me what I had put within its leaves. She held the book close to the side of her head and said, "I see something inside with red spots on it." "Count the spots," I told her; she did so, and said there were five red spots. The card was the five of diamonds. Another card, chosen and concealed in a similar way, was also correctly named; and when a Bank of Ireland note was substituted she said, "Oh now I see a number of heads; so many I can't count them." She sometimes failed to guess correctly, asserting the things were dim, and invariably I found she could give me no information of what was within the book, unless I had previously known what it was myself. More remarkable still, I asked her to go in imagination to Regent Street, in London, and tell me what shops she saw. The girl had never been out of her remote Irish village, but she correctly described to me the shop of Mr. Ladd, the optician, of which I happened to be thinking—referring to some large crystals (of Iceland spar) and to other things in the shop—and when she mentally left the shop she noticed the large clock that overhangs the entrance to Beak Street.

In many other ways I convinced myself that the existence of a distinct idea in my own mind gave rise to an image of the idea in the subject's mind; not always a clear image, but one that could not fail to be recognised as a more or less distorted reflection of my own thought. The important point is that every care was taken to prevent any unconscious movement of the lips, or otherwise giving any indication to the subject, although one could hardly reveal the contents of an optician's shop by facial indications.

This power of "thought-reading," as it has been termed, has often been described by writers on mesmerism, but little credence has been given to it by physiologists or psychologists.

Some assert that this state extends even further; that subjects in this condition are able to perceive occurrences at remote distances which are not known to any present, and yet are subsequently verified. I have had cases of this kind described to me by those whom I esteem as careful and conscientious observers; but as nothing of the sort has ever come under my own observation, I refrain from stating what I cannot vouch for myself. Even as regards the facts I have myself witnessed, I do not pretend that they do more than justify further inquiry, as a large amount of similar evidence must be obtained by well qualified men before these phenomena can be accepted unreservedly. All I wish to urge is, that it is not wise to allow a natural feeling of incredulity on this matter to become a barrier to a possible extension of knowledge.

REMINISCENCES FIFTY YEARS LATER

The word "thought-transference" is apt to be misleading, as it seems to suggest a transmission of ideas between two persons across material space; but space does not seem to enter into the question at all. Here it may be interesting to note that in the first publication of the discovery of this super-sensuous faculty, I called it not "thought-transference," but the *transfusion of thought*. We are now coming back to this idea, for telepathy is probably the intermingling of our transcendental selves or souls. The common and grossly materialistic conception of the soul is that it is limited to the confines and contour of the body. This is surely an erroneous conception if, as we believe, the soul is an *immaterial* entity, not simply a function of the brain. For all we know to the contrary, the human soul may spread through a vast orbit around the body, and may intermingle with other incarnate or discarnate souls. . . .

We must realize that, however trustworthy may be the *evidence* we obtain of supernormal phenomena, the *interpretation* of that evidence may in time alter—as our experience grows wider, and our knowledge of human psychology more extensive and profound. Albeit I am personally convinced that the evidence we have published decidedly demonstrates (1) the existence of a spiritual world, (2) survival after death, and (3) of occasional communications from those who have passed over. . . .

These disputable subjects illustrate the importance of our society [i.e., the Society for Psychical Research] recognizing the fact that a difference of opinion—a *right* and a *left* wing—will necessarily have to exist among its different members. I mean that there are some who have been convinced at first hand, from their own experience, that the existence of certain psychical phenomena—especially those associated with spiritualism—admit of no doubt whatever, and are impatient with those who have not had this experience and are therefore more inclined to be cautious and even sceptical. The former class of our members wish to push forward and perhaps attach less importance to conclusive experimental evidence than they did at first: the latter class wish to go much more slowly and proceed step by step. This difference of opinion, though healthy, naturally leads to a divergence of interest in our subject, and from time to time threatens to break up the solidarity of our society.

2

William James

(1842–1910)

In the paper to follow, William James, the foremost American psychologist of the nineteenth century, writes about the most creative British psychologist of the same period. A difference between the two is that James is remembered today in the literature of psychology, while Frederic Myers is ignored. This is all the more interesting because Myers, beginning in 1891–1892 (Proceedings of the Society for Psychical Research, 7) anticipated much of Sigmund Freud's thinking on the unconscious. The implications of the present paper by James become apparent if one substitutes throughout, Freud's word, unconscious, for Myers's term, subliminal. James predicted—wrongly, as fate would have it—that the problem of the unconscious would henceforth be known as "the problem of Myers."

Myers's thinking is assembled in his masterpiece, Human Personality, and Its Survival of Bodily Death, *which was published posthumously in 1903. The title is somewhat misleading. This two-volume work is a summary of all that was then known about man as a psychological entity, presented and analyzed by a poetic scientist with a view to convincing himself that survival of bodily death might be possible. It depicts the unconscious with a broader brush and brighter colors than Freud chose to use. It is one of the great books of its time, and establishes Myers as the Darwin (or perhaps the Wallace) of the mind.*

The following memorial to Frederic Myers, here abbreviated, appeared in the Proceedings of the Society for Psychical Research, 17 *(1901), 13–23. For a full account of James's intimate involvement with parapsychology, see* William James on Psychical Research *(G. Murphy and R. O. Ballou, Eds., New York: Viking Press, 1960).*

FREDERIC MYERS'S SERVICE
TO PSYCHOLOGY
(1901)

by WILLIAM JAMES

HUMANIST TURNED SCIENTIST

On this memorial occasion it is from English hearts and tongues belonging, as I never had the privilege of belonging, to the immediate environment of our lamented President, that discourse of him as a man and as a friend must come. . . . To me it has been deemed best to assign a colder task, [namely], that I should spend my portion of this hour in defining the exact place and rank which we must accord to him as a cultivator and promoter of the science of the mind.

Brought up entirely upon literature and history, and interested at first in poetry and religion chiefly; never by nature a philosopher in the technical sense . . . ; not crammed with science at college, or trained to scientific method by any passage through a laboratory; Myers had, as it were, to re-create his personality before he became the wary critic of evidence, the skillful handler of hypothesis, the learned neurologist and omnivorous reader of biological and cosmological matter, with whom in later years we were acquainted. The transformation came about because he needed to be all these things in order to work successfully at the problem that lay near his heart, [which], as you know, was that of seeking evidence for human immortality. His contributions to psychology were incidental to that research, and . . . they have a value for science entirely independent of the light they shed upon that problem.

If we look at the history of mental science we are immediately struck by diverse tendencies among its several cultivators, the consequence being a certain opposition of schools and some repugnance among their disciples. Apart from the great contrasts between minds that are teleological or biological and minds that are mechanical, between the animists and the associationists in psychology, there is the entirely different contrast between what I will call the classic-academic and the romantic type of imagination. The former has a fondness for clean pure lines and noble simplicity in its constructions. It explains things by as few principles as possible and is intolerant of either nondescript facts or clumsy formulas. The facts must lie in a neat assemblage, and the psychologist must be enabled to cover them and "tuck them in" as safely under his system as a mother tucks her babe in under the down coverlet on a winter night. Until quite recently all psychology, whether animistic or associationistic, was written on classic-academic lines. The consequence was that the human mind, as it is figured in this literature, was largely an abstraction. Its normal adult traits were recognised. A sort of sunlit terrace was exhibited on which it took its exercise. But where that terrace stopped, the mind stopped; and there was nothing farther left to tell of in this kind of philosophy but the brain and the other physical facts of nature on the one hand, and the absolute metaphysical ground of the universe on the other.

But of late years the terrace has been overrun by romantic improvers, and to pass to their work is like going from classic to Gothic architecture, where few outlines are pure and where uncouth forms lurk in the shadows. A mass of mental phenomena are now seen in the shrubbery beyond the parapet. Fantastic, ignoble, hardly human, or frankly non-human are some of these new candidates for psychological description. The menagerie and the madhouse, the nursery, the prison, and the hospital, have been made to deliver up their material. The world of mind is shown as something infinitely more complex than was suspected; and whatever beauties it may still possess, it has lost at any rate the beauty of academic neatness.

But despite the triumph of romanticism, psychologists as a rule have still some lingering prejudice in favour of the nobler simplicities. Moreover there are social prejudices which scientific men themselves obey. . . . For instance, I invite eight of my scientific colleagues severally to come to my house at their own time, and sit with a medium [Mrs. Leonora Piper] for whom the evidence already published in our *Proceedings* had been most noteworthy. Although it means at worst the waste of the hour for each, five of them decline the adventure. I then beg the 'Commission' connected with the chair of a certain learned psychologist in a neighbouring university to examine the same medium, whom Mr. Hodgson and I offer at our own expense to send and leave with them. They also have to be excused from any such entanglement. I advise another psychological friend to look into this medium's case, but he replies that it is useless, for if he should get such results as I report, he would (being suggestible) simply believe himself hallucinated. When I propose as a remedy that he should remain in the background and take notes, whilst his wife has the sitting, he explains that he can never consent to his wife's presence at such performances. This friend of mine writes *ex cathedra* on the subject of psychical research, declaring (I need hardly add) that there is nothing in it; the chair of the psychologist with the Commission was founded by a spiritist, partly with a view to investigate mediums; and one of the five colleagues who declined my invitation is widely quoted as an effective critic of our evidence. So runs the world away!

I should not indulge in the personality and triviality of such anecdotes, were it not that they paint the temper of our time, a temper which, thanks to Frederic Myers more than to any one, will certainly be impossible after this generation. Myers was, I think, decidedly exclusive and intolerant by nature. But his keenness for truth carried him into regions where either intellectual or social squeamishness would have been fatal, so he "mortified" his *amour propre* . . . and became a model of patience, tact, and humility wherever investigation required it. Both his example and his body of doctrine will make this temper the only one henceforward scientifically respectable.

If you ask me how his doctrine has this effect, I answer: *By co-ordinating!* For Myers's great principle of research was that in order to understand any one species of fact we ought to have all the species of the same general class of fact before us. So he took a lot of scattered phenomena, some of them recognised as reputable, others outlawed from science, or treated as isolated curiosities; he made series of them, filled in the transitions by delicate hypotheses or analogies, and bound them together in a system by his bold inclusive conception of the subliminal self, so that no one can now touch one part of the fabric without finding the rest entangled with it. Such vague terms of apperception as psychologists have hitherto been satisfied with using for most of these phenomena, as "fraud," "rot," "rubbish," will no more be possible hereafter than "dirt" is possible as a head of classification in chemistry, or "vermin" in zoology. Whatever they are, they are things with a right to definite description and to careful observation.

I cannot but account this as a great service rendered to psychology. I expect that Myers will ere long distinctly figure in mental science as the radical leader in what I have called the romantic movement. Through him for the first time, psychologists are in possession of their full material, and mental phenomena are set down in an adequate inventory. To bring unlike things thus together by forming series of which the intermediary terms connect the extremes, is a procedure much in use by scientific men. It is a first step made towards securing their interest in the romantic facts, that Myers should have shown how easily this familiar method can be applied to their study.

MYERS'S CONCEPTION OF THE UNCONSCIOUS

Myers's conception of the extensiveness of the subliminal self quite overturns the classic notion of what the human mind consists in. The supraliminal region, as Myers calls it, the classic-academic consciousness, which was once alone considered either by associationists or animists, figures in his theory as only a small segment of the psychic spectrum. It is a special phase of mentality, teleologically evolved for adaptation to our natural environment, and forms only what he calls a "privileged case" of personality. The outlying subliminal, according to him, represents more fully our central and abiding being.

I think the words subliminal and supraliminal unfortunate, but they were probably unavoidable. I think, too, that Myers's belief in the ubiquity and great extent of the subliminal will demand a far larger number of facts than sufficed to persuade him, before the next generation of psychologists shall become persuaded. He regards the subliminal as the enveloping mother-consciousness in each of us, from which the consciousness we wot of is precipitated like a crystal. But whether this view get confirmed or get overthrown by future inquiry, the definite way in which Myers has thrown it down is a new and specific challenge to inquiry. For half a century now, psychologists have fully admitted the existence of a subliminal mental region, under the name either of unconscious cerebration or of the involuntary life; but they have never definitely taken up the question of the extent of this region, never sought explicitly to map it out. Myers definitely attacks this problem, which, after him, it will be impossible to ignore.

What is the precise constitution of the subliminal—such is the problem which deserves to figure in our science hereafter as the *problem of Myers*; and willy-nilly, inquiry must follow on the path which he has opened up. . . .

One cannot help admiring the great originality with which Myers wove such an extraordinarily detached and discontinuous series of phenomena together. Unconscious cerebration, dreams, hypnotism, hysteria, inspirations of genius, the willing-game, planchette, crystal-gazing, hallucinatory voices, apparitions of the dying, medium-trances, demoniacal possession, clairvoyance, thought transference—even ghosts and other facts more doubtful—these things form a chaos at first sight most discouraging. No wonder that scientists can think of no other principle of unity among them than their common appeal to men's perverse propensity to superstition. Yet Myers has actually made a system of them, stringing them continuously upon a perfectly legitimate objective hypothesis, verified in some cases and extended to others by analogy. Taking the name automatism from the phenomenon of automatic writing—I am not sure that he may not himself have been the first so to baptize this latter phenomenon—he made one great simplification at a stroke by treating hallucinations and active impulses under a common head as *sensory* and *motor automatisms*. Automatism he then conceived broadly as a message of any kind from the subliminal to the supraliminal. And he went a step farther in his hypothetic interpretation, when he insisted on "symbolism" as one of the ways in which one stratum of our personality will often interpret the influences of another. Obssessive thoughts and delusions, as well as voices, visions, and impulses, thus fall subject to one mode of treatment. To explain them, we must explore the subliminal; to cure them we must practically influence it.

Myers's work on automatism led to his brilliant conception, in 1891, of hysteria. He defined it, with good reasons given, as "a disease of the hypnotic stratum." Hardly had he done so when the wonderfully ingenious observations of Binet, and especially of Janet in France, gave to this view the completest of corroborations. These observations have been extended in Germany, America, and elsewhere; and although Binet and Janet worked independently of Myers, and did work far more objective, he nevertheless will stand as the original announcer of a theory which, in my opinion, makes an epoch, not only in medical, but in psychological science, because it brings in an entirely new conception of our mental possibilities.

Myers's manner of apprehending the problem of the subliminal shows itself fruitful in every possible direction. While official science practically refuses to attend to subliminal phenomena, the circles which do attend to them treat them with a respect altogether too undiscriminating—every subliminal deliverance must be an oracle. The result is that there is no basis of intercourse between those who best know the facts and those who are most competent to discuss them. Myers immediately establishes a basis by his remark that in so far as they have to use the same organism, with its preformed avenues of expression—what may be very different strata of the subliminal are condemned in advance to manifest themselves in similar ways. This might account for the great generic likeness of so many automatic performances, while their different starting-points behind the threshold might account for certain differences in them. Some of them, namely, seem to include elements of supernormal knowledge; others to show a curious subconscious mania for personation and deception; others again to be mere drivel. But Myers's conception of various strata or levels in the subliminal sets us to analyzing them all from a new point of view. The word subliminal for him denotes only a region, with possibly the most heterogeneous contents. Much of the content is certainly rubbish, matter that Myers calls dissolutive, stuff that dreams are made of, fragments of lapsed memory, mechanical effects of habit and ordinary suggestion; some belongs to a middle region where a strange manufacture of inner romances perpetually goes on; finally, some of the content appears superiorly and subtly perceptive. But each has to appeal to us by the same channels and to use organs partly trained to their performance by messages from the other levels. Under these conditions what could be more natural to expect than a confusion, which Myers's suggestion would then have been the first indispensable step towards finally clearing away.

Once more, then, whatever be the upshot of the patient work required here, Myers's resourceful intellect has certainly done a service to psychology. . . .

The corner-stone of his conception is the fact that consciousness has no essential unity. It aggregates and dissipates, and what we call normal consciousness,—the "human mind" of classic psychology—is not even typical, but only one case out of thousands. . . . Myers makes the suggestion that the whole system of consciousness studied by the classic psychology is only an extract from a larger total, being a part told-off, as it were, to do service in the adjustments of our physical organism to the world of nature. This extract, aggregated and personified for this particular purpose, has, like all evolving things, a variety of peculiarities. Having evolved, it may also dissolve, and in dreams, hysteria, and divers forms of degeneration it seems to do so. This is a retrograde process of separation in a consciousness of which the unity was once effected. But again the consciousness may follow the opposite course and integrate still farther, or evolve by growing into yet untried directions. In veridical automatisms it actually seems to do so. It drops some of its usual modes of increase, its ordinary use of the senses, for example, and lays hold of bits of information which, in ways that we cannot even follow conjecturally, leak into it by way of the subliminal. The ulterior source of a certain part of this information (limited and perverted as it always is by the organism's idiosyncrasies in the way of transmission and expression) Myers thought he could reasonably trace to departed human intelligence, or its existing equivalent. I pretend to no opinion on this point, for I have as yet studied the evidence with so little critical care that Myers was always surprised at my negligence. . . .

The ultimates of nature,—her simple elements, if there be such,—may indeed combine in definite proportions and follow classic laws of architecture; but in her proximates, in her phenomena as we immediately experience them, nature is everywhere Gothic, not classic. She forms a real jungle, where all things are provisional, half-fitted to each other, and untidy. When we add such a complex kind of subliminal region as Myers believed in to the official region, we restore the analogy; and, though we may be mistaken in much detail, in a general way, at least, we become plausible. In comparison with Myers's way of attacking the question of immortality in particular, the official way is certainly so far from the mark as to be almost preposterous. It assumes that when our ordinary consciousness goes out, the only alternative surviving kind of consciousness that could be possible is abstract mentality, living on spiritual truth, and communicating ideal wisdom—in short, the whole classic platonizing Sunday-school conception. Failing to get that sort of thing when it listens to reports about mediums, it denies that there can be anything. Myers approaches the subject with no such *a priori* requirement. If he finds any positive indication of "spirits," he records it, whatever it may be, and is willing to fit his conception to the facts, however grotesque the latter may appear, rather than to blot out the facts to suit his conception. . . . Myers was primarily a lover of life and not of abstractions. He loved human life, human persons, and their peculiarities. So he could easily admit the possibility of level beyond level of perfectly concrete experience, all "queer and cactus-like" though it might be, before we touch the absolute, or reach the eternal essences. . . .

Frederic Myers was an enormous collector. He introduced for the first time comparison, classification, and serial order into the peculiar kind of fact which he collected. He was a genius at perceiving analogies; he was fertile in hypotheses; and as far as conditions allowed it in this meteoric region, he relied on verification. I am disposed to think [that he] will always be remembered in psychology as the pioneer who staked out a vast tract of mental wilderness and planted the flag of genuine science upon it.

3

Walter Franklin Prince

(1863–1934)

Walter Franklin Prince made major contributions to clinical psychology and to parapsychology. His most important work, "The Doris Case of Multiple Personality," occupies 1,400 pages in Volumes 9 and 10 of the Proceedings of the American Society for Psychical Research *(1915–1916). It is the most complete record of its kind ever gathered, being based upon three years of recorded daily observation of the patient, Doris, whom he legally adopted as his daughter. Curiously enough, despite its scientific pre-eminence, it is less well known than the earlier Sally Beauchamp case reported by Morton Prince (founder of the* Journal of Abnormal Psychology, *and unrelated to W. F. Prince).*

The puzzle of multiple personalities, bluntly stated, is this: Are such "personalities" merely parts of a single personality that have been selected in accordance with Pierre Janet's nineteenth-century theory of hysteria as motivationally explained by neo-Freudian theory, or can they be essentially complete personalities with simultaneously existing consciousnesses living within a single body? Walter Prince's work points to the second alternative.

Like most scientists, Prince had an unwarranted belief in the power of truth. He said in 1915 that "no respectable psychologist today doubts the reality and significance of multiple personality. The facts have passed into the truisms of psychological science."

Indeed they had, but not all truisms are acted upon. The eminent authors of a best-selling American textbook of psychology recently offered the following as a lesson to be learned from multiple personality: "that the typical [normal] personality integrates a number of strands which at different times and under different occasions may cause us to behave in ways that seem very different, and yet reflect certain basic personality needs."

As this passage shows, an unwelcome scientific truth can easily be perceived in a way such that it will be ignored by those whom it might disturb. How else can one explain the fact that this important human potentiality has been overlooked in treating and in theorizing by three generations of psychiatrists and clinical psychologists?

If this situation is now to change, it will be because cases of multiple personality have come to the attention of the public through best-selling books. The most important of these may be Sybil, authored by science writer F. R. Schreiber (New York: Warner Paperbook Library, 1973).

The physician who treated Sybil has written privately that her decision to turn the Sybil story into a popular book was correct because psychiatry has ignored the problems of consciousness in relation to multiple personality and now has decided that it will no longer listen to the psychiatric patient but will only give pills.

It is my hunch that when multiple personality is finally "accepted," subclinical cases will be found to be as common as color-blindness, and an entire new school of psychiatry will come into vogue. I would suppose that ultimately it will become evident that hysterical amnesia provides no true discontinuity between the concepts of mood change and multiple personality.

Walter Prince received a doctoral degree in abnormal psychology from Yale University in 1899. Hence, it was not unnatural that, eleven years later and a year after his wife had begun helping Doris at All Saints Church in Pittsburgh where he was rector, his attention as a lay therapist should have been attracted to the unusual features of her mental illness.

His subsequent relationship to her was described in these words: "Dr. Prince's disposition toward Doris was Christlike in its patient love and sacrifice, but for all these sacrifices he was richly rewarded, not merely by her influence on his destiny, but by her devoted affection and care after he had restored her to health. She was the support, the joy of his declining years."[1]

Although Prince, as a result of his study of Doris, later gave up the Episcopalian ministry and turned fully to parapsychological research, Doris as a patient showed relatively few instances of extrasensory perception.[2] I emphasize her case because I believe that the physiology of psi[3] must be intimately involved with the neural mechanisms of consciousness, and I expect Walter Prince's study of multiple personality (along with split-brain research) to become an important source of clues for the understanding of consciousness.

For presentation here, I have chosen excerpts in which Prince describes the phenomenon of multiple personality in general terms and summarizes the psychic effects he observed in Doris in the period of her illness.

---

1. *Rev. E. Worcestor. Page 12 in* Walter Franklin Prince, A Tribute to His Memory *(by 25 friends). Boston Society for Psychic Research, 1935.*

2. Extrasensory perception *(ESP): Clairvoyance, telepathy, and precognition.*

3. Psi: *A general term for extrasensory perception and psychokinesis.*

THE DORIS CASE OF
MULTIPLE PERSONALITY
(1915)

by WALTER FRANKLIN PRINCE

HISTORY

Divided personality is a phenomenon so remote from the ordinary ken that one feels a kindly sympathy for the man who exclaims "Incredible!", "Absurd!", when the subject is first brought to his attention. It is opposed to "common-sense," which term really means common thought based on common experience. More than that, it is subversive of the psychology taught in the youth-time of men still in active life, for that held the absolute unity of the individual mind. The older type of psychologist revolted against the newer conception of "mental fissures," although offered the comfort that, after all, the fissures may possibly not be so deep, but that unity can be found at the bottom. But no respectable psychologist today doubts the reality and the significance of the phenomena referred to. The old type of physician, too, that talked of the "shamming" and "play-acting" of hysterics, of course scouted the first reported cases of multiple personality. This type has not ceased to exist, for the simple reasons that many do not find time to acquaint themselves with the literature of abnormal psychology, and that, lacking in such acquaintance, few indeed would recognize an actual case if they should meet it in their practice. But the facts are gradually percolating out into medical works and journals to such an extent that the doctor who supposes that the reporters of cases rest their evidence upon the statements of the patients alone, and are therefore on a par with one who should maintain, upon the testimony of a lunatic, that he is rightful heir to the British crown, will soon be as extinct as the dodo.

The layman may be assured at the outset that there is no doubt among the informed regarding the reality of the phenomena of dual and multiple personality. The facts have passed into the truisms of psychological science, and are to be found set forth or referred to as certainties in a large number of authoritative works.

There have also appeared from time to time, particularly during the last thirty years, descriptions and notes based on actual cases, discovered in Europe and America, and yet but few studies worthy of the name have

19

been made, based on single instances. Incomparably the chief of those which exist are, Dr. Morton Prince's "Dissociation of a Personality," and Drs. Sidis's and Goodhart's "Multiple Personality," both American works.

It is probable that in the future, cases of fully-developed dissociation will appear to become much more frequent than they have been in the past.[1] And probably this will be an appearance only, due to increased ability of specialists to bring them to light. For secondary personalities instinctively conceal themselves and seek to avoid detection as a rule, and besides, the distinctive and, once they are known, betraying signs have been until the most modern period misinterpreted, supposed to indicate deception, insanity or demoniac possession. How many victims have been hopelessly immured in asylums as lunatics, how many tortured and put to death as witches in former times, can only be conjectured. A happier period is dawning for the few cases of extreme development, and for the more numerous cases on one side or the other, but near, the boundary line. . . .

The case of Doris Fischer is probably the only one on record in which as early as the third year of the subject's life there appeared a secondary personality, not only existing as a subliminal co-consciousness during the periods when the primary personality was conscious and in control but also alternating as the consciousness in control during the periods when the primary personality was submerged and unconscious.

It is certainly the only one permitted by circumstances to be under scientific observation daily and almost hourly from a period when psychical disintegration was at its extremest stage up to and well past the date when continuity and integrity of consciousness were restored to the primary personality, a duration in this case of three and a half years. Unremitting scrutiny was made practicable by the adoption of the subject into the investigator's family. Thus was it possible, also, to guard her from most of the shocks and strains to which she would otherwise have been subjected, to make constant the application of an experimentally developed system of therapeutics, and to reach so astonishingly swift a cure. It is, indeed, not so much of a marvel that she was restored to psychical integrity in but three and a half years as that this result was attained at all. For when the case was taken in hand two of the per-sonalities (one anomalous, to be sure, in that she did not seem to subtract

---

1. *Dissociation,* as the word is used today, is a splitting or limitation of conscious-ness that may range from benign to pathological. Indeed, division or restriction of attention is a healthy and necessary part of daily living.—Ed.

anything from the mentality or sensory powers of the primary personality) had been in existence for nineteen years, a third had been dominant for five years, a fourth had led her shadowy existence for four years, and the original or primary personality had not in five years summed up as much as three days of conscious living. Besides all this, at the time of the discovery of the central fact of dissociation, a complication of grave and distressing symptoms was in full play. The alternations from one personality to another were sometimes as many as forty in one day. One of the characters in the drama—one might term it tragedy—(Margaret) was at war with another (Sick Doris), attempting to afflict her by bodily tortures, destroying her possessions, undoing her tasks and irritating her with impish derision, though there were brief truces when pity replaced malice. Normal sleep was almost unknown, and night was a phantasmagoria of strange experiences. There were protracted periods of labor in an abnormal condition wherein productivity was more than doubled and brief spaces of catalepsy furnished the only rest. An unusual natural endowment of vitality was almost exhausted, and death was evidently approaching. No wonder that the primary personality (Real Doris), only dimly aware of the sorrows of a life almost wholly shut out from her direct view yet fearing that her own conscious emergences would wholly, as they had already nearly, come to an end, fell upon her knees in thankfulness when she read a note from two of the personalities (Sick Doris and Margaret) informing her that she was to die. And when, after the encouragement of the next following months, Prof. Walker declared that it was unlikely that an almost lifelong condition of such gravity could ever be completely rectified and the patient be restored to entire continuity of consciousness, he said that which was obviously true in the light of psychological science.

CLINICAL IMPRESSIONS

As an easy introduction to the Doris Case I will ask the reader to put himself in my place in the late fall of 1910, when I still supposed that it was one of hysteria only.[2] You are talking with a somewhat stolid looking young woman, with apprehensive manner and nervous laugh (Sick Doris), when suddenly you note what seems to be odd change of mood (Sick Doris sinks into the depths, and Margaret ''comes out''). Though not startling in its abruptness and antithesis (the personalities are on their guard, more or less, to preserve their secret), yet she now has an air of

---

2. That is, classical hysteria, displaying sensory dysfunctions, functional paralyses, and amnesias, but no recognized multiple personality.—Ed.

restrained mischievousness, her demeanor is in some indefinable way more childish, her laugh is freer and her remarks often naïve. Presently the stolid look comes back but with a difference, there is a tendency to chuckle, the signs of nervousness are increased, and in the eyes is a peculiar fixity of regard (S. D. has returned, but M is now more intently watching underneath, and is amused, disturbing the consciousness of S. D.).[3] Later you begin to talk about books or pictures, and suddenly note that the girl is no longer stolid or childishly gay but is following what is said with lips parted in a happy smile and face fairly luminous with interest (Real Doris has taken Sick Doris's place), and you congratulate yourself upon the choice of a subject which has evoked such intelligent appreciation. At another time the transition from reserve and stolidity to the rollicking and humorous "mood" is more pronounced (M. is somewhat off her guard, and is acting more according to her real nature). Gradually you begin to note oddities and contradictions. You expect her to partake of a dish for which she expressed and evidenced fondness yesterday, and she cannot be induced to touch it, but declares that it is not agreeable to her. At the very next meal she devours a quantity of it (S. D. did not know that M. had said she liked the article of food and had eaten it, and M., while aware of S. D.'s refusal and remark, was herself too fond of her favorite dishes to decline them on account of the risk of discovery). Often she repeats a story within a few hours of the first relation, and seems confused when reminded of the fact that she told it before, saying, "O, I forgot that I told *you* that—I thought it was someone else." Not infrequently she contradicts a statement lately made by her, or expresses an opinion at variance with one previously uttered. Sometimes at a "change of mood" there seems to be a hitch in her part of the conversation; she seems for a few moments to be talking somewhat at random. You have not noticed that the moods succeed each other in a certain order when followed by this momentary conversational obscuration. On the whole, she impresses you as being a very mercurial young lady of unsettled mental habits and not uniformly veracious character.

Similar impressions prevail among her acquaintances and even her relatives. Intuitively, as seems to be the rule in these cases, she has felt that she is different from other people, and the group of her personalities has guarded the secret, all except the primary one more or less masking

---

3. The following initials will be used throughout the report for the various personalities: D. stands for Doris, the name of the girl as an individual, without distinction of personalities. M. stands for Margaret. R. D. stands for Real Doris, and S. D. for Sick Doris. S. M. stands for Sleeping Margaret, and S. R. D. for Sleeping Real Doris.

their peculiarities, in proportion as the demeanor of persons with whom she is in company gives token that caution is necessary. Paradoxically, she is in least danger of discovery by those who have known her all her life. They are wholly ignorant of the literature of abnormal psychology, and have been so familiar with her oddities that nothing about her can now surprise them. It is the new acquaintance, known to be well-read and noted to be observant, of whom the group of personalities stands in awe, and with whom they take the most pains, not uniformly maintained nor always successful, to dissemble their individual differences.

When Margaret followed Sick Doris or Real Doris, she came with the knowledge of all the sensory impressions and thoughts of the previous state. The same was true when Sick Doris supplanted Real Doris. But it was otherwise when the alternations occurred in the reverse order. If Real Doris came directly after a Sick Doris or Margaret period, or if Sick Doris followed Margaret, the present personality was utterly ignorant of what had previously taken place. Whatever had been done, said, heard or thought by her predecessor was to her absolutely unknown, except as she could make shrewd inferences from her situation at the moment she "came out." Of course, when the transition was in the order that did not break the mnemonic chain, a conversation, for example, could be carried on across the barrier with perfect ease. But what was the personality to do that came on deck by a sequence that involved amnesia, and found herself engaged in a conversation of whose nature she had no idea whatever? She would do what is always done in cases of this kind, "fish," pretend that she did not hear the last remark of her fellow-interlocutor, appear to have her attention attracted by an object of enough interest to cause her to begin to talk about that, and by various other devices to mark time until with shrewdness developed by practice she was able to get her bearings.

Two of the personalities, the miscalled Sleeping Margaret and Sleeping Real Doris, have not been mentioned hitherto, because they did not figure in the mental manifestations witnessed and misapprehended by the girl's circle of acquaintances. Previously to my discovery of her as the most singular phenomenon in the case, Sleeping Margaret (who must not be confounded with Margaret asleep) had spoken to a human being but twice, and then with such discomfiting results, in each case frightening the auditor out of her wits and causing her precipitate flight, that she had not been encouraged to repeat the experiment. And Sleeping Real Doris (who was by no means equivalent to Real Doris sleeping) was a purely somnambulic personality (corresponding somewhat to the personalities developed in hypnosis by Dr. Morton Prince in the Beauchamp case), and if any of her marvelous "conversation-recitals" were ever attended to by members of the family they doubtless thought that Doris was simply talking, in some weird fashion, in her sleep, and the incident was added to the list of her incomprehensible oddities.

PSYCHIC INCIDENTS

The reader will find in the record incidents of the so-called "occult" order, a few being related to alleged telæsthesia (more commonly named clairvoyance[4]), many to telepathy[5] and a few, mainly involving allegations of Sleeping Margaret, to spiritism. It may be that he will directly be affronted, and demand why these incidents are admitted, unless the writer is credulous and unscientific. A few remarks are necessary here to make my position plain. Formerly I was as prejudiced as anyone could be against all hypotheses admitting what are known as "occult" factors, and as proud of that fact as I am now ashamed of it. For my reason has been sufficiently illuminated so that I now see that, merely as a matter of logic, no hypothesis which comes forward with *prima facie* credentials is forthwith to be expelled as "common or unclean." As a matter of precaution, it is not to be kicked away, with cavalier contempt, without a hearing. The annals of science are too strewn with the skeletons of learned dogmatism not to offer warning to the thoughtful. When one remembers the ridicule and contumely with which what were regarded as the "occult" claims of mesmerism (hypnotism) were treated, he is not inclined to risk adding another skeleton to the desert sands of cocksureness. But I am not in this work advocating any occult theory whatever, but only recording the actual data in the case. There can be no intelligent question of my duty as a historian of the facts. It makes no difference whether the facts please my intellectual and æsthetic palate or that of my readers; it is none of my business in what direction the facts may seem to point. I am but the witness who is to "tell the truth, the whole truth, and nothing but the truth." It may be that the seemingly "occult" facts have a non-occult signification, but whether or no, they must have *some* significance, and the record would be defective, perhaps fatally so, with them omitted. The useless facts of one generation, which have interest only for the intellect, often become useful ones in the next. Many a "hardheaded" man formerly muttered disdainfully, "What's the use of studying bugs and flies?" but now even the ivory-enclosed intellect is aware that

---

4. *Clairvoyance*: The transfer of information from objects or objective events to a brain by other than known physical energy.—Ed.

5. *Telepathy*: Direct brain-to-brain transfer of information.—Ed.

intimate knowledge of flies and bugs is leading to successful war against some of the worst diseases of men. Residual mysterious facts of psychology, which are often omitted or glossed over in scientific reports, will be, judging from the past, the very keys of some citadel of knowledge,—if not of one, then of another. Some day every scientific reporter will add to his litany some such franchise as this: "From the dishonesty that suppresses facts, from the cowardice that will not utter them, from the dogmatism that cannot see them, Good Lord deliver us!" . . .

On a number of occasions M. obtained information, sometimes of a complex character, which if not acquired by telepathy I confess inability to account for. One instance only will be summarized here, not because it is the best but because it can be given in short compass. On the evening of Nov. 29th, 1911, M., after looking awhile into my eyes with an intent and curious expression, exclaimed, "You wrote to a man named Prince today—to Dr. Prince. . . . You wrote about Doris. . . . You asked him how someone was getting on." The fact is that I had that afternoon, without acquainting anyone of my intention, written to Dr. Morton Prince for the first time. I did write chiefly about Doris. I did not ask how anyone was getting on, but I did very distinctly debate in my mind whether to ask him if "Miss Beauchamp" was still mentally stable. I took pains to make it impossible that anyone should see me write either the letter or the address on the envelope, as I did not want the girl to suspect that I was writing about her, mentioned to no one that I had written, and while alone put the letter where no one could possibly get at it. M. told not only to whom I had written, and what I had written about, but also specified a thought which had not been set down in black and white at all. When she made one of these announcements, it was always after she had gazed steadily, with a look of interested amusement, into my eyes. Her own claim was that she saw, not what I was consciously thinking of at the moment, but what was "passing like a parade down underneath." And it was true that what she revealed was always something that I had thought of not long before. She never made an incorrect announcement of the kind. Nor did she ever manifest any desire to "show off" in this or other matters, and appeared to regard them as mere games, in no way remarkable.

When R. D., before her mother's death, was away from the house, she often had a subjective vision of the latter engaged in one way or another, and on her return would inquire and find that the mother had been so engaged at the time. There can be no doubt of her absolute confidence that such were her frequent experiences, nor does she have the feeling of most other people that there is something *outre* and bizarre about them. I leave it to others to say that these are mere hallucinations of memory. Knowing as I do the mentality of the girl, I do not believe that the explanation is here, wherever it may be found. M. also, it was alleged, had clairvoyant and veridical visions, though no such sophisticated terms were employed by the personalities. Similar claims were made in regard to S. D. Should telepathy pass the gauntlet of science there would be no particular difficulty in admitting a visual type of telepathy, though that description would not agree with the views of the personalities. One instance said to have been experienced by S. D. was carefully canvassed, as is set forth in the Record. I am far from saying that the evidence is sufficient to establish the validity of a claim of this sort, in fact I do not think it much stronger than would be required for the condemnation of a man to the gallows.

4

William McDougall

(1871–1938)

William McDougall, a Fellow of the Royal Society, is accepted by academic psychology today, with some ambivalence, as a brilliant British–American pioneer. His most important contribution to psychology may prove to have been the sponsorship he gave to Drs. J. B. and L. E. Rhine at Duke University from their parapsychological beginnings in 1927. This historic role was indicated in the first issue of the Journal of Parapsychology *in 1937 by his appearance as co-editor with J. B. Rhine.*

*The here-given excerpt from William McDougall's 1920 presidential address to the Society for Psychical Research (*Proceedings, 31, 105–123) *discusses the unwillingness of psychologists to support psychical research—an unwillingness that continues to this day. In his view, "if the Society [for Psychical Research] consisted only of its right wing, [then academic psychologists] would come in and co-operate cheerfully and profitably." Although McDougall does not admit the connection, he comes closer to an explanation of psychologists' reluctance when he says in his next paragraph: "Pandora's Box has been opened" by the findings of parapsychology.*

Similarly, his belief that the firmly established reputability of physical science was what allowed physicists of the stature of Nobel prizewinners Lord Rayleigh and Sir J. J. Thomson to associate themselves publicly with the Society for Psychical Research, fails to explain why the leaders of experimental physics today, almost without exception, have turned their backs to the evidence for psi phenomena. The unwillingness of Western man to accept evidence for a direct connection between consciousness and the physical world is a far darker topic than we are willing to concede.

THE MISGIVINGS OF PSYCHOLOGISTS
(1920)

by WILLIAM McDOUGALL

I will not attempt to express my sense of the great honour you have done me in electing me to the presidency of this Society. That sense is much accentuated by the fact that my predecessor in this chair,[1] whose loss we all deplore, was so great a man; a man of science so great that his name will remain among those few which the English people will ever cherish with pride and gratitude. Our Society was fortunate indeed in being able for many years to claim him as a member, and still more fortunate in that he consented to occupy this chair before he was called away.

In looking with mingled pride and humility at the list of former Presidents of the Society, I cannot avoid remarking that one only of them was primarily and professedly a psychologist. I mean of course William James, the man who more than all others has been for me the shining leader, the perfect exponent of scientific candour and courage.

I notice also that but few other names of professed psychologists appear on our roll of membership. I am moved by these facts to offer some slight apology and explanation on behalf of my professional colleagues; for surely they, beyond all other men of science, should have felt the call to support, if only by passive membership, the work and reputation of this Society. They, by special knowledge and training, are or should be better equipped than any others to evaluate the work of the Society, to criticise it, or, better still, actively to cooperate in it. The fact that the great majority of them stand aloof requires some consideration; for it is capable of being, and in some quarters has been, interpreted in a sense detrimental to our work. It may be said: Here is a body of men on whose judgment the public may best rely in forming its opinion about psychical research, and that judgment seems to be adverse; for the bulk of them do not support the work, even to the small extent of joining the Society. This conclusion would, I think, be false. The explanation of the fact is in the main to be found in a different direction.

---

1. The physicist, Lord Rayleigh. —Ed.

An open mind towards the phenomena which the Society investigates is far commoner, I am sure, among men of science, than appears to the general public. This opinion, which I venture to express in this highly responsible position, is founded not only upon my personal contacts with men of science, but also upon the fact that only one scientific creed logically permits the deduction that these alleged phenomena do not and *cannot* occur. That creed is dogmatic materialism: and although that creed can still claim a few confident exponents, it is distinctly out of fashion at the present time. However materialistic may be the dominant habit of thought among men of science, there are but few of them who will confess to a whole-hearted acceptance of materialism as a philosophic creed. The bulk of them are sufficiently well educated to know that as such it is untenable; and also to know that from it alone can they logically deduce the impossibility of the alleged phenomena. The grounds of the aloofness of so many men of science from the work of our Society, in spite of their minds being more or less open to conviction in its sphere, are many and complex. It would perhaps not be altogether unprofitable to attempt to describe and examine them. But for my present purpose I wish to point out one only of them, one by no means discreditable to those who are influenced by it. I mean a sense of responsibility towards the public. Men of science are afraid lest, if they give an inch in this matter, the public will take an ell and more. They are afraid that the least display of interest or acquiescence on their part may promote a great outburst of superstition on the part of the public, a relapse into belief in witchcraft, necromancy, and the black arts generally, with all the moral evils which must accompany the prevalence of such beliefs. For they know that it is only through the faithful work of men of science during very recent centuries that these debasing beliefs have been in large measure banished from a small part of the world; they know that, throughout the rest of the world, these superstitions continue to flourish, ready at any moment to invade and overwhelm those small areas of enlightenment. They know that such overwhelming of those areas must plunge their populations back among the grovelling fears and the cruel and hateful practices which have been the scourge and torment of mankind since that remote age when the race became endowed with the two-edged and dangerous weapon of imagination. Now the psychologists, just because they of all men must be regarded as best equipped to judge of these difficult matters, feel this responsibility more acutely than any other class of scientific men. Further—they feel a great responsibility for the reputation of their own science and are afraid of doing it an injury. Any physicist, like the great physicists who have adorned and strengthened this Society, may display an active interest in psychical research without the least risk of injury to the reputation of his science. Physical science stands firmly established in the esteem of all men; for it is clear to all that it has provided the material basis of our civilisation. Psychology stands in a very different position. It is only beginning to assert its position among the sciences; the general public and even some of our universities still regard its claim to be a science, and a science of high practical value, with doubt and suspicion. In face of this situation the academic psychologist is rightly cautious. His attitude may, I think, be succinctly and concretely expressed by saying that he is afraid of the left wing of our Society, and that, if the Society consisted only of its right wing, he would come in and co-operate cheerfully and profitably. But both wings are necessary to our Society; we cannot hope to fly to any good purpose on one alone. It has been the great virtue of our Society that, in spite of differences of opinion, sometimes acute, it has kept the allegiance of men and women of so widely different views in respect to its problems. My own conviction is that the risk I have indicated must be run. I myself belong very decidedly to the right wing; but I recognise the importance of the left; I recognise also the right of its members to their opinions, and I esteem the driving power and the freedom of speculation which come from the left as essential to the success of our work.

The importance of the work of our Society seems to me to justify the taking of some risk. But that work does not really add to the risk of relapse into barbaric superstition; rather it is our best defence against it. For Pandora's box has been opened, the lid has been slightly lifted, and we are bound to go on and to explore its remotest corner and cranny. It is not only or chiefly the work of this Society that has raised the lid a little and exposed us to this danger. The culture of Europe has for a brief period rested upon the twin supports of dogmatic affirmation and dogmatic denial, of orthodox religion and scientific materialism [respectively]. But both of these supports are crumbling, both alike sapped by the tide of free enquiry. And it is the supreme need of our time that these two pillars of dogmatism shall be replaced by a single solid column of knowledge on which our culture may securely rest. It is the policy of sitting on the lid of the box that is risky; a danger and threat to our civilisation.

I have said that I belong to the extreme right of our Society, and I fear that I may shock and hurt some of our members of the left by the following remark, which nevertheless, I feel I am bound to make. It is conceivable to me that we may ultimately find the box to have been empty from the first, as empty as some of our dogmatic critics assert it to be. Even then I should maintain that the work of our Society in boldly exploring its recesses and showing its emptiness to the world had been of the very greatest value. But I do not anticipate this result, though I do not dread it. As regards our positive conclusions and their value I will say only this, I believe that telepathy[2] is very nearly established for all time among the facts recognised by science, mainly by the work of this Society. If and when that result shall have been achieved, its importance for science and philosophy will far outweigh the sum of the achievements of all the psychological laboratories of the universities of two continents.

As regards the other main lines of enquiry of our Society,[3] I confidently hold that nothing hitherto established by science or philosophy can be shown to imply that these enquiries must have a purely negative result. Our conclusions must be founded eventually upon just such collection and critical sifting of the empirical evidence as our Society has resolutely pursued for nearly forty years. During these forty years a whole generation of devoted workers has passed away. But what are forty years in the great procession of knowledge! Even though it were clear that four hundred years will be needed for the attainment of definite conclusions, we ought not to shrink from the task, or falter by the way. The supreme importance of the problems before which we stand would justify an indefinitely great expenditure of time and energy upon them. For the interests of our culture and civilisation demand that the present chaos of conflicting opinions and prejudices shall be replaced by clear and definite knowledge.

2. Direct brain-to-brain communication. —Ed.

3. Inquiry into the possibility of spiritual life after bodily death. —Ed.

5

Upton Sinclair

(1878–1968)

Upton Sinclair is known today as the American Charles Dickens whose many novels exposed social evils in the United States in the first half of the twentieth century. Perhaps in the future, he will be better remembered as a lay scientist who, with his wife as his subject, performed one of the most important series of experiments in the early history of parapsychology. There had been many other picture-drawing experiments before his,[1] but none so extensive or so fully reported.

The first publication of Mental Radio, *coming as it did in 1930 shortly before J. B. Rhine's first book in 1934, served to strengthen and complement Rhine's card-guessing research. Sinclair's work remains to this day a major obstacle for those who wish to deny the reality of extrasensory perception.[2]*

For presentation here, I have selected some passages that reveal the cast of mind of Sinclair and his wife and their ideas about the possible meaning of their experiments. I have skipped over the drawing evidence that the Sinclairs gathered.

---

1. See Part 2 of Bulletin 16 *(1932) of the Boston Society for Psychic Research.*

2. Current editions: Clothbound: Springfield, Illinois: C. C. Thomas, 1962. Paperback: New York: Macmillan, 1971.

EXCERPTS FROM *MENTAL RADIO*
(1930)

by UPTON SINCLAIR

SETTING FOR A SCIENTIFIC ADVENTURE

If you were born as long as fifty years ago [i.e., before 1880], you can remember a time when the test of a sound, common-sense mind was refusing to fool with "new-fangled notions." Without exactly putting it into a formula, people took it for granted that truth was known and familiar, and anything that was not known and familiar was nonsense. In my boyhood, the funniest joke in the world was a "flying machine man"; and when my mother took up a notion about "germs" getting into you and making you sick, my father made it a theme for no end of domestic wit. Even as late as twenty years ago, when I wanted to write a play based on the idea that men might some day be able to make a human voice audible to groups of people all over America, my friends assured me that I could not interest the public in such a fantastic notion.

Among the objects of scorn, in my boyhood, was what we called "superstition"; and we made the term include, not merely the notion that the number thirteen brought you bad luck, not merely a belief in witches, ghosts and goblins, but also a belief in any strange phenomena of the mind which we did not understand. We knew about hypnotism, because we had seen stage performances, and were in the midst of reading a naughty book called *Trilby*; but such things as trance mediumship, automatic writing, table-tapping, telekinesis, telepathy and clairvoyance—we didn't know these long names, but if such ideas were explained to us, we knew right away that it was "all nonsense."

In my youth I had the experience of meeting a scholarly Unitarian clergyman, the Rev. Minot J. Savage of New York, who assured me quite seriously that he had seen and talked with ghosts. He didn't convince me, but he sowed the seed of curiosity in my mind, and I began reading books on psychic research. From first to last, I have read hundreds of volumes; always interested, and always uncertain—an uncomfortable mental state. The evidence in support of telepathy came to seem to me conclusive, yet it never quite became real to me. The consequences of belief would be so tremendous, the changes it would make in my view of the universe so revolutionary, that I didn't believe, even when I said I did.

But for thirty years the subject has been among the things I hoped to know about; and, as it happened, fate was planning to favor me. It sent me a wife who became interested, and who not merely investigated telepathy, but learned to practice it. For three years I watched and assisted in this work, day by day and night by night, in our home. So I could say that I was no longer guessing. Now I really know. I am going to tell you about it, and hope to convince you; but regardless of what anybody can say, there will never again be a doubt about it in my mind. I *know*! . . .

* * * *

THE QUESTION OF FRAUD

I have now given nearly all the 65 drawings [out of a total of 290] which I call "successes," and about half the 155 which I call "partial successes." This, I think, is enough for any purpose. No one can seriously claim that such a set of coincidences could happen by chance, and so it becomes necessary to investigate other possible explanations.

First, a hoax. As covering that point, I prepared a set of affidavits as to the good faith of myself, my wife, her sister, and her sister's husband. These affidavits were all duly signed and witnessed; but friends, reading the manuscript, think they use up space to no purpose, and that the reader will ask no more than the statement that this book is a serious one, and that the manuscript was carefully read by all four of the persons mentioned above, and approved by them as representing the exact truth.

That a group of persons should enter into a conspiracy to perpetrate a hoax is conceivable. Whether or not it is conceivable of the group here quoted is something of which the reader is the judge. . . .

How about the possibility of fraud by one person? No one who knows Mary Craig Sinclair would suspect her; but you who do not know her have, naturally, the right to consider such an hypothesis. Can she be one of those women who enjoy being talked about? The broaching of this idea causes her to take the pencil away from her husband, and you now hear her own authentic voice, as follows:

> I happen to be a daughter of that once very living thing, "the Old South," and there are certain ideals which are in my blood. The avoidance of publicity is one of them. But even if I had ever had a desire for publicity, it would have been killed by my actual experiences as the wife

of a social crusader. My home is besieged by an endless train of persons of every description, who travel over the place, knocking on doors and windows, and insisting upon having a hearing for their various programs for changing the nature of the universe. I have been driven to putting up barriers and fences around my garden, and threatening to flee to the Himalayas, and become a Yogic mistress, or whatever a Yogic "master" of my sex is called.

Jack London tried to solve this problem by putting a sign on the front door which read, "Go to the back door," and on the back door one which read, "Go to the front door." But when I tried this, one seeker of inspiration took his seat halfway between the two doors, and declared that he would remain there the rest of his life, or until his wishes were acceded to. Another hid himself in the swimming-pool, and rose up from its depth to confront me in the dusk, when, as it happened, I was alone on the place, and went out into the garden for a breath of air. A third announced that he had a million dollars to present to my husband in person, and would not be persuaded to depart until my brother invited him to go downtown to supper, and so got him into a car. Having faithfully fed the hungry millionaire, my brother drove him to the police-station, where, after a serious talking-to by the chief, he consented to carry his million dollars away. A fourth introduced himself by mail as having just been released from the psychopathic ward in Los Angeles, and intending to call upon us, for reasons not stated. A fifth announced himself by telephone, as intending to come at once and shoot my husband on sight. Yet another, seven feet tall and broad in proportion, announced that he had a revelation direct from God, and had come to have the manuscript revised. When politely asked as to its nature, he rose up, towering over my none too husky spouse and declaring that no human eye had ever beheld it, and no human eye would ever be permitted to behold it. Such experiences, as a continuing part of a woman's life, do not lead her to seek publicity; they tend rather to develop a persecution complex.

Speaking seriously, I consider that I have every evidence of the effect of people's thoughts on each other. And my distrust of human nature, in its present stage of evolution, is so great, that the idea of having many persons concentrate their attention on me is an idea from which I shrink. I agree with Richet that the fact of telepathy is one of the most terrifying in existence; and nothing but a deep love of truth had induced me to let this very personal story be told in print.

Next, what about the possibility of unconscious fraud? This also is a question to be frankly met. All students of psychology know that the subconscious mind has dubious morals. One has only to watch his own dreams to discover this. A person in a trance is similar to one talking or walking in sleep, or a drunken man, or one under the influence of a drug. But in this case it must be noted that my wife has never been in a trance. In these mind-reading tests, no matter how intense the "concentration," there is always a part of her mind which knows what she is doing. If you speak to her, she is immediately "all there." When she has her mental pictures, she sits up and makes her drawing, and compares it with mine, and this is a completely conscious act.

Moreover, I point out that a great deal of the most impressive evidence does not depend upon Craig alone. The five drawings with her brother-in-law, Figures 1, 16, 17, 18, 19, constitute by themselves evidence of telepathy sufficient to convince any mind which is open to conviction. While it would have been possible for Craig and Bob to hoax Dollie and me, it could certainly not have been done without Bob's connivance. If you suggest that my wife and my brother-in-law may have been fooling me, I reply that there is a still greater mass of evidence which could not have been a hoax without *my* connivance. When I go into my study alone—a little sun-parlor at the front of a beach-house, with nothing but a couch, a chair and a table—I certainly know that I am alone; and when I make a drawing and hold it before my eyes for five or ten minutes, I certainly know whether any other person is seeing it. This covers the drawings presented as Figures 2, 20, and 21, with four others told about in the same series. It seems to me these seven cases by themselves are evidence of telepathy sufficient to convince any open mind.

Furthermore, there are the several score drawings which I made in my study and sealed up in envelopes, taking them to my wife and watching her lay them one by one upon her body and write down more or less accurately what was in them. I certainly know whether I was alone when I made the drawings, and whether I made the contents of the envelopes invisible, and whether my wife had any opportunity to open the envelopes before she made her drawings. Of course, I understand the familiar conjuring trick whereby you open one envelope, and hide it in your palm, and pretend to be describing the next one while really describing the one you have seen. But I would stake my life upon the certainty that my wife knows no sleight-of-hand, and anyhow, I made certain that she did not open the first one; I sat and watched her, and after each test she handed me the envelopes and drawings, one by one—the envelopes having previously been numbered by me. She would turn out the reading-light which was immediately over her head, but there was plenty of light from other parts of the room, enough so that I could look at drawings as they were shown to me. Often these tests were done in the daytime, and then all we did was to pull down the window-shades back of the couch.

It should be obvious that I stand to lose much more than I stand to gain by publishing a book of this sort. Many have urged me not to take the risk. It is the part of prudence not to believe too many new and strange ideas. Some of my Socialist and materialist friends are going to say—without troubling to read what I have written: "Sinclair has gone in for occultism; he is turning into a mystic in his old age." It is true that I am fifty-one, but I think my mind is not entirely gone; and if what I publish here is mysticism, then I do not know how there can be such a thing as science about the human mind. . . .

FRIENDS AND FELLOW SOCIALISTS

October, 1929. At my wife's insistence, I have held up this book for six months, in order to think it over, and have the manuscript read by friends whose opinions we value. A score or more have read it, and made various suggestions, many of which I have accepted. Some of the reactions of these friends may be of interest to the reader. . . .

There came to me a letter of warning from a good comrade, T. H. Bell of Los Angeles, an elderly Scotchman who has grown up in the Socialist movement, and known the old fighters of the days when I was a child. He begged me not to jeopardize my reputation; so I thought he would be a good test for the manuscript, and asked him to read it. Some of his suggestions I accepted, and the work is the better for them. But Comrade Bell was not able to believe that Craig's drawings could have come by telepathy, for the reason that it would mean that he was "abandoning the fundamental notions" on which his "whole life has been based."

Comrade Bell brought many arguments against my thesis, and this was a service, because it enables me to answer my critics in advance. First, what is the value of my memory? Can I be sure that it does not "accommodate itself too easily to the statement Sinclair wishes to believe?" My answer is that few of the important cases in the book rest upon my memory; they rest upon records written down at once. They rest upon drawings which were made according to a plan devised in advance, and then duly filed in envelopes numbered and dated. Also, my memory has been checked by my wife's, who is a fanatic for accuracy, and has caused me torment, through a good part of our married life, by insisting upon going over my manuscripts and censoring every phrase. Also Bob and Dollie and my secretary have read this narrative, and checked the statements dealing with them.

Next objection, that I am "a man without scientific training." The acceptance of that statement depends upon the definition of the word "scientific." If it includes the social sciences, then I have had twenty-five years of very rigid training. I have made investigations and published statements, literally by thousands, which were criminal libels unless they were true and exact; yet I have never had any kind of libel suit brought against me in my life. As to the scientific value of the particular experiments described in this book, the reader can do his own judging, for they have been described in detail. I don't see how scientific training could have increased our precautions. We have outlined our method to scientists, and none has suggested any change. . . .

I think that if you will go back and look over those drawings as a whole, you must admit that the objects were as varied as the imagination could make them. I do not see how any one could choose a set of objects less likely to be guessed than the series which I have numbered from 5 to 12—a bird's nest full of eggs and surrounded by leaves, a spiked helmet, a desert palm-tree, a star with eight double points, a coconut palm, a puppy chasing a string, a flying bat, a Chinese mandarin, and a boy's foot with a roller-skate on it. None of these objects has any relationship whatever to my life, or to Craig's, or to our common life. To say that a wife can guess such a series, because she knows her husband's mind so well, seems to me out of all reason.

Next, the point that some of the cases are not convincing by themselves. I am familiar with this method of argument, having encountered it with others of my books. Let me beg you to note that the cases are *not* taken by themselves, but are taken as a whole. . . . Any one who wants to can go through the book and pick out a score of cases which can be questioned on various grounds. Perhaps it would be wiser for me to cut out all except the strongest cases. But I rely upon your common sense, to realize that the strongest cases have caused me to write the book; and that the weaker ones are given for whatever additional light they may throw upon the problem,

If you want to deal fairly with the book, here is what you have to explain. How did it happen that at a certain agreed hour when Bob at Pasadena drew a table-fork and dated and signed the drawing, Craig in Long Beach wrote: "See a table-fork, nothing else," and dated and signed her words? If you call this a coincidence, how are you going to account for the chair, and the watch, and the circle with the hole in the middle, and the sense of pain and fear, and the spreading black stain called blood, all reproduced under the same perfect conditions? I say that if you call all this coincidence, you are violating the laws of probability as we know them. I say that there are only two possible explanations,—either telepathy, or that my wife and her brother-in-law were hoaxing me.

But if you want to assume a hoax, you have to face the fact that my wife a few days later was reproducing a series of drawings which I made and kept in front of my eyes in a separate room from her, in such a position that she could not see them if she wanted to. If I thought it worthwhile, I could draw you a diagram of the place where she sat and the place where I sat, and convince you that neither mirrors, nor a hole in the wall, nor any other device would have enabled my wife to see my drawings, until I took them to her and compared them with her drawings. The only way you can account for that series of successes is to say that I am in on the hoax.

My good friend and comrade, Tom Bell, does not suggest that I am in it; but others may say it, so I will answer. Let me assure you, there is no reason in the world why I should take the field on behalf of the doctrine of telepathy—except my conviction that it has been proved. I don't belong to any church which teaches telepathy. I don't hold any doctrine which is helped by it. I don't make any money by advocating or practicing it. There is no more reason why I should be concerned to vindicate telepathy, than there is for my coming out in support of the Catholic doctrine of the Immaculate Conception, or the Mormon doctrine of Urim and Thummim, or the Koreshan doctrine that the earth is a hollow sphere and we live on the inside of it.

I assure you I am as cold-blooded about the thing as a man can be. In fact, I don't like to believe in telepathy, because I don't know what to make of it, and I don't know to what view of the universe it will lead me, and I would a whole lot rather give all my time to my muckraking job which I know by heart. I don't expect to sell especially large quantities of this book; I am sure that by giving the same amount of time and energy to other books I have in mind, I could earn several times as much money. In short, there isn't a thing in the world that leads me to this act, except the conviction which has been forced upon me that telepathy is real, and that loyalty to the nature of the universe makes it necessary for me to say so. . . .

A Shared Substratum of Mind?

"What is the use of it?" some will ask. I reply with another question: "What was the use of the lightning which Franklin brought down from the clouds on his kite-string?" No use that Franklin ever knew; yet today we make his lightning turn the wheels of industry, and move great railroad systems, and light a hundred million homes, and spread jazz music and cigarette advertising thousands of miles in every direction. It is an axiom of the scientist that every scrap of knowledge will be put to use sooner or later; get it, and let the uses wait. The discovery of the cause of bubonic plague was made possible because some foolish-minded entomologist had thought it worth-while to collect information about the fleas which prey upon the bodies of rats and ground squirrels.

I know a certain Wall Street operator who employed a "psychic" to sit in at his business conferences, and tell him if the other fellow was honest. I believe it didn't work very well; perhaps the circumstances were not favorable to concentration. Needless to say, Craig and I have no interest in such uses to be made of our knowledge. What telepathy means to my wife is this: it seems to indicate a common substratum of mind, underlying our individual minds, and which we can learn to tap. Figure the conscious mind as a tree, and the subconscious mind as the roots of that tree: then what of the earth in which the tree grows, and from which it derives its sustenance? What currents run through that earth, affecting all the trees of the forest? If one tree falls, the earth is shaken—and may not the other trees feel the impulse?

In other words, we are apparently getting hints of a cosmic consciousness, or cosmic unconsciouness: some kind of mind stuff which is common to us all, and which we can bring into our individual consciousness. Why is it not sensible to think that there may be a universal mind-stuff, just as there is a universal body-stuff, of which we are made, and to which we return?

6

L. L. Vasiliev

(1891–1966)

L. L. Vasiliev, the Soviet Union's foremost parapsychologist, is little known in America. At the time of his death, Vasiliev was Professor of Physiology at the Institute of Brain Research in the University of Leningrad, a corresponding member of the Soviet Academy of Sciences, and holder of the Order of Lenin.

His work in parapsychology, carried out from 1921 to 1938, is reported in his book, Eksperimentalnie Issledovaniya Mislennovo Vnusheniya, *from which I shall present excerpts.*

Several features of this book deserve mention. It is a Soviet document whose publication in 1962, in the time of Khrushchev, was ordered by the Editorial Council of the University of Leningrad. The book reveals that from the beginning of their research the Russians had a surprising knowledge of Western parapsychology—the East-West window must have been fitted with one-way glass. Even so, it is evident that, although Vasiliev and his co-workers drew inspiration from the West, they built their scientific opinions upon their own work and not upon ours.

They began with the belief that ESP is a form of electromagnetic radiation (radio waves)—a comfortable, materialistic assumption. Over a period of years, by careful and diligent experimentation, they proved that this is not true, and they developed a psychological sophistication as to the nature of the phenomenon. For us, the message of their work is this: Vasiliev was a first-rate scientist, and we must assume that there are others like him in the Soviet Union who have read his book.

A comparison of Vasiliev's method of experimenting with that of Upton Sinclair reveals a striking difference between Soviet and American approaches to extrasensory perception. As judged from his book, Vasiliev engaged in empirical exploration of the characteristics of ESP with little apparent concern for the prior question: "Does it occur? Is there a real phenomenon of the purported kind?" Sinclair, on the other hand, in his presentation and in his experiments, was almost totally absorbed by the question: "Does this unbelievable phenomenon really happen? How can I convince myself and others?"

One might ascribe Vasiliev's casual acceptance of ESP to his personal experience with it as a child, or one can speculate that he was constrained by political considerations to ignore the philosophic enormity of the phenomenon. I rather doubt, however, that either of these factors was the ultimate determinant of his experimental approach. I think we are in the presence of a cultural discrepancy and that resulting differences in method—often quite subtle—in all of the natural sciences will be found between Western Europe and the Soviet Union.

This discrepancy might be thought of as between an indigenous culture and one that was in some measure acquired. Admittedly, in all non-Western, technologically sophisticated countries there are scientists who have been wholly Westernized, but, for the most part, scientists in those countries do not perceive science within a Cartesian world view. It is in the latter context that ESP is an enormity—and only in that context, moreover, that Western science could and did flourish as a self-sufficient philosophic endeavor.[1]

What has happened in the USSR since the 1962 publication of Vasiliev's book? There is reason to believe that the Soviet government, having set aside its ideological fear of basic novelty, is intensively investigating psi phenomena. In 1973, the authoritative ideological and scientific Soviet journal, Voprosi Filosofi, *published what was, by its own claim, a position paper from the Presidium of the Soviet Association of Psychologists. In their conclusion, its four eminent authors said:*

> There is a definite need to organize the scientific research work into the areas of real occurrences described in parapsychology . . . and to do it at the Institute of Biophysics . . . and at the Institute for Problems of Information Transmission of the Academy of Sciences. . . . The Psychological Institutes of the Academy of Sciences and of the Academy of Pedagogical Sciences and other psychological institutions should also review the possibility of the strict scientific investigation of these phenomena. . . .
>
> It seems to us that attention of serious scientific organizations to the phenomena described in parapsychology will help reveal their true nature [and] will block the road to charlatans who are profiting by the quite natural curiosity of the general public.[2]

Since 1973, open sources of information about parapsychology in the USSR have dried up. On June 11, 1977, Robert Toth, correspondent for the Los Angeles Times, *was arrested and detained for receiving a*

---

1. By "Cartesian world view" I mean a dualism in which mind and body interact and in which mind is the province of religion but not of science. Operationally, Descartes' dualism was a materialistic monism. Later, when religion went out of fashion, scientists escaped from the necessity of dealing with mind by declaring it an impotent epiphenomenon of the brain. This neo-Cartesian stratagem is discussed by Charles Honorton in his essay, "Parapsychology and the mind-body problem," later in this book.

2. I have reported this document more fully in a paper listed in the bibliography appended to this book.

parapsychological document from a laboratory chief of the Institute of Medical-Biological Problems (New York Times, June 12, 1977). Although the interpretation of this event remains obscure, the indisputable fact of its occurrence tells something about the status of parapsychology in the upper levels of the KGB and raises a question as to how that status was reached.

Vasiliev's book has been translated twice into English, once in England in 1963 in cooperation with the author under the aegis of Anita Kohsen and C.C.L. Gregory, and once by the United States Government, presumably at the request of the Central Intelligence Agency.

My excerpts from Vasiliev's book were selected to display the administrative history of the Soviet effort, one kind of experiment they have done, and the growth of Soviet scientific understanding of this field. Although the original book is heavily documented, for simplicity I have omitted all references to notes and appendices. Page numbers refer to the American translation (available from U.S. National Technical Information Service as Joint Publications Research Service Report No. 59163*).*

PARAPSYCHOLOGY IN THE SOVIET UNION
(1962)

by L. L. VASILIEV

HISTORICAL SUMMARY

In this book are submitted experimental studies of telepathic phenomena which I pursued over a period of 40 years, with several interruptions, partially alone, but more often in collaboration with colleagues. I carried out these studies at the Leningrad Institute for Brain Research, first at the suggestion of Professor V. M. Bekhterev, founder of the Institute, and then independently after his death in 1927, on my own.[1]

I joined the Brain Institute as a beginner in physiology in the fall of 1921, at the time when V. M. Bekhterev along with the well-known animal trainer, V. L. Durov, was enthusiastically engaged in experiments with trained dogs involving mentally suggested movements. Bekhterev attributed much importance to this work and devoted a comprehensive article to a description of it in the *Proceedings of the Institute*. I was fortunate enough to participate in some of these experiments.

During those same years, Bekhterev published the results of his mental suggestion experiments with an 18-year-old girl who had an astoundingly acute susceptibility (guessing which object was thought of out of 7 to 12 set on a table). To continue and broaden experiments of this type, in the spring of 1922 he founded a special commission for the study of mental suggestion at the Brain Institute. . . .

The members of this commission concentrated primarily on investigations of two categories of phenomena: mental suggestion in human experiments and [the supposed] psychophysiological effect of magnetic fields on hypnotism. The results were reported to V. M. Bekhterev who deemed them noteworthy and included papers by commission members on the program of the Second All-Russian Congress on Psychoneurol-

---

1. Bekhterev's achievements in animal conditioning were recognized in his time as comparable to those of Pavlov. That he is less well known today may, in part, be the incidental result of his choice of terminology to describe his work. See, pp. 21–22 in G. A. Kimble: *Hilgard and Marquis' Conditioning and Learning*, New York: Appleton-Century-Crofts, 1961.—Ed.

ogy, which convened in 1924 at Petrograd [Leningrad]. On January 8, at a morning meeting of the section on hypnosis, suggestion, and psychotherapy, the following papers were delivered by the commission:

(1) "Present Status of the Question of Mental Suggestion in Other Countries," by A. K. Borsuk.

(2) "Investigation of Intercerebral [telepathic] Induction and Perception Phenomena" (results of the commission's experimental work), by V. A. Poderni.

(3) "On the Psychophysiological Effect of Magnetic Fields" (results of the commission's experimental work), by L. L. Vasiliev and V. N. Finne. . . .

There was a special item in the resolution adopted by this congress noting the need for further investigation of so-called mental suggestion. . . . The All-Russian Congress of Psychoneurologists not only recognized the scientific significance of the work done by the commission but also favored expanding it. The commission itself, however, had ceased to exist by that time (it was closed in late 1923, i.e., just before the congress convened).

Implementation of the resolution adopted by the congress was assigned to the Society of Neurology, Reflexology, Hypnology, and Biological Physics at the Brain Institute. At a plenary session of the society in March 1926, chaired by V. M. Bekhterev, the following papers were delivered:

(1) "On the Subject of Long-Distance Direct Thought Transmission" (experimental), by A. K. Chekhovskiy.

(2) "Biophysical Bases of Direct Thought Transmission" (theoretical), by L. L. Vasiliev.

The paper by Professor Vasiliev, which proposed a materialistic approach to the phenomenon of mental suggestion, was published in a popular form in the journal, *Vestnik Znaniya* (No. 7, 1926). . . .

In October 1926 the society appointed a special commission for more systematic development of the question of mental suggestion and related biophysical problems, and named it the Experimental Commission for Hypnology and Biophysics. V. M. Bekhterev was the president of this commission. . . . Its members executed the following experimental and methodological works:

(1) Objective methods were developed for analysis and monitoring of cases of "spontaneous" manifestation of mental suggestion (I. A. Borichevskiy).

(2) Hundreds of experiments were performed referable to phenomena of so-called "guessing visual images" (G. V. Reyts).

(3) Experimental investigations of pseudorecognition phenomena (I. A. Borichevskiy).

(4) A series of experiments were conducted dealing with "recognition" with subject P, which yielded negative results (G. V. Reyts and A. V. Dubrovskiy, at the suggestion of Bekhterev).

(5) Experiments were conducted to develop the effect of myoneural overexcitation (according to Charcot) during hypnosis by the method of combined (conditioned) reflexes (L. L. Vasiliev, V. A. Poderni, and V. A. Finne).

(6) Various experiments were performed involving pin-pricking of different parts of the body with simultaneous recording of respiration, pulse, and blood pressure (Vasiliev and Dubrovskiy, with reference to the demonstrations of To Rama).

(7) Experiments were performed dealing with the influence of hands on a mobile metal pointer [Ouija board] (Vasiliev and Dubrovskiy, at the suggestion of Bekhterev. . . .

In 1932, the Bekhterev Brain Institute, now headed by Professor V. P. Osipov, the well-known psychiatrist (it must be stated that he did not concede that there was a possibility of existence of telepathy), was given the assignment to begin an experimental study of telepathy in order to determine, if possible, its physical nature; at what electromagnetic wavelength "the brain radio" works, i.e., transmission of information from one brain to another brain, if such transmission really exists. It must be noted that in those years (1923–1933) the experiments of the Italian psychiatrist, Cazzamalli, gained wide renown; he presumed to have discovered cerebral radio waves in the range of centimeters and meters. The investigations of Cazzamalli were considered a firm corroboration of the electromagnetic theory of telepathic phenomena.

The director of the Brain Institute accepted this assignment. I was charged with scientific supervision of the project. Under the dome of the institute building an isolated area was assigned for a special laboratory equipped with all the necessary apparatus for physical and physiological tests. The work was done by a team of scientists: I. F. Tomashevskiy (physiologist), A. V. Dubrovskiy (medical hypnologist), and R. I. Skariatinym (physicist-engineer). Another physiologist, G. Yu. Belitskiy, participated in one of the series of experiments. Authorities on radio engineering of those days were among our consultants in the physical part of the work. One of them (Academician V. F. Mitkevich) accepted the possibility of telepathy and conducted experiments on mental suggestion himself, using a simple technique that he developed. Another consultant (Professor M. V. Shuleikin), on the contrary, was sceptical about the problem and submitted all our tests to rigorous criticism. His criticisms were very beneficial to our project. In their efforts to satisfy the sometimes petty demands of this strict critic, the working team of the laboratory spared no effort to continuously improve the experimental set-up.

These studies were pursued for five and one-half years (up to 1938). In this time much experimental material was accumulated and written by the authors in the form of three reports:

(1) "Psychophysiological Bases of the Telepathic Phenomenon" (1934).

(2) "Physical Bases of Mental Suggestion" (1936).

(3) "Mental Suggestion of Motor Acts" (1937).

The principal result of these studies concerned the physical nature of the factor that transmits mental suggestion. The result was unexpected even for the researchers. Contrary to electromagnetic theory, the most thorough shielding by metal of the "agent" who was sending the mental suggestion, or of the "percipient" receiving it, did not degrade in any way the transmission of nonverbal suggestions in all cases when it could be distinctly manifested without any shielding. This unexpected and, at first, confusing result cast doubt on the validity of the electromagnetic theory of telepathic phenomenon.

During World War II and thereafter, of course, our investigations of mental suggestion were interrupted. . . . In 1956, I established a correspondence with R. Warcollier, president of the Paris International Metapsychological Institute, from whom I obtained some information about the status of parapsychological research abroad.

In 1959, Gospolitizdat published my brochure entitled *Tainstvennye Yavleniya Chelovecheskoy Psikhiki* [*Mysterious Phenomena of the Human Psyche*] (Moscow) in a large printing. One of its chapters ("Does a Brain Radio Exist?") deals with a brief description of the history and present status of the problem of telepathy, which had not been mentioned for about 20 years in the pages of the Soviet press. Publication of this pamphlet played its role: articles began to appear in the newspapers about "biological radio communication". . . .

In late 1959 and early 1960, a member of the Paris Metapsychological Institute, R. L. Kherumian, sent me two articles from French popular science journals. These articles described in detail a sensational experiment of mental suggestion [supposedly] conducted in the summer of 1959 on board the American atomic submarine, Nautilus.

This experiment showed—and herein lies its principal

significance—that telepathic information can be immediately transmitted through sea water and a metal-enclosed submarine, i.e., through media that usually hinder radio communication considerably. They completely absorb short radio waves and weaken long waves considerably, whereas the factor, still unknown to us, of transmitting mental suggestions passes through them readily. This result was obtained by the Americans 25 years after our above-mentioned experiments of the 1930s and corroborated them completely. The advantage of the American experiment over ours was only that the telepathic effect traveled over a larger distance and overcame more significant obstacles (the enormous thickness of water plus the metal shell of the submarine).

Such an unexpected confirmation by foreign researchers of our 25-year-old experiments prompted me to report them to wide circles of scientists (the first paper was delivered on 21 April 1960 at a Leningrad conference dedicated to Radio Day at the Scientists' Center). Our old investigations had not lost any of their interest. Rather the contrary was true, with the passage of time their significance increased. They withstood the most rigid test, the test of time. I had many occasions to repeat my paper in Leningrad and Moscow, and each time it inspired lively interest in the audience.

Should one recognize that telepathic phenomena are a reliably established fact or not? One thing is obvious: they can no longer be ignored; they should be investigated. At the present time the investigation of mental suggestion is being pursued all over the world. In the Soviet Union we should be informed as to what has been done and is being done on this score abroad and, furthermore, we should acquire our own experience in this matter.

This is why the Leningrad University deemed it opportune to organize a special laboratory at the Physiological Institute, biological faculty, in 1960, to investigate telepathic phenomena under the guidance of the present author, and to have this book published.

Its contents consist of the integrated and newly edited reports of studies referable to the 1920s and 1930s which I pursued along with my colleagues, . . . In essence this is a monographic presentation of many years' experimental investigation of mental suggestion pursued using three principal investigative methods: motor, sensory, and especially hypnogenic. Of primary importance are the experiments to test the elecromagnetic theory of mental suggestion using a metal-shielded ''agent'' (person sending) or ''percipient'' (the individual perceiving the suggestion). [pp. 2–7]

THE RADIO THEORY OF TELEPATHY

This scientific materialistic hypothesis is believed to have been first voiced by E. Houston in the 1890s. The conceptions of this author were based on the phenomenon of electrical resonance [i.e., radio transmission] discovered by Hertz shortly before, in 1888. The neuropsychic process associated with bioelectric current in the sender's brain [supposedly] induces electromagnetic waves of a specific length (radio waves of the brain) in the environment which reach the percipient's brain and cause in him an analogous neuropsychic process. To put it more briefly, the phenomenon of thought transmission can be reduced to a process of "intercerebral electromagnetic induction."

Further elaboration of this concept was encouraged, on the one hand, by the strong development of radio engineering, and, on the other hand, by the accumulation of knowledge on bioelectric currents that are inseparably related to the process of excitation of brain cells and nerve conductors.

In our country Academician V. M. Bekhterev . . . did not question the existence of telepathic phenomena and was the first among Russian scientists to expound the electromagnetic hypothesis to interpret them. The teaching on electromagnetic radiation of the brain was the working hypothesis for our investigation and as such made it necessary to consider it on a deeper and more critical level. [p. 15]

*   *   *   *

All that we have discussed in this chapter indicates that, although it is supported by some observational facts, the electromagnetic hypothesis of mental suggestion is faced with several difficulties and contradictions that are far from having been removed. Nevertheless, when we started our investigations, we were governed by this hypothesis. At that time we did not yet question its validity. [p. 28]

It is significant that Hans Berger, the famous contemporary electrophysiologist and discoverer of the electroencephalographic method, rejected [the radio theory of telepathy]. Who, it would seem, more than he, should be an ardent proponent of the electromagnetic hypothesis? In a small book published in 1940, Berger develops the hypothesis of "psychic energy" as a factor transmitting telepathic information. He became interested in this matter following a few cases of spontaneous telepathy that had occurred in his life, and he personally conducted many mental suggestion tests with 200 subjects.

[Berger came to believe] that the changes in electric potentials in the brain are too small to explain the transmission of telepathic information—in some cases over enormous distances. He tried to show that the electric voltage generated by brain cells is transformed into psychic energy that can spread over any distance and pass through any obstacle encountered on its way. Berger viewed this process as a dissemination of waves similar to Hertz [i.e., radio] waves but not identical to them. He divides the telepathic process into three stages: (a) electric processes in the brain are converted into "psychic energy"; (b) this energy is propagated in space; (c) when it reaches the percipient's brain it is again converted into electric energy that induces physiological processes and related psychic experiences corresponding to the experiences of the telepathic sender. [p. 170]

A Sleep-Induction Experiment

The most important experiments of the book (Chapters 6–8) are concerned with hypnotic suggestions to fall asleep or to waken, given from a distance beyond the range of sensory perception—in a few cases from 7.7 km or more.

In some of these experiments the rhythmic squeezing of a rubber balloon strapped to the hand of the test subject caused the movement of a pneumatic stylus on a time-versus-amplitude recorder located at the end of a hose in another room. The squeezing stopped when the subject fell into hypnotic sleep and resumed upon waking. A separate stylus was used to record the times of command to sleep or to waken.

In the years 1933–1934, 260 sleep/waken experiments were performed—mostly with one or the other of two psychoneurotic patients suffering with dissociative reaction (i.e., hysteria). Sleep induction failed in only six experiments, and wakening failed in only 21. Of the 260 experiments, 194 were instrumented as just described. Of the instrumented experiments, comparisons of command-response time intervals for the sender and subject (1) in the same room, (2) in different rooms, (3) in different rooms with electromagnetic screening of the sender, and (4) in different rooms with electromagnetic screening of both sender and subject, showed a statistically suggestive additional response delay for condition (2) compared to (1), but none for (3) compared to (2), nor for (4) compared to (3).[2]

---

2. These results suggest that hypnosis is a psychokinetic phenomenon in which the brain of the subject is controlled by the command of the

Because these results, although quite definite, were contrary to expectation, Vasiliev and colleagues repeated this work in 1935–1936 with a new room arrangement, new subjects, and a new protocol.[3]

An intensity of purpose in the experimenters is shown by the sender-shielding chamber they built of 3 mm lead for some of the 1935–1936 work. One-way signalling into the chamber was done by a direct-current magnet on the outside whose field entered through the lead to operate an iron armature with switch contacts controlling a battery-powered lamp (to avoid leaks along feed-through wires). The trough holding the edge of the lead-shielded lid was sealed to a depth of 4 cm with mercury, which, however, eventually dissolved a hole through the lead and was replaced by lead filings.

The foregoing description is not offered here as evidence for the reality of the phenomena but to suggest to the sceptical scientist that the Vasiliev book might be worth his attention. For present purposes, I have selected the following noninstrumented, hand-logged experiment that is of unusual psychological interest.—Ed.

Experiment on 20 April 1934; subject Federova arrived at the laboratory at 0930 hours and was taken to room *A* for a rest before the experiment. At this time, Professor Vasiliev entered room *B*, into which Tomashevskiy also arrived, having been with the subject previously. Conferring about the conditions for the next experiment, they developed the following plan: The subject would be placed in chamber No. 1 in room *B*; Tomashevskiy would remain with her as an observer; Vasiliev, who had never before put the subject to sleep either mentally or verbally, was to pretend that he was leaving the laboratory; actually, he would move to room *A* in order to start mental suggestion at a moment not known to the observer (Tomashevskiy).

This plan was then executed. At 0955 hours the subject was moved from room *A* to room *B* and entered the chamber with Tomashevskiy. Vasiliev pretended to leave the laboratory and went to the distant room *A*. Throughout this experiment, the observer interrogated the subject,

---

experimenter—an idea that may add a new dimension to the Barber-Hilgard controversy. (See, E. R. Hilgard: The domain of hypnosis, American Psychologist, 1973, 28, 972–982.)

3. The subject, isolated in bed, was allowed to fall asleep while rhythmically pressing the balloon, with or without a distantly given suggestion to sleep. Whether a suggestion was given was determined by a randomizing wheel after the subject was isolated. A t-test comparison of time to fall asleep for 27 trials without suggestion (17.7 ± 1.86 minutes) versus 26 trials with suggestion (6.8 ± 0.54 minutes) yields a p-value of less than 10^{-5}.

entering his questions and her answers in the log. At 0958 hours the inductor (Vasiliev) began mental suggestion of sleep. At 1000 hours the subject sank into a hypnotic trance.

Subject: That's enough.

Observer: Who put you to sleep?

Subject: You—today he is putting me to sleep well.

Observer: Who is putting you to sleep?

Subject: Tomashevskiy.

Observer: What else comes to mind?

Subject: Vasiliev is poking into my head—the minute I fell asleep, I thought of him, and immediately he poked into my head.

At 1018 hours it occurred to the inductor (Vasiliev) to transmit the image of a bird, which he imagined as a condor or vulture. At approximately the same time, the observer posed the following question to the subject: "Tell me what comes to your mind."

Subject: He is showing well.

Observer: Who is he?

Subject: Vasiliev, his eyes are bulging.

And immediately after this:

Subject: A rooster—now I see him. He is sitting at a table, a round one (the inductor was indeed seated at a round table). He is the one who took everything away from me.

Observer: Who put you into the hypnotic trance?

Subject: That means he is the one who put me—he has immobilized me.

At 1035 hours the inductor walks to the subject's room and enters the iron-shielded chamber, No. 2. At 1040 hours the inductor begins to mentally waken the subject.

Subject: Wait a bit—he is winding the ball [of string—a symbolic reference to coming out of trance]. That's enough—Professor Vasiliev, stop it—oh, well, I'll have to wake up—I don't want to—well, all right, that's enough.

At 1041 hours:

Subject: I'm fed up—Vasiliev is there (pointing in the direction of the shielded chamber), sitting there—poor thing, he's trying hard—and I did hear him.

At 1043 hours the subject wakes up. At 1043 hours and 30 seconds, the inductor undertakes mental suggestion of sleep a second time (immediately after the subject woke up, which is contrary to the usual practice).

Subject: Something is not right.

She falls asleep at 1046 hours.

It appears to us that the significant elements in this experiment are not only that the subject recognized the inductor (though, we repeat, in the two years that he has known the subject, he has never tried to put her to sleep) but also the fact that throughout the experiment the subject accurately described the inductor's behavior and his whereabouts.

These phenomena could be attributed either to the percipient's ability to recognize the inductor according to the nature of the energetic influence picked up from him or the ability to pick up the contents of the subconscious of the observer, who, in this instance, being busy questioning the subject and making entries in the log, was far from conscious suggestion of anything whatsoever to the subject. [pp. 139–141]

ON THE NATURE OF TELEPATHY

To sum up all that was discussed in the [preceding] chapters, we arrive at the following main facts and conclusions:

First, we must conclude that there must be preliminary screening of sensitive subjects to conduct experiments to determine the psychophysical nature of the telepathic phenomenon. This is mandatory to obtain convincing enough results.

Second, we find that the "hypnogenic method" we developed, including the subject's own statements and objective recording of his reactions, is quite suitable for further experiments, since the results obtained by this method are distinct and unequivocal.

Third, we can conclude that it is not mandatory for the experimenter to know where the subject is and what his environment is. But apparently the experimenter must know the subject personally and clearly visualize his image for telepathic transmission to take place.

Fourth, it must apparently be assumed that the distance between the experimenter and the subject has no perceptible effect; but this does not mean that the law of inverse square of distance does not apply to this case.

Fifth, we note that thus far no one has succeeded in establishing any physical indicator of brain-generated radiations that transmit telepathic information. We have not corroborated Cazzamalli's statements and his experiments with recording of electromagnetic waves of the human brain.

And, finally, sixth, we see that, contrary to some data in the literature, metal shielding between the experimenter and the subject does not prevent the telepathic phenomenon. Hence we have to conclude that, if thought transfer at a distance does occur by radiation of electromagnetic energy from the central nervous system, such electromagnetic energy should be sought in the kilometer range of electromagnetic waves or beyond soft x-rays; but both assumptions are improbable.

These are our conclusions. As one can see, the objective of future research will be more complex, and it will turn from the area of purely psychological experimentation to that of psychophysical experiments, which should either confirm the hypothesis of the electromagnetic nature of telepathic transmission or, having rejected it, should seek a kind of energy, unknown as yet, that would be characteristic of the higher form of matter represented by the human brain. [pp. 146–147]

Does the percipient know that the command he has executed (for example, the card he has called) is indeed the same command that the sender mentally suggested? And, can the percipient state who precisely was the sender?

According to our data and those of S. Ya. Turlygin, such a possibility exists, but this is denied by many contemporary authors. They stress that lack of feedback in both directions is characteristic of telepathy. It is supposed that the inductor does not know or feel whether or not the percipient has received the suggested command, and the percipient does not know whether his response is the one suggested by the sender or, indeed, who is playing the part of sender.

We believe that in most experiments this is so, but that it can also be otherwise. Some telepathic senders maintain that when a test is successful they experience a unique "feeling of success." For example, the psychotherapist, Dr. K. D. Kotkov, describes his experience during mental suggestion of sleep in the following words: "I had a strong wish for the young girl (percipient) to fall asleep. Finally this wish changed into certainty that she was asleep and into some unique sort of ecstasy of success. I would send a signal at such a time and stop the experiment."

Moreover, our best percipient, Federova, [in a number of experiments] "sensed" when the inductor began to "work" and so stated without error. Apparently, the hypnogenic method of mental suggestion enhances demonstration of two-way communication between inductor and percipient. Experiments involving the use of other mental suggestion methods failed to demonstrate the two-way nature of the telepathic process for some undetermined reasons. [p. 165]

[Certain] facts and their interpretation create the impression that "telepathic giftedness" is not a phenomenon that is subject to progressive evolution; rather it is a primitive property that man retained from his zoological ancestors and that is revived in some mentally or nervous-system-deficient individuals in the form of distinctive atavism. We find our best subjects for mental suggestion tests among psychoneurotics and even mentally retarded individuals. . . . This question cannot be considered definitively answered. Cases of spontaneous telepathy can be found in the biographies of prominent people. Heightened telepathic faculty is sometimes observed as a transient, temporary phenomenon in healthy children, young women and men; like the temporary organs, it appears, only to disappear without a trace. [p. 168]

I have had occasion to hear the following critical statements repeatedly: "First supply us with incontrovertible evidence of the reality of mental suggestion; then study and describe its properties, its physical nature, and so forth." It can be anticipated that the same objection will be made with regard to this book. The present author cannot agree with this objection: such a policy would not accelerate but would slow down progress in the field.

Granted that any test I have performed, taken individually, is not sufficient to establish the fact of mental suggestion, but the entire series taken as a whole . . . shows that it is highly probable that mental suggestion does exist. This is enough to justify further research on this phenomenon without waiting for universal acceptance. It is precisely in the course of such investigations that all the conditions necessary and sufficient for continuous experimental induction of mental suggestion phenomena could be found, and this will serve as the best evidence of their real existence. [p. 8]

7

Rosalind Heywood

(1895–1980)

If we are collecting opinions about parapsychology, surely we must go to those who have directly experienced its phenomena. As in the study of history, secondary sources are suspect. A parapsychologist's analysis of psi occurrences may have enlightened him, but it can give us only hearsay evidence of their flavor. Collected, factual descriptions of well-authenticated ESP incidents may convince us that the phenomenon occurs, but they are of little value if what we seek is personal knowledge of its subjective aspects. It might even be argued that for a true understanding, one should examine exclusively the opinions of those who know psi phenomena firsthand—but that would be another book than the one I have chosen to assemble.

For our present purpose the usual limitation of psychic individuals is that they are not unbiased observers. They live in a society where prevailing doctrine denies the reality of their experience. Merely for ego survival, they must develop special psychological defenses.

They may want to use their abilities to help others or to support themselves financially, and this forces them at once into an unusual and sometimes degrading relationship with their subculture. In a search for understanding, they may view themselves as gifted by the Deity and perhaps as His representative. They may evolve for their special abilities, pseudoscientific explanations that overlay and distort their experiences.

If they are of above-average intelligence, so that unsophisticated escape hatches from social reality are closed to them, they may deny their extrasensory experiences and suppress their latent powers. Psychic ability does not flourish among the well-educated in our culture.

We would like to consult psychic persons who accept their special ability but are not dominated by it—"psychics" who, despite their handicap, live successful, ordinary lives. There may have been many such persons, but only one, to my knowledge, has given a full account of her way of life.

How does psi manifest itself when it is accepted as a natural occurrence, like sleep—and as hardly more mysterious? What is the flavor of psi in everyday living that is undistorted by theatrical obligations, a belief in spirits, the suspicion of one's friends, or fear of the unknown? In such an environment, how would it feel to be a well-educated psychic with exceptional intelligence, unusual courage, and unquenchable zest for living? I can think of no more tantalizing psychological question. The answer will be found in the excerpts to follow, from the The Infinite Hive, the autobiography of Rosalind Heywood, my friend through three decades.

I have long regarded this book as the most important extant primary source of information about the subjective nature of spontaneous psi. Mrs. Heywood's account has an added interest because over the last 40 years she interacted personally with nearly all of the leaders of English parapsychology and with many of the intellectual leaders of England. Because we are in search of understanding rather than personal conviction, I have chosen excerpts from Mrs. Heywood's book to show her personality, the quality of her intellect, her attitude toward her psychic experiences, and the nature of those experiences, but not especially their evidential force.

The popular image of ESP as a kind of supernatural stage magic is a caricature, titillating to the ignorant and repulsive to the scientifically sophisticated. Incidents of spontaneous ESP are in reality infrequent, fleeting, and usually ambiguous even with so outstanding a psychic as Mrs. Heywood. In the laboratory, most experimenters find ESP impossible to produce dependably. If it were otherwise, there would be no controversy.

It is axiomatic that nearly all psychics who commit themselves to serving a clientele must eventually resort to fraud to supplement their sporadic abilities. It is likewise true, in an age of "publish or perish," that those who commit themselves to a research career in parapsychology, more than in any other field of natural science, will be under pressure to reason fallaciously and to lower their evidential standards—if indeed they were not attracted to the field as romantic individuals to begin with. All this cannot affect the reality of psi phenomena, but it does provide a ritual stamping ground for the shamans of orthodoxy. For the open-minded, Heywood's matter-of-fact autobiography will provide a true perspective of the subtle challenge of these prodigious phenomena.

The Infinite Hive is currently available in British Commonwealth countries from Penguin Books. An earlier American edition of the work may be found in libraries under the title, ESP: A Personal Memoir. My excerpts are taken from Chapters 4-9. To avoid a disjointed presentation, I have omitted ellipsis marks except where needed to warn of a change of topic.

AUTOBIOGRAPHY
(1964)

by ROSALIND HEYWOOD

CHILDHOOD

One needs something to trigger off a backward flight across the years and this was provided for me last winter by my host at dinner, a famous novelist. "You must have been hell when you were a child," he said suddenly, with feeling, between two mouthfuls of duck.

Famous novelists do not make that sort of remark without reason, and I gave it a good deal of thought. That he was right soon became painfully clear, but it also struck me that being hell could perhaps have stimulated the acute sense of solitude and longing for "real communication" which started young and still endures today. Such longing was absurdly exaggerated and obviously doomed to frustration in outer life. So too was my other basic longing. This was for "Something Central"—though I did not know what that Something was or where to look for it. And I often ran after very false gods.

The first voice to be heard from the distant Edwardian world of my childhood is our aged Nanny's, "Naughty girl! What you want is a good licking!" The first picture is of my own legs and arms flailing in protest against the vast silk handkerchief which would be tied over my shrieking mouth to protect the tender ears of grown-ups. But perhaps the fault was not all mine. She had been my father's Nanny too, and, so my mother told me in after years, could never quite forgive me for being a girl. Also she may have needed to lick something since in her youth her young man had vanished to America and had never been heard of again. I do not think she was unkind to me, but she did not encourage what she called Namby-Pambyness. Nor, in his very different way, did our devoted father. He was our God as well as our father, tall, handsome, impersonally just and a famous cricketer. When he smiled his delightful smile and said "Not bad," (it was not necessary to add, "for a girl") our young hearts swelled like Christmas balloons. He took for granted that Fusses Are Never Made, and this, together with Nanny's disapproval of namby-pambyness, made us take stoicism as a Law of Nature, so much so that my young sister once walked for miles uncomplaining while an upthrust shoe nail bored a hole in her foot, and I said nothing when a table crashed on mine with such force that on going to bed I found a toe-nail adrift in my sock.

Our mother would have died for us, but to confide to her was out of the question. We sensed that she was frightened of Nanny, if we ailed she got really anxious, and there was also a second Law that she must *never* be worried. We were told that in her youth some doctor had diagnosed— I suspect erroneously—that she "had a heart."

A third Law in our upright and ordered world was "Black is Black and White is White." Any grey between was not envisaged. This Law held in the books which penetrated our nurseries and schoolrooms, and even when I reached the stage of novel reading. Fortunately, in the end Good Whites always triumphed over Bad Blacks, and the novels also informed me that all earthly troubles ceased with the ringing of marriage bells. These two dicta took a good deal of unlearning; and the process might have been disastrous had I not later on been fortunate enough to marry an extremely long-suffering husband.

A fourth Law was "Little Girls must not ask Why?" This was very frustrating as I seemed to have been born with that bad word on my lips. I was also born lacking the love for dolls, needles and thread which all nice little girls were assumed to feel as a matter of course. What I felt, on the contrary, especially after I had learnt to read, was, "Why waste time sewing silly petticoats for the silly creatures when a book could open the door on to splendid worlds filled with Knights, Genies, Mohicans, Treasure Islands and Black Panthers? And why, anyway, mustn't little girls ask why?" I never could get a sensible answer to that. . . .

Since questions were not in order, whenever possible one had—one just *had*—to try and find out for oneself. And thus, eventually, I found a use for a doll. Church bored me horribly. I wanted to run about, and the choir sent knives right through me by singing out of tune, but one Sunday my attention was caught by another intriguing statement, that worms could destroy dead bodies. I had wept over a dead rabbit and recoiled, feeling sick, from a dead hen, which had been mauled by a fox and was horribly smeared by its own eggs; but how could tiny soft worms, which did not seem to have any teeth chew up even their fur and feathers, much less the huge hard bodies of grown-ups? (In those days women in English country houses were all firmly encased in whalebone.) But—if one buried that new doll with its silly flapping eyelids, that would give the worms a chance to show what they could do! The result of this exciting experiment was negative. After a restless week, exhumation disclosed that they had done nothing at all, and so I learnt that a statement made in Church could be inaccurate. I also learnt, though being very sensible people my parents did not say much, that it was not really done to turn smart new dolls into mildewy wrecks in attempts to test the truth of Holy Scripture.

It was at about the age of five, when I heard Fairy Stories for the first time, that I began to realize the awful hidden dangers that menaced us children. Of course one could never be so namby-pamby as to ask grown-ups for protection from them, and yet how readily, how gladly, I know too late, our parents would have given it. As it was, they seemed quite unaware that the more predatory inhabitants of Fairyland, about whom they so kindly read to us, did not obey the rules and remain there, but that every night after dark their sinister powers were unleashed in our world too. Almost worse, there was the Tiger which hung on the staircase wall. Every evening after tea my young sister and I were scrubbed, brushed and buttoned into white muslin frocks with blue sashes, and then sent down to spend an hour in the drawing-room with our parents. This would have been delightful but for the fact that to reach the drawing-room we had to run the gauntlet of the Tiger's snarling fangs, which hung at the most convenient height to crunch off our heads; and however safe a haven was Daddy's knee, there was always the awful knowledge that the only way back to the nursery was past those fangs again.

Another thing that grown-ups did not appear to know was that some people had nasty Insides. The worst of these was a parlourmaid whom my innocent mother held in high esteem. She had cold, opaque, brown eyes and a mouth like a bilious cod, and I did what I could to get rid of her, even to pouring a bucketful of water from an upper window on to her smartly-capped head. This failed in its object. All it achieved was to earn me an afternoon locked in the box room to meditate on my sins. In the end the parlourmaid vanished rather quickly, her nastiness having, I supposed, at last become apparent to grown-ups. Nothing, of course, was said to us children and nobody related that nastiness to my own bad behaviour. . . .

But there was one person of whom I was not aware, either inside or out, and this seemed odd, for my mother read to us about Him and prayed to Him every morning, and the whole household, except Alice, the cook, visited Him every Sunday. His name was God, He lived in the sky, He had made me and everyone else and He kept an eye on all of us all the time. Moreover, He could do anything whatever He liked. That being so, it seemed a pity that He had not made me good like my young sister, who did not have unpopular ideas but was quite content to ride a hobby horse or play with the dogs or a ball all day. My mother assured me lovingly that, if I prayed to Him, He would help me to improve, but for a long time, in spite of all my prayers, He gave no sign of His existence and I did not improve at all. However, one day after a bout of special wickedness, in despair I prayed "fit to bust," as Nanny would have put it, and then for one ecstatic moment I found myself caught up into a warm and shining world where I was no longer a Naughty Girl, and there was no need at all to cry. But He did not keep me there and He never did it again, so I grew bored with prayers. . . .

When I was eleven the glorious impossible happened: our father was sent to India to reorganize its geographical survey and he decided to take his family with him. Like cumulus, stupendous visions billowed inside my head: Whales, Mountains, Elephants, Parrots, Maharajahs, Palms! Eventually all these wonders did materialize, though for the most part on the far side of an invisible security curtain. In our Calcutta garden, for instance, there waved palms just like those which supplied the Elephant's Child with bananas.

"Can we explore the garden, please?"

"No, dear, there might be snakes."

A tarantula on the stairs was some consolation, so was a banded krait on the Maidan, but it was almost more than human nature could bear when a lovely Maharanee in a glittering saree asked if we children could visit her, and the answer was, No.

During the hot weather the family migrated up the Himalayas to Darjeeling. We children had never seen a mountain before. Now, right at our feet, rivers of billowing treetops poured down to steamy sub-tropical valleys miles and miles below, and beyond them the mountains climbed again, ridge after ridge, until they were lost in a blue and dreamlike nothingness.

"Look, children, there are the Snows," said our father, pointing we thought towards the nothingness. For a long time we could not see them. We had not looked high enough. Then at last, towering against the cobalt sky, we saw Kanchenjunga, white, shining, inviolate, all but the highest mountain in the world. I could not—and cannot—formulate what moved me almost beyond bearing in the Hills. It was as if some wind of the spirit blew down on the childish creature and touched something in it awake, so that it could never be quite so childish again. One night after our return to England when our mother came as usual to kiss me good night, I had not been quick enough to dry the nostalgic tears from my face. "What's the matter, darling?"

"Nothing, nothing at all."

"But there must be something!" She looked hurt.

"It's leaving the Hills," I mumbled and, as I had foreseen, her look changed to one of bewilderment. What could there be to regret in that land of dirt and disease and thieves and heathen ways? Some years ago I went to an international dinner party in Eaton Square expecting witty, pleasant talk but not "real communication." I found myself sitting next to an explorer who had just returned from Tibet and to him, surprisingly, I also found myself daring to mutter a little of what as a child the Hills had meant to me. After a pause he said the two words that of all others I would have chosen to hear. They were "Those Presences!"

It was soon after our return from India—I was just thirteen—that I realized that in some intangible way I was at times aware of lesser presences in certain places. Some were grim and sad and I felt that if only I could *see* them they would be less unnerving. One was in my bedroom in my grandfather's house which overlooked Dartmoor. By day it was a gay little room, facing south, with a wall-paper festooned with blue ribbons and pink roses. But at night it was a very different place. Then a mysterious invisible Somebody shared it with me—and I didn't know who that Somebody was! Because of its presence I undressed in the nursery, leapt blindly from the door into bed, pulled the blankets over my head and kept well under them until a friendly housemaid flung open the curtains to the blessed morning sun. Had the Somebody been mentionable to a grown-up I might have learnt that my mother and aunt had both independently seen the apparition of an old woman standing at the foot of the bed, but, needless to say, they both kept this to themselves until years later after my grandfather's death. I suppose they assumed that children were not aware of what I am sure they called "these things."

I also felt invisible presences in another aunt's house in Norfolk—melancholy frightening presences—but again, not until I was grown-up did I learn that to her they were not invisible, but she often saw them and took them in her stride.

GROWING PAINS

My father wisely decreed that for the two years we were to be in India I need have no schooling, but could send for any books I liked from the Calcutta Club. The child was too young, he said, for them to do her harm. This enabled me to gulp down a very mixed diet of books with the indiscriminating joy that a mastiff gulps down meat, and the Indian servant who fetched and carried them got quite a lot of exercise. At thirteen I was sent back to England to live with an adored uncle and aunt and be instructed, along with their sixteen-year-old daughter, by a very Parisian governess.

My cousin I humbly revered, not only for her great age but because of her prowess at tennis, climbing trees and handling spirited horses. In lessons she had just been promoted to something called geometry, of which I had never heard, and instead of learning my history dates I listened enthralled while the governess tried to expound to her a delightful puzzle called the Pythagorean theorem. And I saw, I *saw* what it was getting at! "Please, may I learn that too?" I burst out at last.

"No," said the governess coldly, "you are too young," and later my cousin conveyed subtly that it was not done to be too much interested in that sort of thing. I felt ashamed.

When I was fifteen and a half, adventure once more beckoned. My father was sent to run the Geographical Section of the War Office and the family moved to London, which to me was a Mecca, swarming with artists, musicians, writers and romantic Ruritanian foreigners. That my family would be unlikely to gravitate to such exotic individuals did not occur to me, and my dazzling visions seemed about to come true when my parents decided that I had had all the general education that a girl could need, and told me that they would provide a Bechstein—with their narrow means a most generous gesture—if I wished to concentrate on learning the piano. Did Christian wish to enter Paradise?

What I thought were the Gates of Paradise were the grimy doors of 194 Cromwell Road, and behind them sat a fat and red-faced archangel, the well-known pianist, Mathilde Verne, who had been a pupil of Clara Schumann's and in her youth had actually played to Brahms. Unfortunately for her own pupils she enjoyed playing on their nerves as much as she did on the piano, and by a velvety finger-tip touch of approval she would sweep them up to the skies, just for the fun, apparently, of casting them thence with a crash into the nethermost pit. Here my early training came in useful. I was cowering in the pit one day when she remarked reflectively, "You know, you are the only pupil I have never managed to make cry."

I shall die before you do, I thought. But why should anyone want to make anyone cry? Nevertheless she did open to us the minor heaven of chamber music where isolated young creatures could play themselves into a joyful unity. Here, at last, were moments of real communication.

It was perhaps due to the stimulus of extreme panic that at the age of seventeen I experienced the inner linkage of joint performance in visual terms. Mathilde never did things by halves and to launch the child prodigy, Solomon, she took the Queen's Hall and engaged Nikisch, no less, to conduct. And then, to show what she could make of even sub-human material, she decreed that amateur pupils should play a Mozart concerto for two pianos. I arrived for the one rehearsal under

Nikisch just in time to see her turn purple, tear at her curly black hair and shriek, "My God! I forgot to tell him there were amateurs playing. He will refuse to conduct!"

Even his kindly message that he too was an amateur did not prevent my knees from playing the drum on the underside of the piano keyboard until, on looking up to begin, I saw miraculously stretched from him to every player, including me, a shining cord. Owing to my cord, something not me played with zest and assurance and entirely out of my class. At the end he bent down and clapped and said, "Bravo! Bravo!" But I knew dimly, though he did not seem to, that he was congratulating himself, not me.

From now on the turmoil of adolescence in a creature totally ignorant of both psychology and physiology made me hell, merry hell, not only to my parents but to myself. Even the joy of music turned to inchoate longing for I knew not what, and to wake up in the morning from vanished celestial mansions to the muddy swamp of this "solitude called life" became intolerable. Even to listen to footsteps walking down the street at night would drive me crazy. "What's the point," I asked my bewildered mother, "of all this talk about sisters and cousins and aunts and cricket, of keeping bedroom drawers tidy and mending underclothes with invisible stitches?"

She tried pathetically to explain that nice girls liked their clothes and drawers to be in apple pie order, to which I replied that clearly I was not a nice girl. She tried again. In her youth she had not only done, she had thought what her mother wanted, because she loved her.

"I love you too," I replied, "but I don't order my thoughts. They come. And I still want to know why mending petticoats is more worth while than practising Bach?"

"Well, music *is* only entertainment, isn't it," she said, more puzzled than ever. I froze. We were a million miles apart. . . .

Not that my own parents disapproved, in principle, of things of the mind—my father even read Tennyson and Browning—but such things did not seem to have any connection with real life. I began to read Browning too and got quite a kick out of the fact that his wife, Elizabeth, and my grandfather were first cousins. It was exciting to have a run-away poetess in the family. But I got no change when trying to coax romantic tit-bits out of my tiny lace-capped Irish grandmother about the time she and grandpapa had spent with the Brownings in Florence. "I was very fond of Baa," she said. "You never could have told she was 'clever.' But Robert *would* stand on the hearthrug and *talk*!"

Soon after my seventeenth birthday my parents sent me to visit an aunt, and while with her, as a preliminary sortie into grown-uphood, I was to stay up to dinner, and play tennis and croquet with some "nice" young men.

On reaching the station the maid went to buy my ticket and I took the chance to skip across to the bookstall. Lying on it was a small green book called *The Riddle of the Universe*. It was by somebody called Ernst Haeckel, price one shilling. *That* was what I wanted! And by good luck I had a shilling. There was just time to buy the book and slip it under my coat before being placed in the "Ladies Only" carriage, where I could read it safe from interruption or inquiry. My poor mother! No bomb could have smashed more effectively the framework on which she had so carefully moulded her daughter's life. Here at last was the truth. There was no God. Beauty was a snare and a delusion, which merely served to conceal that the universe was a soulless mechanism, clanking round and round for ever and ever to no purpose at all. That night I stared at the stars from my bedroom window and could almost hear their rusty gearwheels creaking. Gone was any hope of finding that Central Something, and—my all-wise parents lived in a fool's paradise!

There was no one, of course, to whom I could possibly speak of this appalling discovery, so I hid *The Riddle* among my underclothes, shyly played the prescribed croquet and tennis with equally shy young men, said "Thank you very much" to my aunt and returned home. . . .

However, the young and healthy are very resilient, and whether or not there was any point in the universe, after a few months my little whirlpool gave an occasional gurgle. It was now, my parents decided, time for me to "come out." In other words, my hair would be done up in puffs and rolls, three feathers would be planted in it and I would be taken to bow the knee before my monarch. That this tribal initiation would change me, in the twinkling of an eye, into a grown-up as wise, balanced, decorous and kind as my parents I took for granted, and it was a shock to find that after it I was as unworthy a daughter and as much hell as before. The young men I now met at balls provided a second shock. They would all, I had assumed, be brilliant and witty and would dance like swallows, but, on the contrary, they appeared distressingly earthbound. Most of them stepped, rather painfully, on my toes, and their talk, what there was of it, seemed limited to cricket or killing things.

HUNCH AND HEALING

I cannot tell whether the incidents recorded in this chapter involved any faculty akin to ESP on my part, though the first two in hospital suggest that it may have been exercised by two sick people. That my actions in a number of difficult situations were more intelligent than my ignorant childish conscious self could initiate, I have little doubt. If so, they may illustrate that on such occasions I tapped something superior to that self. . . . The impulses to constructive action which seemed to be out of my class I shall label Orders—for want of a better word—but by this I mean no more than that they were confident and not initiated by my conscious self. Like ESP-type experiences, they emerged unexpectedly out of the blue.

To me the 1914 war came as a thunderbolt out of a clear sky. Hitherto I had taken little notice of politics, assuming that they were matters to be left to clever men. Anyway, my simple schooling had conveyed that the world in which we lived, a world of boring security guaranteed by the perfect and all-powerful British Empire, would last for ever, and it never occurred to my father to mention serious matters to his daughters. . . .

[There was] an appeal in *The Times* for voluntary nurses, as the professionals were too few to cope with rising casualties. I was appalled, for my world went green at the sight of a cut finger, and I was sick at the smell of vomit. My parents were appalled too. "You're far too young, you've led far too sheltered a life!"

The casualty lists grew longer and longer and at last they let me go—without a maid—for an interview with the matron at Barts. "What reason," inquired that starchy potentate, "has a child like you to think she would be any use?"

"None," I quavered, "but you could always kick me out."

On my second day at Barts the sister gave me a lamp to hold for a first dressing after a thigh amputation. Layer after crimson layer was stripped off and at last the spongy mess was laid bare. The patient shrieked, and I found myself in the kitchen with my head between my knees. The Matron had been right. I wished I were dead. Then came the Staff Nurse's voice, blessedly indifferent. "Don't worry, Nurse. People usually do that the first time."

She too was right. That patient's shriek, not curtseying in feathers, had been my initiation into something approaching grown-uphood, for now, for the first time I think, I learnt to look at other human beings, the patients, as themselves and not solely in relation to ME. I fell in love with the lot of them, their courage, their childlike simplicity, their sense of fun. One plump creature, who had lost both legs gave me most gay and helpful instructions when I was promoted to doing his dressings, and when he was convalescent he discovered that he could elicit roars of laughter from his fellow patients by bouncing up and down the ward on his back side.

After three months at Barts I was drafted to Milbank Military Hospital, and was at once put on night duty to care for a Sister who had meningitis. Since most of the time she lay unconscious, I took the chance, crouched in a dimly lit corner, to read *The Brothers Karamazov*. All went well until I reached the argument between the sick man, Ivan, and the Devil, at which point, to my horror, my patient leapt up, pointed a trembling finger at the foot of the bed and addressed the Devil herself. Very startled, I flung down the book and ran over to her, whereupon to my great relief, she fell back unconscious once more. I knew nothing about telepathy but it seemed clear enough that in such situations one's mind should be kept on milder topics than devils, so rather shakily I decided to write a letter to my young sister about a new spring hat. That, fortunately, aroused no response from the sick nurse.

A few weeks later I was set to watch a man who was gravely ill and delirious after a severe operation. He appeared quite unconscious of my presence, and I felt desperate because there seemed no way to reach and comfort him. This desperation may perhaps have enabled a confident inner Order to emerge to consciousness. The Order was *"Think* him quiet." I was much surprised but remembered the sick Sister and tried to obey, and, to my even greater surprise, he at once fell into a quiet sleep. Naturally enough, in view of my raw ignorance, a little later the Staff Nurse moved the screens to see how he was doing, and woke him up. I was able to think him asleep again, but soon afterwards the Ward Sister came rustling in and woke him once more. I tried a third time, but it did not work. Then, suddenly, the tossing and delirium ceased, he looked at me with quiet, rational eyes—he was obviously an educated man—and said calmly, "It's no use concentrating any longer, Nurse. I shall not be going to sleep again." Then the rational man vanished and the agonizing delirium began once more. If this is how death comes, I thought, it is even more terrible than I had imagined. But suddenly his face lit up. "It's Annie!" he cried, gazing in joyous recognition at someone I could not see, "And John! . . . Oh, the Light! . . . The Light! . . ."

Soon afterwards he died. I was impressed by the fact that so soon after he had appeared to be aware of my thoughts he also appeared aware of invisible presences. Could they, I wondered, in some unknown sense be "real"? In the light of *The Riddle* it seemed almost inconceivable; but still I could not be sure that they were only created by his fevered imagination. . . .

In the spring of 1917 Milbank buzzed with rumours that a draft of nurses was to be sent to Macedonia. Olympus! Centaurs! The Argonauts! Socrates! Alexander! Winged feet took me to the Matron's Office and in my excitement I addressed her as if she were merely human. "Oh, Matron, I know I'm not senior enough, but please, *please,* put my name down on the list for Salonica."

To my astounded delight she picked up a pen and did so then and there. I did not tell my horrified parents how my name had got on the list—the first time, apart from hiding *The Riddle,* that I had had the strength of mind to keep any action of mine from them. . . .

For our hospital, the Q.M.G. in Macedonia had chosen a plateau site halfway up Mount Hortiach, thinking that, being high, dry and windswept, it would be more or less mosquito-free. But the mosquitoes thought otherwise and, no one knew why, we soon held the record for malaria of any hospital in the command. Round us the mountains exuded a brooding sadness and past and present seemed to co-exist. Across the bay towered Mount Olympus, and a mile down the valley thin and hungry refugees from Asia Minor threshed their meagre corn with half-starved oxen, just as their ancestors had done in Old Testament days.

Our hospital was a dysentery centre; but an enemy almost as grim as that dreary disease was boredom—the boredom of long weeks of convalescence, made slower by the malaria which blanched the men's blood to water, and unbroken by games, gramophones, books or visitors. Even the food was tasteless, and there was nothing to look at but the barren hills. More than medicine, a nurse had to purvey comfort, to greet each man in the morning and tuck him up at night as if he were the only apple of her eye. One night in the rush of settling in a convoy I forgot a semi-convalescent patient until, at 3 a.m., my lantern caught the flicker of his lonely eyes. "A rigor again?" I whispered.

"No, Sister, but you didn't say good night. How could I go to sleep?"

Sometimes Orders created problems for me. A nice boy was dying of blackwater fever. Five doctors clustered round his bed, and when they left the senior among them said to me, "You can do what you like, Nurse. We can do nothing more."

I felt helpless and desperate, but Orders did not hesitate. "Ask him what he wants more than anything in the world." I knelt down, took his fingers in mine and did so. His answer—I could hardly hear it—was "A red rose, Sister."

"You shall have one tomorrow," I heard myself saying, "I promise."

Had I been mad? What miracle could produce red roses on those arid

hills? But the miracle had been prepared by destiny. The hospital despatch rider had been a patient in my ward and I happened to know the
Quartermaster General. So the despatch rider added to his mail for
G.H.Q. a shameless S.O.S. "Please, somehow, get a red rose *at once*,
or one of my men will die."

In a few hours he rode up the mountain again with a miraculous bunch
of roses which the Q.M.G. had obtained from the garden of a Greek
magnate. They were scented like an English garden and almost as black
as night. When I went on duty the boy was still just alive. I held them
under his nose. "Here are your roses. Smell them."

He half opened his eyes, almost smiled, and—against all reason—he
got well.

But Orders were not always so novelettish. One man was dying
because he would not take nourishment. "It's no good telling me to use
my will," he muttered, "I have no will. I became a drug addict in
Persia. I tell you, I'm going to die."

"Nag him," said Orders. "Nag! Nag! NAG!" This was entirely
contrary to my instinctive approach to a sick man, but I obeyed. At last
he wailed, "Oh, I'll eat anything, anything, if you'll only go away!"

In three week he was eating hospital stew as if he liked it. . . .

In Macedonia I had a stroke of luck. For the first time I met someone
far more knowledgeable and intelligent than myself who was willing to
talk to me about such problems. This was Vivian Usborne, the Senior
Naval Officer—though he was not so senior in years, being the
youngest and, it was said, the gayest Captain in the Navy. He talked a
little of the Society for Psychical Research, but I took for granted that
this was a body far too remote and august for such as I; it was only
twenty-one years later, in 1938, that I found that ordinary people were
allowed to join it. Later still, soon after the Second World War, Vivian
died and I had an experience which I do not know how to interpret. He
appeared to return from his last voyage to tell me that the conclusion he
and I had finally come to, that death was the end, was quite mistaken.
But that incident belongs further on in Chapter XIV.

INTERLUDE

It was raining cats and dogs when, early in 1919, I arrived home in
London. My loving family welcomed me with arms wide open; but to
me—it was quite unjustified—they seemed to be living in a goldfish
bowl, cut off from the real world where men and women could be cruel
and unjust, where love stories did not always end "happy ever after"
and where the sick could die because those caring for them did not care

enough. The gulf between my family and me widened when I discovered that in Macedonia I had not been as invisible as, being the youngest and humblest of V.A.D.s, I had unthinkingly assumed. Exaggerated rumour had reached home about the innocent safety valves by which my two particular friends and I had sought, when off-duty, to forget the sadness of the wards. We had gone riding over the mountains with gay young officers, knowing very well that V.A.D.s were not allowed to ride. We had slipped across the Aegean in a torpedo boat and climbed quite a way up Olympus on the backs of strong-minded mules. And I, with a young archaeologist, had climbed up the dome of Salonica Cathedral and taken photographs while clinging like a monkey to the cross at the top. Though we did not know it, these childish escapades had caused a good deal of amusement in the Command and had earned us the indulgent nickname of The Three Disgraces: but though my parents were sensible people and said very little, I did not feel that such behaviour really accorded with their orderly outlook.

Unfortunately rumour had also linked with mine the name of one of our escorts—and unfortunately rumour was right. Purple mountains and blue seas and orange sunsets, iris and asphodel and oleander, set against a background of war, pestilence and death, could end for the young in one thing only—romance. Early in 1918 I dived into my first love as a dolphin dives into the sea, with, though I had no idea of it, a *hero* I had myself invented, all-wise, all-beautiful and all-entertaining. The young man I cast for this exacting role was a French officer of Scottish descent who was doing liaison work with the British. All would have been well but for the fact that he was an idealist and that his Catholic family had married him off to the daughter of a neighbouring landowner just as the war began. This and my Puritan upbringing drove us to behave with a frustrating virtue which may have led to my first exterior visual hallucination.

In September 1918 Alex was sent on a mission to Paris, and on waking one morning after he had gone I saw him, just for a fleeting moment, standing in bright daylight in the entrance to my tent. A little later the same thing happened in reverse. He wrote to me from Paris that I had come into his room, sat down at his side and taken his hand. As is frequent in such cases, I was in no way startled or even surprised at my hallucination. Nor, which is far more odd, was Alex at his, though he was a shrewd and incisive soldier who would have laughed in theory at the idea of anything so absurd as ESP. Yet he reported my appearance in Paris when he knew I was in Macedonia as a plain statement of fact. "You," he wrote, "were here."

There is no evidence, of course, that I was there. A more plausible explanation is that both his hallucination and mine were self-created. But why did we create them? Was it merely frustration, or was this the only way that our conscious minds could be told of subconscious telepathic interaction between us?

The end of this ordinary little romance is short. Fairly soon Alex and I did the only thing our outsize consciences made possible. We broke apart. (He was killed in the Second World War, but I had no awareness of it.) After the break I was too busy wallowing in my own selfish misery to notice the miseries of other people, but from this bout of egoism I was rescued by the care-free giggles and romps of some very young debs at a dance.

Silly creatures! What did they know about life? And—what on earth was I doing cavorting about in silks and satins when the men I had nursed and loved had come back to unemployment and despair and hunger, instead of the world fit for heroes to live in, to which I had so hopefully drunk with them?

Shame landed me in a London University course for social workers. Its students had to spend half their time gaining practical experience, and to do this I was sent to a branch of the Charity Organization Society in the East End. It was good to meet the men again, but I was appalled at the conditions in which I found them. The C.O.S. personnel were painfully competent and, according to their lights, kind and well-meaning; but my ears went back at their calm assumption that—provided the recipient was moral and deserving—the Almighty had empowered them to dole out as charity (horrible debasement of a beautiful word) the succour which I felt to be everyman's due from his fellows as a matter of course.

As it was, I mutinied because the elderly Committee jibbed at providing irons for the seaman's skinny crippled little daughter, on the ground that her subnormal mother had run away with another man. "Would you have found that a sufficient reason," I asked, "had the crippled legs been yours?"

This was impertinent, but it got the irons; and at the end of the course they offered me a permanent job. I refused it, explaining as politely as I could that all I appeared to have done when working for them was to wangle help for the sick which they should have had by right. . . .

I was still naive enough to get a violent shock at the terrible plight of so many of my fellow countrymen; and yet more naïve in believing that among the thousands of Great Writings by Great Men which I found on the shelves of the College library some would expound how such wrongs could be put right. The library had the effect on me that the smell of fish has on a kitten, and I read voraciously far more than I could digest. "Education," said my coach austerely, "does not consist in gobbling facts but in trying to exercise your judgemnt about them. Try yours on this."

This was J. S. Mill's *Essay on Liberty*. That evening I scurried home from the C.O.S., rolled myself in a rug in my unheated bedroom and exercised my judgment till the sun rose. I ended frozen and in tears. The argument was doubtless as clear as daylight; but, try as I would, there was one place where I could not make it follow. Evidently my father's dictum that women had no judgment had been a just one after all. But when next day I abjectly confessed to failure, my coach replied peacefully, "Of course you couldn't make it follow at that point. It doesn't."

It will be hard for the sophisticated to believe that I was still so naïve that a cosh between the eyes could not have knocked me out more neatly. If a mere girl could detect a flaw in a great man's argument—then, obviously, reason would have to go the same way as religion. Life was no more than a quicksand. *Nothing* could be trusted. However, this shocking discovery gave a fillip to my own little critical faculty, which was usually smothered under respectful hero-worship, and I began to doubt whether the socialist Utopia, so enticingly preached by my coach and the good-looking G. D. H. Cole, was more desirable than the Establishment upheld by my family and the C.O.S. Were the working men I knew, lovable as they might be, much more intelligent or disinterested than my parents? And would they relish being pushed and shoved doing just what the Webbs thought good for them? As for me—this horrifying thought came into focus gradually—was the only way to avoid doing actual harm to do nothing at all until at last I died?

I should not have included this childish episode but for the fact that in the end it too ministered to my ferret-like urge to find out something more about the real nature of human beings. How could anyone help anyone if they didn't know what kind of animal they were trying to help? To begin with, however, my loss of faith in the various efforts to benefit mankind which I had recently seen in action induced a kind of numbed passivity which must have made me worse hell than usual for my long-suffering family to live with. I took for granted that this passive mood would last for life, but one afternoon, about a year after Alex had said good-bye to me, I was shaken into a turmoil by the sudden conviction that he, although invisible, was standing in front of me—just there, quite close! A few days later I heard that he had come over to the French embassy on a two-day job and on that afternoon had been asking mutual friends for news of me. "I'm not dead yet," I thought morosely, and redoubled the killing-off process. This progressed according to plan for another year, and then, when dining out, I met a brisk young British officer, whom I had run into three or four times in Macedonia, and who had been very kind to me. Dysentery and malaria had hit him hard, and on our way home from dinner the friend with whom I was staying remarked casually, "Well, he looked a pretty scarecrow, didn't he!"

I stared at her in astonishment. "You wouldn't talk like that if you knew I was going to marry him," I thought. . . .

The brisk young soldier did marry me [1921], and thereafter until shortly before the Second World War the ordinary wife and mother kept her foot on the head of the inquiring ferret—but only just, and it often snapped and bit.

CLASSIFYING MY EXPERIENCES

My experiences divide roughly into two kinds: a passive awareness, usually fleeting and on the fringe of the mind, of apparent presences or of situations not perceptible via the senses; and an inner prompting to action or comment on behalf of other people, which seems either beyond my normal capacity, or absurd in the light of facts known to me at the time, but turns out to be relevant in the light of other facts learnt later on. As I said earlier, for want of a better word I have called these promptings Orders, though I do not thereby want to suggest that they must come from outside myself. I do not know where they come from, except that it is not my conscious self.

Some of my experiences were unverifiable and could well be labelled fantasy, but others corresponded with the thoughts or feelings of other people, and a very few with events that had not yet taken place. At first it seemed best to record them in chronological order, and thus indicate trends; but when I tried to do so, there were no trends; the experiences varied according to circumstances. Moreover, if listed chronologically they would be no more than a patternless string of anecdotes—and anecdotes by the dozen are an excellent soporific. Yet it is still by the dozen that they are needed in a field-naturalist's search for clues as to process, agency, motivation, encouraging or inhibiting conditions—in fact for anything which might suggest an experimental situation in which ESP might be coaxed to appear to order. It seemed then a better plan to group the experiences into classes. But this also created a difficulty: most experiences fall into two or more. A telepathic signal, for instance, can emerge to consciousness as a waking exterior hallucination, a sensation, an inner voice or image, a dream, a scent, or a simple urge to action. Nor was it always possible to decide whether an impression was telepathic or precognitive, or even whether a simple impulse to action beyond my conscious capacity might not after all be due to no more than subconscious inference or to a bit of information read long before and then forgotten. . . .

MARRIAGE AND ESP

In 1959 my husband engaged a new secretary, a brisk and sensible girl. One morning soon afterwards when busy typing, I felt an urge to run upstairs and speak to him, although I had no reason to do so and wanted to get on with my work. As I walked into his study I heard him say to the secretary, "I told you so."

"Told her what?" I asked.

He laughed, "That you'd come if I called you mentally," he said. I glanced at the girl. Her eyes were round with shock. What sort of employer had she come to—Aleister Crowley?

This little incident was a typical example of the many correspondences between my reactions and his situation, or vice versa, which had long since convinced us that some sort of subconscious extra-sensory linkage existed between us. We should not, of course, expect them to convince an outside investigator, for he could dismiss each one separately as a chance coincidence, or as the result of expectation.

The interest, if any, of the correspondences which I shall give lies, not in their mainly trivial content, but in the possible implication that my husband and I are in subconscious telepathic contact with each other. And if us, then surely others; we are not exceptional people. It may be then that even if signs of it never emerge to consciousness—or at least are never recognized—many other married couples, parents and children, teachers and pupils, and co-enthusiasts or co-workers, are also linked beneath the surface in a similar fashion. . . .

Because it seems possible that the mutual impact of my husband's marked personality and my own, which was very different, may have stimulated our embryonic ESP, I will begin by trying to sketch our early surface reactions to each other as I saw them.

In me marriage soon melted the frozen coma induced by the preceding years of frustration and disillusion, but my grandiose adolescent ideas of service to mankind and the search for the ultimate were now for the time replaced by positively ferocious service to my new and delightfully immediate Godlet. Fortunately for me—and for him—he quite liked being served, and as he had just been sent to the Staff College I also obtained thereby some mental nourishment. To begin with I was allowed to type his essays and to draw maps and plans of battles. On one of my maps his mentor wrote, "Just what Nap would have liked," and my cup was full. Then one glorious day my Godlet threw down before me some enormous tomes on Nap's strategy and said, "Read these and see if I am interested." My cup ran over.

This sort of thing was scarcely my natural diet, but it taught me two very useful lessons. One was that if you did not say exactly what you meant the worst could happen—even to tangling up at a crossroads two divisions on the march. This struck deep, for I pictured the result as much like a skein of wool on which a kitten had been at work. The second lesson was the old Staff College maxim: "There are four courses open to the enemy. He will always take the fifth." In other words, keep a look out for possibilities beyond the obvious ones.

For our first summer vacation we planned to drive down thorugh the apple orchards of Normandy to stay with my Godlet's uncle amid the vineyards of Anjou. . . .

In Anjou that year the weather was abnormally hot, and although the scent from the towering conifers cunningly grouped round the chateau was quite intoxicating, it was soporific as well. With the warmest generosity *la Famille* took me to their hearts—was I not the young bride of *"notre cher cousin"*? But they had come from Paris to relax, and relax they did.

My husband, who had been working all out, naturally sank into this feather bed of family devotion and good living with a sigh of enjoyment. I thought that I too was enjoying myself, but in fact I grew a little bored and perhaps somewhat "liverish." This led to an odd experience, which, though unverifiable and not telepathic, may still be indicative of an ESP-prone temperament.

One hot night my husband was peacefully sleeping while I wriggled, restless and wide awake, at his side in the great carved bed. At last the excessive peace became unbearable. "I can't stand it," I thought, "I shall wake him up to make love to me."

Before I could carry out this egoistic idea I did something very odd—I split in two. One Me in its pink nightie continued to toss self-centredly against the embroidered pillows, but another, clad in a long, very white, hooded garment, was now standing, calm, immobile and impersonally outward-looking, at the foot of the bed. This White Me seemed just as actual as Pink Me and I was equally conscious in both places at the same time. I vividly remember myself as White Me looking down and observing the carved end of the bed in front of me and also thinking what a silly fool Pink Me looked, tossing in that petulant way against the pillows. "You're behaving disgracefully," said White Me to Pink Me with cold contempt. "Don't be so selfish, you know he's dog tired."

Pink Me was a totally self-regarding little animal, entirely composed of "appetites," and she cared not at all whether her unfortunate husband was tired or not. "I shall do what I like," she retorted furiously, "and you can't stop me, you pious white prig!" She was particularly furious because she knew very well that White Me was the stronger and could stop her.

A moment or two later—I felt no transition—White Me was once more imprisoned with Pink Me in one body, and there they have dwelt ever since. It is only quite lately that I have become aware, though I seldom remember it, that I can deliberately identify myself with White Me and watch without feeling them—that is the point—the desires and repulsions that must inevitably toss all Pink Me's around. If Freud ever struck such cases perhaps they helped to lead him towards the concepts of Id and Superego; but they seem to be rare, certainly more so than the experience of simply seeing one's double, as reported, for instance, by Goethe. One point may be of psychological interest. On other occasions when I have been aware of duality in myself, the split seemed to be because a hidden part of me wanted to act on information which the conscious part did not possess. But here the wills of White Me and Pink Me were entirely opposed. I felt as Swedenborg once wrote: "It was strange that I could be of two minds, quite separate at the same time."

One of my adolescent illusions, fostered by Victorian novels and the harmonious lives of my parents, had been that with marriage came total companionship and agreement on every subject. But I had not reckoned with my own questioning, critical, rebellious temperament, so very unlike my mother's, and it did not turn out quite that way. My husband told me recently that it had been a bad shock to him to find that I would not take his word for things. At the same time I over-did the hero-worship, and he was patience itself while I slowly and reluctantly woke up to the fact that no one human being could have all the contradictory attributes, virtues and interests with which I insisted on crediting him. His way of dealing with me was just to go on quietly being himself and doing what did interest him. What emphatically did not was the verbal tennis which was my favourite sport, mainly, I think, because it gave me a flickering illusion of real communication. The result was that for about two years I treated him to a monologue, until one day, to my great surprise, I found I had run dry. An experiment seemed indicated; at luncheon I would not speak till he did. "What's the matter?" he asked comfortably, peeling his apple after a silent meal.

"Nothing. But I've told you everything I've ever felt or done."

"Oh, that's all right," he said kindly, "I like your babble.". . .

Our surface interests, except for music, were different too. He did not share my passion to discover what made my fellow men tick, preferring to use his hands to make more docile machinery tick himself. Work apart, his hobbies were to invent gadgets, to tinker with cars in order to drive them faster than their makers had designed them to go, and to play golf. And yet, safely hidden behind this competent man of action I soon discovered a mystically minded intuitive, who took ESP in his stride and had no apparent wish to pester nature with petty questions merely because she did not always conform to Newtonian science. I well remember when first he told me of a hunch which saved his life. He was working at a forward artillery observation post on a hill top which was being heavily bombarded. Nevertheless, he kept his companion on the job until, suddenly, he 'knew' that the moment had come. "Now!" he cried. "Drop everything and clear out."

They just got away as a shell fell slap on the post. An investigator would have to say, "Chance," but I knew what he meant by "knowing." So the story set me off once more on my usual stream of questions: How? Why? What is time? and so on. To a man of his intuitive-cum-practical temperament it must have seemed the twittering of a sparrow, and a tiresome sparrow at that. How tiresome I only realized forty years later when, as a joke, I told the family of my host's remark that I must have been hell as a child. "Not half as hell as you were as a bride," he broke in with feeling.

So much for background. I will now give a few illustrations of the type of correspondence which led us to suspect telepathic interaction between us. The most elementary correspondences were between my sensations and his—or his thoughts about them, I do not know which. This resembled Mrs. Severn's impression that her lip was cut about the time her husband's lip was gashed by a tiller,[1] and it was first brought to our notice in 1927 by an absurd incident in which my sensations corresponded with his thought. We were living in a romantic but chilly converted barn in a Sussex village, and my husband, having just been appointed Military Attaché in Turkey, was going regularly to London for Turkish lessons. One cold winter's day he said to a casual acquain-

1. *Proceedings of the Society for Psychical Research*, 2, 128.

tance in London that he could not get his feet warm. "Oh, yes, you can," said the man, "Just concentrate on the idea that they are warm and they will become so."

My husband was amused, but he will always try anything once and during the afternoon he concentrated diligently. It was to no avail. His feet remained as cold as ever. Those were the days before the blessed invention of fur-lined boots for women, and my feet used to feel like twin icicles when I took my small boy for walks on the freezing cliffs. But not so that afternooon. For no apparent reason they burnt like furnaces, and it was not until I heard my husband's joke about his abortive effort to warm his own feet that I wondered if he had succeeded with mine instead. (I always wish I knew whether mine really became hot or whether I only thought they did.)

Such correspondences have continued throughout the years, but obviously they can only be striking to other people if they occur when my husband's bodily or mental state changes suddenly and it is possible to check the correspondence in time. This will only happen very occasionally. It last did so in 1960. While getting the breakfast I unexpectedly felt so very ill and depleted that the idea struck me, "Well, I'm growing old, perhaps I'm going to die." Then I thought muzzily, "At least I'd better try and get Frank's breakfast first," and somehow carried on. A few minutes later my husband came down in his dressing gown, flopped on to a chair and confessed, rather shamefacedly, that he had nearly fainted as the result of too long and too hot a bath. He had never done this before. . . .

Now to turn to my husband. He does not appear to reproduce my bodily sensations, but with mental impressions the traffic between us is two-way; the difference being that he seems to respond to my wishes only if they are ardently directed towards him, whereas I may pick up his situation even when I am not at the time in his thoughts. The next two incidents illustrate this difference.

The background to the first is that in 1949 by a stroke of fate due to the war, our main source of income went down the drain, and I was flagging with worry and overwork. We had sold our house at Sunningdale but a friend had kindly lent us a cottage at Sunninghill, and one Friday night my husband went down there for a week-end's golf. I said I would join him on the Saturday afternoon as I had an appointment in the morning, but it fell through and I set off early instead. It was very hot and I felt exhausted and was in consequence unreasonably discouraged when, owing to an exhibition at Olympia, three successive Green Line buses arrived at Victoria unexpectedly full. After waiting in the hot sun for over an hour I took a bus by a circuitous route to Englefield Green, about four miles from the cottage. On getting out of it I thought I was going to faint, and stumbled, full of self pity, to a telephone kiosk by the roadside, hoping against hope that my husband had arranged to play golf in the afternoon and would be free to come and fetch me. When there was no reply to my call, tears of fatigue began to trickle down my cheeks. Like a child I longed for his support and comfort. In fact, if ESP is encouraged by emotional fuel, on this very trivial occasion it was there in plenty.

Then my luck turned. A passing motorist kindly gave the drooping object a lift to the Sunninghill crossroads, five minutes' walk from the cottage, and as I got out of his car my husband drove up from Sunningdale.

"What an extraordinary coincidence," I cried enraptured.

"It's not a coincidence," he said. "We played early and as we were walking in from our game I felt suddenly that you needed me, here, at once. I had just accepted a drink from my opponent, but I cried off, saying that after all I had to meet you."

Two points about this incident may be worth noting: his impression was not in accord with rational inference, for there was not a bus from London at that hour in the morning, and anyway I had said I would come in the afternoon; and he went to the place where I was, rather than to where I had been when I longed for him to fetch me.

In contrast, here is a case where I responded to his annoyance over a minor mishap, although it was not one he had expected me to remedy. For a time during the 1939-45 war he was a Deputy Director at the War Office and he used to come home to Sunningdale to sleep whenever possible. One dark wet November evening my mother and I were sitting quietly together after tea and I broke the silence by saying, *à propos* of nothing, "Frank has no torch. I must take him one to the station."

My mother was not pleased; even in her old age she was full of fears for her children, though never for herself. "He always takes a torch," she protested. "It's absurd to walk all that way in the rain for no reason at all."

I did not want to annoy her; in fact, I found it hard to stand up to her; yet the conviction that my husband needed a torch to get home in the blackout was strong enough to make me brave her continued protests— and the weather—and walk to the station. It was worth it. On getting out of the train he exclaimed spontaneously, "I am glad to see you. My torch gave out as I left the War Office and I wasn't at all looking forward to that long walk in the dark without one."

I do not remember ever having taken such apparently irrational, not to say inconvenient, action when it was not needed.

By the time we were sent to Washington in 1934 my response to his wishes if they were directed towards me had become so commonplace that, since the Embassy staff were not encouraged to make outgoing calls, when he wanted to speak to me he sent me a mental message to telephone him. That, it will be noted, was a valid situation, and all went admirably until he began to talk about how well I responded. This gave me a reputation to keep up, I became self-conscious, and for a short time took to imagining that he wanted me when he did not. But that died down when I ceased to think about it.

The natural reaction to this type of anecdotage is likely to be, "Very well, if you think you have a permanent link with your husband, why not demonstrate it to order?" And the only answer I can give will seem foolishness to those who do not share this kind of experience. First, there seems to be a kind of complementarity between my conscious and my subconscious receiving level, with the result that conscious attention and effort inhibit the emergence of ESP-type impressions. So does anxiety to please, much as anxiety to win at tennis is inclined to make me play badly. Apparently I must feel carefree, and the impression must be unexpected, except on a very few unpremeditated occasions when something inside me has said, "Now! Now's the moment; Try now."

Another impediment to experimentation with my husband is that he would only undertake it dutifully to please me, and I would be aware all the time that he would far rather be doing something else; not a situation, as any experient will agree, which is likely to lead to success. In fact, it seems that for him, as for me, the situation usually needs to be a valid one—we must really *want* to communicate at moments when sensory methods of doing so are not available.

8

Gardner Murphy

(1895–1979)

How is it possible for a giant to stand with one foot in orthodoxy and one in heresy and yet never lose his professional balance? Gardner Murphy was president of the American Psychological Association and of both the American and British psychical research societies. Throughout a long and distinguished career in contemporary psychology he was strongly supportive of parapsychology. How did he manage to achieve respectability in both fields?

The answer may lie in his careful conception of the relation between parapsychology and psychology, as set forth in the following essay. He believed that parapsychology has two aspects, one psychological and one "philosophical." As he cogently argues, motivational, gestalt, and genetic principles apply to the experimental findings of parapsychology. Psychical research has "a primary matrix of psychological assumptions and data which carry us a considerable part of the way towards" an explanation.

By the word "psychology" Gardner Murphy means contemporary psychology in "its most systematic and scientific form . . . in which memory, association, and other more complex processes are conceived to be partially derivative from relatively simple sensory and motor responses." By this narrow definition of psychology, the phenomena of parapsychology lie elsewhere, in another realm entirely. What is the nature of this realm? Murphy rejects mind-body dualism and says only that the realm is "out there," somewhere, as an island. As he explains, the phenomena of parapsychology are nonpsychological because they are "transpatial," "transtemporal," and "transpersonal."

The last part of his essay is devoted to the difficulties of erecting a bridge to the island beyond our present comprehension. Theory building will be slow. No single span can reach so far. He suggests that until theoretical understanding has been achieved, scientific acceptance of the experimental facts of parapsychology by the Establishment may not be forthcoming.

The essay, presented here in an abridged version, will be found in its entirety in the Proceedings of the Society for Psychical Research *in 1953 (50, 26–49).*

THE NONPSYCHOLOGICAL PROCESSES
OF PARAPSYCHOLOGY
(1953)

by GARDNER MURPHY

THE PARADOX OF THE BLIND PROFESSION

I believe that a historical study of the relations between psychology and psychical research[1] will reveal a strange paradox. On the one hand, professional psychologists are in general disinclined to touch the problems of psychical research. In so far as we can tell from questionnaire inquiries, from their subscriptions to journals, and from their degree of familiarity with research, it would appear that most psychologists belong in one or the other of two main groups. First, there are those who find in psychical research a serious metaphysical and professional threat. The potential mind-body dualism which appears to them to be inherent in most psychical phenomena strikes them as scientifically beneath their dignity, and this means that they "know in advance" that the data cannot exist. The second group are those who remain agnostic regarding the phenomena, attempt no general dogmatism, but are disinclined to give their effort to anything as bizarre, as far off the main track of science, and as likely to betray them as belonging to the "lunatic fringe" of the intellectual world. I quote here from memory an excellent summary of a personal position by B. F. Skinner, an exceptionally able and clear-headed leader of one wing of experimental psychology: "Of course there might be something there, but I don't care to gamble on anything as far from the realm of science in which I feel competent, anything that seems to me a priori so unlikely to yield a constructive scientific result, as long as there are so many interesting and important problems with which I can cope in my laboratory."

There is of course a third small group who believe that psychical research is important, and a fair number who believe that many significant facts are well authenticated. Without attempting to indicate any

---

1. *Parapsychology* I would regard as the scientific study of the mind-body (i.e., consciousness-brain) problem. Gardner Murphy would presumably not have phrased it that way (See below). *Psychical research* is an older name for parapsychology.—Ed.

certainty as to the number, I would call attention to the fact the Lucien Warner found by a questionnaire addressed to the Members of the American Psychological Association a dozen years ago that very few of this group accepted extrasensory perception as a fact. He has just conducted a follow-up study, finding that the proportion has not greatly changed [1952]. This small group tends for the most part to be familar with and to give credence to experimental findings primarily, and to lean rather heavily upon the work of the Duke University laboratory. The number of professional psychological subscribers to the *Journal of Parapsychology* at the time when I was one of its editors was fourteen [1939-1941]; a nation-wide advertisement directed to American psychologists to try to induce a few more to subscribe produced not one single additional subscription.

Within the group who have a positive orientation there are certainly not more than a few dozen in the world who might be called broadly familiar with the history and range of the phenomena of psychical research.[2]

The other face of the paradox lies in the fact that almost every problem, in fact I would venture to say *every* problem, in psychical research involves a straightforward problem in psychology. Indeed it has been so recognized from the very beginning. Human interests, motives and habits must be considered in relation to every phenomenon of telepathic interchange, or of apparent communication. The processes of memory and thought are typically studied not only to see in what way the paranormal event transcends what could be comprised within the ordinary psychology of the individual, but one tries to see *how* these processes operate when the paranormal is present. Nowadays the personality as a whole, so far as it is known, is regularly brought into relation to the fact that psychical phenomena occur with some persons and not with others, or depend upon interpersonal relations involving intimacy, affection or other dynamic interchanges. Moreover, the comprehensive theories of psychical phenomena, such as those of Myers among the pioneers, or of Tyrrell (8) or Carington among the moderns, are psychological theories worked out in terms of conceptions of conscious and subconscious, and conceptions of dissociation, learning, memory, emotion, will; and in the case of Carington, the whole classical association theory (1).

We then have psychical research constituting a psychological discipline, in which as a matter of fact we find over the years that new psychological discoveries, whether from experimental psychology, from

---

2. Still true in 1981.—Ed.

psychoanalysis, or from projective testing are regularly brought in as technical adjuncts to the tasks which psychical research pursues. . . .

THE METAPHYSICS OF A DISTINCTION

What do we mean by the word "psychology"? I believe we should use the term strictly, and refer to psychology in its most systematic and scientific form, including that unified modern psychology which studies contact with the world of physical stimulation through the sense organs, a psychology in which memory, association, and other more complex processes are conceived to be partially derivative from relatively simple sensory and motor responses. The whole realm of genetic, comparative and physiological psychology gives us a rich and unified scientific system in which psychological phenomena are brought into intimate relation with the physiological and physical events in the life of the organism. Psychoanalysis, for example, is rapidly merging into this psychology at many points, e.g., through the physiology of instinct and the learning process and through psychosomatic medicine. Psychologists need not of course espouse a metaphysical monism or any kind of ultimate theory as to mind-body relations; but in actual practice they regard psychological events as at least in part the derivatives of biological, and ultimately of physical, events. The psychologist who uses his psychology in coping with the data of psychical research is grateful for the whole rich field of experimental, clinical, child, and comparative psychology, and as a matter of fact would regard himself as derelict in his duty if he did not utilize every possible clue from the physiological and physical sciences.

When we say, therefore, that psychical research comprises events which are more than psychological, we mean that this comprehensive and systematic psychology, including and utilizing much from the physical and biological sciences, cannot at present offer any coherent attempt at an explanation. When, for example, an act of will is reported as altering the movement of a falling die or determining the region upon which the die comes to rest, the assumption is that something more than psychology is at work. This is a *vis a tergo*, something which, while deriving from the psychological world, moves from it into the realm of the physical and causes a physical effect. Yet as soon as we are certain that there is more here than psychology, we use psychology to the limit to explain the form of the results! Efforts, for example, have been made, notably by J. B. Rhine, to show that psychological laws are evident in psychokinesis; laws, for example, in relation to motivation, to interest, to boredom or negativism, to freedom from psychological interference. The "decline curves,'' whether they appear in a day's work, a record sheet, in a half sheet or even in a single run, relate to the psychological structure rather than the physical structure of the task. We have then a consistent view that psychology must be given all the work to do which it can possibly bear. Yet psychology will not ordinarily be regarded as sufficient for the whole job, because the psychology which we know today is one which does not know how to cope with the interrelations of the organism and environment except in physical terms. In the same breath, therefore, it is necessary for the student of psychokinesis to prove two things: first, that the phenomena are psychological and second that there is also a process at work which is not psychological.[3]

There are probably many who believe that we have manœuvred ourselves into a difficulty by assuming a false conception of psychology. Instead of the psychology of today, anchored on physiological, evolutionary and psychopathological evidence, they may favour an essentially dualistic (Cartesian) conception of mind and body, or one of the more or less dualistic systems which C. D. Broad would include under "substantive vitalism." *I must indicate my reason for rejecting all such dualism* [emphasis added]; for I think that if we are really to use psychology it must be the kind of psychology which the last hundred years—since evolutionary theory, experimental psychology and psychoanalysis—have given us. The older view of course *may* by sound; but to say that this kind of dualistic system represents a usable psychology, and to court all over again the enormous difficulties involved in having a nonbiological control-system operate constantly to produce the physical and even the biochemical processes of individual behaviour, is apparently to add to, rather than substract from, the metaphysical difficulties. For example, if we have some sort of nonphysical control of the organism, such as some of the vitalists have assumed, then we must put these principles to work in the control of growth, repair, reproduction and other life processes, so well differentiated from non-life processes. Then, however, we must introduce a *separate* set of nonphysical concepts to explain paranormal activity. We thus need a *double* dualism, one invented ad hoc to explain life itself, another invented ad hoc to explain the paranormal. (To say, as some have done, that there is paranormal activity in *every* normal process seems to me simply to create hydra-like difficulties in order to escape the relatively few and clear difficulties which are based on our present ignorance).

---

3. *Psychokinesis* (PK): An influence exerted by a brain on an external physical process, condition, or object by some means other than known physical energy.—Ed.

I believe, then, that we can adequately summarize the situation by saying that in psychical research we have a primary matrix of psychological assumptions and data which carry us a considerable part of the way towards the explanation of all the authenticated phenomena, from apparitions and hauntings to telepathic and precognitive transactions, and the physical phenomena as well. But we need a good firm bridge to the paranormal, which lives on an island at some distance from the *here and now* where we pass most of our lives. It is an open question at least whether the bridge which will ultimately connect psychology with psychical research will prove to be the same one which today begins to connect descriptive psychology, the psychology of our own immediate experience, with the psychology of the organic biological system. Let us not prejudge this issue.

Psychological Concepts in Parapsychology

From the present viewpoint, therefore, psychical research might be regarded as a combination of two huge enterprises, the first being psychological, the second essentially philosophical, in the sense that it seeks by all the methods known to man to find a way of bridging a gap in nature for which we have at present no adequate conceptual approach. My own chief task in this chapter is the psychological rather than the philosophical. It may be wise to map out three typical ways in which contemporary psychology might offer clues to the phenomena of psychical research.

1. In accordance with the whole dynamic emphasis of the psychology of recent decades, under the influence of the evolutionary theory, the cultural approach and psychoanalysis, we may first stress the problems of *motivation*. We are impressed with the fact that in the great majority of spontaneous cases of telepathy, a preoccupation of the percipient with the activities of the agent is obvious in the record. In some cases the percipient consciously seeks to make contact. . . . In other instances, which are probably more common, he does not consciously orient himself towards the agent; but since he is a person devoted to and preoccupied with the agent, it does not seem to be too far-fetched to assume that he is chronically and unconsciously sensitized to the agent's doings.

In a third group of instances, the agent seems to be impressing himself upon the percipient rather than the percipient's striving to receive from the agent. This difference in relative activity is certainly important, but there is good reason to believe today (as Mrs Sidgwick maintained) that agent and percipient are connected by a deep channel of reciprocal influences, such that the conception of formal movement from one to another is a less effective way of defining the situation than is the conception of interchange. . . .

[Motives] probably segregate themselves according to psychological level; and it is quite likely that the motives which are important under laboratory conditions are quite different from those which are important in spontaneous cases, with the result that relatively superficial layers of personality are involved in the former, deeper layers of the personality in the latter.

Everything that we know about the psychology of motivation ought to be useful in relation to the study of motives which figure in paranormal occurrences. There has long been emphasis upon *unconscious* motivation as predisposing the percipient to one or another type of experience, which then may undergo some form of disguise or elaboration before reaching the conscious level. Freud himself pointed out thirty years ago the possibility that telepathic phenomena encountered in psychoanalytic practice are of this sort. . . .

Again, the phenomena of *conflict* between motives are full of significance for psychical research. There is a good deal of evidence, for example, in systematic displacement effects and in consistent missing effects, that there are unconscious motives which interfere with paranormal contact with a specific target; and it becomes not altogether implausible to suggest that one set of motives is struggling to guide the cognitive responses in the direction of the target while another set is striving to draw them away. In the case of consistent below-chance scoring it is reasonable to follow Rhine in believing that both such factors are chronically at work. A person cannot consistently miss unless in a certain sense he is oriented to the target and unless at the same time he is oriented to miss the target. To make sense out of consistent subchance scoring, what is really needed from the psychological point of view is the conception of motives and of motive conflict. Without these conceptions it is hard to see what could be done. . . .

2. Our second psychological clue is the principle of *organization*. Ever since J. B. Rhine showed the systematic form of decline curves in ESP (6), and later in PK, there has been much to suggest the rather characteristic picture of a relatively high scoring level at the *beginning* of a task. A particularly pretty piece of evidence in the matter of organization is one appearing in a study by J. B. Rhine, dealing with "segment salience" and "run salience." This is a study of precognition, in which, in a general way, the scores are furthest from chance at the beginning and end of runs; to this fact the term "run salience" is applied. When, however, picture cards are inserted after each five ESP cards which have

to be called in the routine task, these picture cards being different and interesting and breaking up the otherwise rather monotonous sequence, the effect is to increase deviation from chance just before and just after the interpolated card. The result is to break up the run of 25 into 5 subruns of 5 each, in which we find that the first and the last items in each run of five tend to be furthest from chance expectation. This gives, when visualized, a sort of long loop (run salience) with a series of little scallops (segment salience), both run salience and segment salience being present in the same experiment and often in the same subject.

It is of course conceivable that all of these decline and salience effects are due to wandering interest or at least to the disappearance of that first fine flush of enthusiasm and naive simplicity of orientation which may often characterize "beginner's luck"; so that even these effects would be due to motivation. It is entirely possible also that the U-curves (success at beginning and end) are due to the recovery of interest towards the end of task, as in the case of the "end spurt" found in curves of work. There is at least, however, a large likelihood that we are dealing here with the relative ease of seeing that which comes first and that which comes last in a presentation. Under conditions of brief exposure in the tachistoscope, we expect people as a matter of course to see the first and last letters of a word somewhat better than they see the middle. The same is of course true of temporal exposures. It is the first and last items, whether in brief or long series, that are best registered. There is a host of material from memory experiments indicating these laws of position, and at least some suggestive evidence that they are related to certain formal attributes of the nervous system or of the very process of perception itself. . . .

3. When we come to [our third major principle, that of] *individual sensitivity,* we must distinguish between the problem of constitutional (hereditary) predisposition and the broader question of the *present* personality make-up in respect to sensitivity, regardless of whether this be considered to be "constitutional," "acquired," or both. . . .

There is a considerable number of cases of spontaneous experiences running in certain family lines; even a few cases where the sharing of a specific paranormal experience suggests an actual biological similarity in sensitivity among the percipients. There are a few cases of sensitives whose parents, children or other relatives have shown similar sensitiveness. Certainly the most striking is that of Mrs. and Miss Verrall, whose paranormal abilities, expressed through automatic writing, were studied over many years.

There have been some interesting—indeed some rather quaint—theories about racial and national differences in psychic predisposition, as for example the suggestion that the reason why the Poles, among all the Catholic nationality groups of Europe, are the richest in mediumship, stems from the fact that Poland was the only country essentially untouched by the Inquisition and therefore the only one in which there was no rooting-out of sensitives. I believe that anyone at all familiar with the complexities of the problem of heredity and the problem of family and national characteristics will do nothing in response to any such argument but maintain a generous yet nevertheless very firm scepticism.

In the absence of anything like direct evidence, I believe that the biologically oriented psychologist would say that the theoretical likelihood of an inheritance factor in *family* lines large enough to produce real similarities in paranormal sensitivity is very good, and that we are all ready for experimental and statistical investigation of the problem, comparing the relative success of persons of various degrees of blood kinship when tested by comparable methods. One might, for example, use a technique like the one recently used by Eysenck (3) to demonstrate the inheritance of neuroticism among certain London children—comparing identical twins with fraternal twins of the same sex.

In fact, we know of no psychological attributes which do not reveal *any* constitutional aspects whatever. Sometimes they are not large enough to be measured in a way that yields results which are socially important. In some cases the results obtained from measurement *are* of great social importance. This has sometimes led to the naive idea that some traits are inherited and others acquired. All the evidence of modern genetics is that every characteristic of the living organism, whether plant or animal (and that this holds true with a vengeance in the case of a creature as complex as man) is the unfolding of constitutional predispositions under the specific influence of a lifetime of physical and social forces, so that the intact organism is not a mosaic of hereditary and environmental fragments, but a unitary whole in which nevertheless a certain slant or loading has been given by congenital predispositions. . . .

THE TRANSPHYSICAL ASPECTS OF ESP

I have attempted to indicate that we make contact through the sensory processes and through the extrasensory processes in essentially the same way; that as far as psychology is concerned the basic dynamics are the same in the two areas. Everything which helps us, for example, to perceive clearly at the level of normal perception helps us to perceive clearly at the level of extrasensory perception; examples are strong motivation, favoured position in the organization of a task, and a dissociative tendency. To state the problem in the broadest possible way, the question is whether there is *any* process whatever in the psychology of the living individual which operates in the case of paranormal activities which is not also operative constantly as a necessary aspect of normal everyday psychology. This question suggests another: Do paranormal phenomena occur only when in addition to our ordinary normal psychology there are realized certain special conditions of an unknown sort which bring about contact between the individual and the environment?

On another occasion (4) I argued that there were at least three respects in which paranormal processes differed from normal ones. I urged that they were transpatial, transtemporal and transpersonal. . . .

We tend to believe that distance between target and subject is unimportant in paranormal processes; but this is of only secondary importance if we know, as we do, with some degree of certainty that we are not dealing with any of the types of physical energy with which contemporary physics is concerned. Of course what the physics *of the future* may reveal none of us should be foolish enough to try to predict; this is perhaps one of the reasons for being a little hesitant about insisting so strongly today that we know we are dealing with psychic or spiritual factors rather than physical ones.

All sorts of possibilities occur here. It may turn out that what we call physical factors are indistinguishable from what we call spiritual factors; it may turn out that the physical factors are special classes of psychical or spiritual factors; it may turn out that there are many different classes of phenomena intermediate between what we call the physical and the spiritual. Metaphysical theories have become richer rather than poorer as a result of the extraordinary *volte-faces* of physics in the last fifty years. We are safe, however, in emphasizing that the present problem is the *reality of a transpatial relationship between agent and target* in so far as the *physics of today* is concerned.

The second point, about transtemporal relationships, may also need a little clarification. We may regard the functions of the living organism, with its typical processes of growth, decline and dissolution, as following a four-dimensional time line similar to the four-dimensional time lines of other events known to physics. We have, however, in the case of paranormal phenomena, contacts with events which belong unmistakably at a point on the time line not capable of being perceived under normal conditions. Several ingenious theories, such as those of Saltmarsh, have suggested that this is due to the fact that instead of dealing with a zero duration of time we ought to think of a "specious present" or "blurred now"; something like the conception of indeterminacy which would make clear that an event is not really an event of zero duration but is a definite time-consuming process. While it is true that most of the experiments in precognition have dealt with very short time intervals, there are a number of spontaneous cases which seem to involve intervals of hours, days, or weeks; and if the specious present has to be stretched to comprise more than the ordinary moment which we experience subjectively as now, it is hard to see how it is very useful anyhow. . . .[4]

In the matter of transpersonal communication, I did not [in 1949] at the time of my address to the S.P.R. (4) mean much more than had been suggested in the twenties by Mrs Sidgwick (7) in her idea of two-way flow between persons in paranormal contact. I think I am willing to go a short step further than that at this time. I feel myself moving in the direction of belief that the phases of individuality which interact in such cases are phases comprising more than the personal or I-centered consciousness with which we are ordinarily concerned. Whether they correspond well to Myers's subliminal, I do not know (5); and whether light is thrown upon them by the Indian conception of the Atman I likewise do not know. I am prepared, however, to say that I believe the transpersonal aspect of these events is as important as the transphysical and transtemporal, and that I believe that a great deal of blindness in psychical research has resulted from the tradition of the Western world—earlier so largely Platonic and in recent centuries so largely individualistic—which has tried to make a sharp clear jewel out of the individual personality utterly separable from its environment. I believe, as a matter of fact, that a large part of the motivation which has maintained our system of religion and ethics, and a large part of the motivation which has supported psychical research, has been related to the conception of the unlimited value of unique sharply defined self-sufficient individuality, which is so precious in itself that we can hardly bear to think of its undergoing radical change even in life, and dissolution of which in death appears to us to cast a blemish upon the fair name of the universe as a whole.

THE NATURE OF FUTURE THEORIES

Whether the transpatial, the transtemporal, and the transpersonal are aspects of the same thing I do not know. . . . If this be the case, it would be likely that the same basic discovery which would reveal the manner in which we may transcend one of these three kinds of limitation would likewise lead to the discovery of the means of freeing ourselves of the

---

4. *Precognition*: The gaining by a brain of information that will be created by random external future events.—Ed.

other two. The more attractive, naturally, are the "dimensional" theories beginning perhaps with Ouspensky or Dunne, and continuing through Smythies and the commentators upon his theory. What we are all impelled to do is to find one basic scientific operation which will carry us all the way over the gulf; that is, which will carry us from normal psychology to the full-fledged expression of the paranormal.

Now it may be worthwhile to recall that scientific discoveries in general are not of this type. For the most part, the bridging of straits and bays is done with multiple span bridges, not with one-span bridges. The transition from pre-Darwinian to Darwinian evolution, which looked at one time as if it could be made in a single step, has turned out to involve a fantastically complicated set of intermediate concepts relating to the nature of the gene, the fundamental unit of heredity, relating also to the nature of growth and adaptation, together with the recognition that many of the basic principles emphasized by Darwin were unsound. . . .

I might express my scepticism about the "one step" efforts to span the gulf by asking a very simple question, which is parallel to the one we are asking in psychical research: How likely is it that somebody during the twentieth century will discover one clear principle which brings into orderly relationship the world of subjective experience and the world of physiological activity? No psychologist at all familiar with the complexities of the problem and of the history of the attempts at their solution is likely to believe that the answer can be "dreamed up" by some brilliant genius. It has taken dozens of years since the beginnings of experimental psychology and since the beginnings of modern quantitative experimental biology to give us the rudimentary fragments which we now possess as to the intimate relations between specific psychic structures— perceptions, memories, and so on—and specific organic processes. Is it likely that we shall soon see with a tremendous flash of insight the whole complex towering unitary reality? . . .

The very fact that we recognize the length of the road to be traversed may be a reason for reminding ourselves that research is a very fundamental part of our undertaking and is not to be crowded out by our speculative systematic efforts at unified theory, no matter how brilliant. There is certainly a place in every science for a certain quota of pure speculation. This is a healthy thing. In psychical research Myers's theories, for example, though today frequently appearing to be emotionally coloured and at times fanciful, nevertheless had healthy effect in the clarification of issues, in sensitizing readers to the reality of certain phenomena and in suggesting the necessity of certain types of investigation. The Carington hypothesis (1) is an example of one in recent years which seems to me to have been very fruitful.

I would stress, however, one aspect of the Carington approach which is not shared by most of the speculative systems. Carington's theory was so formulated that it was possible to gather empirical data to test its various aspects. . . . In all science a theory which is not capable of being tested is likely to have very limited utility in comparison with theories which prompt definite empirical tests. It is of some interest that some, though not all, of the dimensional theories of the paranormal (cf. Dunne) do suggest not only new ways of looking at accumulated material, but new types of experiments which might be carried out. I urgently hope that some at least of my readers may be willing to forgo the hope that before long a brilliant theoretical solution of the relations of the normal to the paranormal will be achieved, for the sake of the more modest and pedestrian aim of securely establishing an adequate theory by means of a series of logical steps, each of which can be satisfactorily tested, modifying the later steps as one goes along in the light of the data from the earlier steps.

From such a point of view we could then hope that we could use all the psychology, physiology and physics that we know, and all that we ever shall know, to help in establishing a firm base from which to throw our bridge across the chasm. We shall need for this purpose a wide familiarity with modern science, both physical, physiological and psychological, in so far as it may provide research tools or working concepts to suggest the nature of the chasm and what lies on the other side; and at the same time a free and bold philosophical spirit which will constantly ask how our whole present approach may be biased by the intrinsic cultural loading of outlook from which we all suffer.

J. B. Conant (2) has pointed out in a recent volume that *established ways of thinking in science are never overthrown by the establishment of clear facts which obviously refute them.* Such established theories are overthrown only when the newly established facts are organized into a new system which is so plausible, so coherent and so convincing that it washes away the foundations of the older system. Psychical researchers are likely to complain that their facts are ignored by other scientists. If Conant is right, there is nothing surprising or unusual about such rejection. Perhaps after one or two of the units in a pontoon bridge have been put down and we have the beginnings of an empirically tested theory, we shall be able to convince our colleagues that we know where we are going, and they may be willing to look at our facts. Perhaps, however, we shall have to get the pontoon bridge carried all the way to the other side before a coherent system is established to replace the current system, so congenial to our everyday modes of thinking. Perhaps we can use a little psychology on ourselves, in helping ourselves to understand the degree to which we and our colleagues are bound by preconceived conceptions of the world; perhaps we can use a little psychology on our colleagues in finding ways to administer small doses of factual material to them which may make them gulp with wide-opened eyes and a slight expression of startle without repudiating the dish altogether. . . .

REFERENCES

1. Carington, W. *Telepathy*. Methuen, 1945.
2. Conant, J. B. *On understanding science*. 1950.
3. Eysenck, H. *The Journal of Clinical Psychology,* 1952, *8. The scientific study of personality*. Routledge and Kegan Paul, 1952.
4. Murphy, G. Psychical research and personality. (Presidential address) *Proceedings of the Society for Psychical Research,* 1949, *49*, 1–15.
5. Myers, F. W. H. *Human personality*. (2 vols.), 1903.
6. Rhine, J. B. *Extrasensory perception*. 1934.
7. Sidgwick, E. M. Phantasms of the living: An examination of cases reported since 1886. *Proceedings of the Society for Psychical Research*, 1922, *33*, 23–429.
8. Tyrrell, G. N. M. *Science and psychical phenomena*. Methuen, 1938. *The personality of man*. Pelican Books, 1946.

9

Louisa E. Rhine

(1891–   )

The unconscious nature of psi[1] phenomena is their singly most important characteristic. With rare exceptions, those who experience these phenomena have no direct subjective indication of their ocurrence. The central nervous system concommitants of the psi process, whatever they may be, do not directly enter awareness, although they may indirectly do so via various psychological mechanisms.

*Those of us who know Dr. Louisa Rhine think of her first, not as the wife of J. B. Rhine and the mother of their children, but as a leading parapsychologist by her own accomplishments. In these excerpts from a longer paper covering other topics (*Journal of Parapsychology, 35, 34–56*), she discusses the unconscious nature of psi phenomena in spontaneous cases and in the laboratory and gives us a look at some of the clues that must be accommodated in future theory.*

---

1. Psi *is a general term for the phenomena of parapsychology, i.e.,* extrasensory perception and psychokinesis.

THE UNCONSCIOUS NATURE
OF ESP AND PSYCHOKINESIS
(1971)

by Louisa E. Rhine

It can scarcely be said at what specific date the recognition of the psi process as an unconscious one occurred. It probably was assumed as soon as telepathy and clairvoyance were recognized as mental processes. But it began to be mentioned when the tendency was noticed for hits to be grouped rather than scattered at random over the record pages, thereby creating position effects. For instance, in 1941, in the first paper on position effects (2), the author said that "the unpredictable nature of ESP . . . due, perhaps, to the lack in the subject of any consciousness of its functioning . . . has so generally been observed that any slightest departure from it . . . is properly regarded as a phenomenon in itself." The paper then presented evidence of a "pattern tendency" of hitting in which the beginning and end of runs of ESP tests showed more hits than the middle calls, resulting in what was called terminal salience.

When, by 1950, the fact was emphasized that the difficulty experimenters faced in their tests arose largely because unconscious processes were involved, specific projects to study them were undertaken. The study of spontaneous cases of psi to see what light they could shed was one of them, and the more detailed study of negative deviations, or target avoidance, was another.

THE FORMS OF SPONTANEOUS PSI EXPERIENCE

The study of a large collection of cases that seemed to involve psi had been initiated at the Parapsychology Laboratory of Duke University in 1948. The general objective of the study was to get suggestions about the way psi operates that could be tested for validity in the laboratory. Since in experimental testing the need to by-pass the unconscious nature of the psi process was recognized, one of the first objectives of the study was to find a viewpoint which would bear on the problem. One kind of case of frequent occurrence that seemed to do so was the "conviction case" (6), the kind in which the person not only "knew" a correct item of information with no sensory reason for doing so, but was also convinced it was true, and took action accordingly even though without logical reason.

It seemed that conviction cases were instances in which the ESP message somehow had been made conscious. Consequently they were examined to see if the persons betrayed any method by which the transfer into consciousness had been accomplished. However, no such indication could be found. The persons simply believed without any reason. It was noticed incidentally, however, that instances of conviction were more likely to be expressed in experiences that occurred when the person was awake than when he was dreaming. This observation led to a study of the forms that psi experiences take in consciousness.

Before 1950 emphasis in psi research had been on establishing and distinguishing the types of ESP as classified in terms of kind of target material involved. No particular attention had been paid to the manner in which psi was expressed. But now the cases in the collection at the Laboratory were grouped according to the form they took in consciousness, regardless of the type of target involved.

About one thousand cases were used in this study, a report of which was published in 1953 (7). The cases fell into four reasonably distinct groups. Two of them occurred when the person was awake, and they were in the form either of hallucinations or of intuitions. When the person was asleep, his dreams were either realistic or unrealistic in form. In addition, a few cases involved inexplicable physical effects that coincided meaningfully with the emotional crisis of a human being. These were classed as presumptive instances of spontaneous psychokinesis (PK) and, accordingly, as a fifth form of spontaneous psi manifestation.

Each of the four ESP forms included instances in which the person had secured a complete idea (for instance, "John is dead."); but they also included many in which the information was incomplete "Someone dear to me is dead." "Something has happened to John."). Or the idea might even be nonexistent, with only a strong emotion or compulsive action to mark the occurrence. These various kinds and degrees of incompleteness were especially numerous in the waking experiences of the intuitive form.

The recognition of the forms that psi may take emphasized the fact that practically all experimental work has involved the intuitive form, since it is the most likely to be called forth by laboratory procedures. The study also emphasized the fact that ESP has no specific consciously recognized form of its own. It uses those that are common in mental life:

intuitions, dreams, hallucinations. This in turn explains why ESP is difficult to recognize. In experiments the presence of ESP must be shown by statistical evaluations; and in spontaneous cases it can only be recognized, and that only tentatively, by the peculiar or unusual nature of the information so secured.

The recognition of these forms of psi permitted new glimpses into the probably nature of the psi process (8,9). Of course, the process must begin with the accessibility of the specific item of information. This occurs unconsciously and in some manner that is the principal unknown of the psi process. Tyrrell called this part of the process Stage I, and the rest, Stage II (12). Stage II is the stage in which the information is manifested. This is accomplished in ESP by the ordinary psychological processes . . . and in PK by unexplainable physical effects (10). . . .

TARGET AVOIDANCE

Almost from the beginning of ESP testing, the phenomenon of target avoidance was noted. Even Estabrooks in 1927 reported a series of tests with a negative score deviation. For many years negative deviations were recognized mainly as a nuisance that often thwarted the experimenter and prevented a successful outcome to an experiment.

It was soon noticed that negative deviations tended to occur when for some reason the subjective conditions were less than optimum, and also that they tended to occur in the middle rather than the beginning and ending of runs or series, thus creating the salience ratios already referred to. By 1941 the salience ratio was recognized as a method of evaluation (2). In 1950, according to J. B. Rhine's "Mid-Century Inventory" (3), target avoidance was recognized as one of the concomitants of the unconscious operation of the psi process; and in 1952 the thinking about it was crystallized in a *Journal* article (4). A summary in that article of the various instances of significant negative deviations over the history of experimental psi tests provided the basis for an analysis of the possible kinds of psychological explanation of the effect. The general deduction was that all of them were at least partly the outcome of the fact that the process is unconscious—that unconsciousness is at least a common contributing condition.

The earliest tentative explanation for target avoidance was that it represented unconscious negativism on the part of the subject, that even though consciously the subject might be trying to hit the targets, he unconsciously wanted to miss them. Some of the instances in which negative deviations were obtained seemed explainable in this way; for example, Schmeidler's finding that disbelievers in ESP tend to score negatively. But not all of the evidence fitted this explanation; for instance, cases in which a subject regularly scored positively in the first half of the runs of a series and negatively in the last half, or positively at the ends and negatively in the middle. This effect was particularly noticeable if the runs were relatively long. It did not seem, though, that the subject's motivation would change in each part of a run in that way. Therefore another explanation seemed called for.

The fact that target avoidance seemed to occur when circumstances were less than optimum suggested that under strain or other disturbance the subject might make some change in the way of proceeding that produced hits, as if the "orientation" necessary for hitting was very unstable and easily destroyed by even slightly unfavorable influences. . . .

On the matter of devising a practical method by which experimenters could by-pass the cancellation effect which resulted when systematic hitting and missing tended to occur in the same experiment, a suggestion came from the fact that when a test was designed to compare two situations in a single experiment, the subjects often scored positively on one part and negatively on the other. It was as if the matter of contrast or comparison itself led to the opposite *directions* of scoring. This suggested that experimenters might plan their tests to include such contrasts (two-aspect tests) and so to "drain off" the avoidance effect into one part of the experiment and then [apply a statistical null test to the difference between the two parts] (5). . . .

The study of spontaneous cases had revealed little about the target avoidance problem, for if a case were "avoided", no evidence would exist to show a sign of it. Yet, in the intuitive cases, the form most analogous to that of experimental tests, there was a strong tendency for the complete information to fail to reach consciousness. In the incomplete cases a greater or smaller degree of blocking at the threshold was very often indicated. This blocking effect may be a condition that leads to target avoidance in experimental tests, for in them the subject continues to respond and thus the [systematic] errors pile up until they become statistically significant.

Still another method of evaluation had been introduced, the variance method, by which the presence of psi could sometimes be noted in data that, without it, appeared to be meaningless (1,11). . . . This test showed whether scores varied in distribution around the mean more than they should by chance or less than they should by chance. . . .

[Target avoidance is evidently the result of cognitive error based on the subjective conditions of the test. It is these that cause psi scores to fluctuate.] "In a word, *it is psi that is stable*, and psychological factors that are the source of uncertainty." (5, p. 29) Target avoidance has implications for a much wider area than parapsychology alone. As the author [J. B. Rhine] said in that same article (p. 34), "Similar unconscious cognitive error might occur over the entire range of subliminal functions of life . . . and especially if the individual is forced into reaction by his environment. I am much inclined to think we are dealing with a *general unconscious tendency to judgmental error*. . . .

The difficulty of psi research can now be seen to be caused mainly by the unconsciousness of the phenomenon and the consequent difficulty of controlling it. In fact, control in the strict sense may well be impossible. As J. B. Rhine said in his "Mid-Century Inventory" (3, p. 242): "It may be that the very nonphysical nature of psi phenomena . . . forever bars it from *conscious* control. Consciousness itself . . . *may* be limited to sensory interaction with physical stimuli, and the derivatives of sensation (such as memory and imagination). Extrasensory perception may, by the very nature of the case, not lie within the range of conscious experience, even while its cognitive content may be at least partially convertible to awareness."

REFERENCES

1. Carpenter, J. C. Scoring effects within the run. *Journal of Parapsychology*, 1966, *30*, 73–83.
2. Rhine, J. B. Terminal salience in ESP performance. *Journal of Parapsychology*, 1941, *5*, 183–244.
3. Rhine, J. B. Mid-century inventory of parapsychology. *Journal of Parapsychology*, 1950, *14*, 227–243.
4. Rhine, J. B. The problem of psi-missing. *Journal of Parapsychology*, 1952, *16*, 90–129.
5. Rhine, J. B. Psi-missing re-examined. *Journal of Parapsychology*, 1969, *33*, 1–38.
6. Rhine, L. E. Conviction and associated conditions in spontaneous cases. *Journal of Parapsychology*, 1951, *15*, 164–191.
7. Rhine, L. E. Subjective forms of spontaneous psi experiences. *Journal of Parapsychology*, 1953, *17*, 77–114.
8. Rhine, L. E. Psychological processes in ESP experiences. Part I. Waking experiences. *Journal of Parapsychology*, 1962, *26*, 88–111.
9. Rhine, L. E. Psychological processes in ESP experiences. Part II. Dreams. *Journal of Parapsychology*, 1962, *26*, 172–199.
10. Rhine, L. E. Spontaneous physical effects and the psi process. *Journal of Parapsychology*, 1963, *27*, 84–122.
11. Rogers, D. P., and Carpenter, J. C. The decline of variance of ESP scores with a testing session. *Journal of Parapsychology*, 1966, *30*, 141–150.
12. Tyrrell, G. N. M. The "modus operandi" of paranormal cognition. *Proceedings of the Society for Psychical Research*, 1946–49, *48*, 65–120.

10

J. B. Rhine

(1895–1980)

Beyond a doubt, J. B. Rhine will be acknowledged as the greatest leader in the first one hundred years of parapsychology. The vigor and experimental direction of the field today are the outgrowth of his work at Durham, North Carolina. In the following paper he gives his view of the history of parapsychology in relation to American psychology over the sixty years from 1892 to 1951. In a longer version and under another title, this paper was delivered as an invited address on September 4, 1967, at the Annual Convention of the American Psychological Association in Washington, D.C., and was later published in the Journal of Parapsychology *(32, 101-128).*

J. B. Rhine received the doctor of philosophy degree in plant physiology at the University of Chicago in 1925. In 1926 he and his wife went to Boston to work with William McDougall at Harvard and with W. F. Prince at the Boston Society for Psychic Research. They followed McDougall in 1927 to Duke University, where the laboratory experiments for which they are best known were carried out. With Rhine's approaching retirement from the University, he established in 1962 at Durham the Foundation for Research on the Nature of Man and its operating subsidiaries, the Institute for Parapsychology and the Parapsychology Press.

PSYCHOLOGY AND PARAPSYCHOLOGY
(1967)

by J. B. RHINE

A parapsychologist who reviews the history of psychology since the founding of the American Psychological Association must be expected to give main attention to the controversy between the two areas of study. The issue could not possibly be avoided; it is one of the outstanding clashes in the history of science. I shall attempt, therefore, to outline the vigorous contest that has lasted down through this period (which I shall divide into four sections: three sections of twenty years each and one of fifteen years). . . . [The last is omitted in this condensation.]

AMBIGUOUS BEGINNINGS: 1892–1911

Two Meetings in 1892

The review must begin, of course, with the historic meeting called in 1892 by President G. Stanley Hall at Clark University, at which twenty-six psychologists met and organized the APA, an organization which last numbered a thousand times the size of the original group. The emphasis at the founders' meeting naturally was academic and professional; it represented for the most part the American university world of psychology of that time. Although there were a number of men in the group (among them, William James, Josiah Royce, James Hyslop, and Stanley Hall himself) who had already been active in the investigation of psychical research (as parapsychology was called at that time), there is no record that the subject was even mentioned in the organization of the association. Hall's interest had declined by then; but Hyslop was to give many of the later years of his life entirely to the American Society for Psychical Research, and James was to say years later that he thought the most important research of the next fifty years would be in that field. Quite evidently a lively enough interest remained with some of the APA founders, but psychical research just did not seem to belong to the schedule of academic psychology as the organizers of the APA saw it. Psychology in American institutions had already taken shape along lines that did not include psychical research; and there is no indication that even its psychologist friends expected things to be otherwise.

Interestingly enough, however, another psychological meeting occurred that same year in which psychical research did figure rather prominently. The second convention was an international affair, a much larger one indeed: the Second International Congress of Psychology. When it met at University College in London for three days in August of 1892, it too was a distinguished assembly, with an attendance of around three hundred. The psychological leaders of the day were there in force. Von Helmholtz, Ebbinghaus, Hitzig, and Münsterberg were among the Germans; Richet, Janet, Binet, and Bernheim were there, among others, from France. Four Americans read papers.

Yet, odd as it may seem today, the man who presided over this notable gathering was none other than the President of the Society for Psychical Research himself, Professor Henry Sidgwick, the Cambridge philosopher. Nor was this any sort of mere accidental association. One of the leading events of the London convention was a psychical research report, Sidgwick's own paper on the Census of Hallucinations, which he had been authorized to prepare by the preceding Congress three years before. This was a systematic collection and analysis of reported hallucinations coincident with death, experiences suggesting a telepathic basis of exchange.

Some impression of the atmosphere of the Congress may be gathered from a quotation from Sidgwick's later report to the SPR: "The severe taboo long imposed upon the subjects with which we deal has been tacitly removed. . . . We cannot but feel that this forward step had been achieved more rapidly than we had any good ground to expect." Quite evidently, then, psychical research had its day in court at this international gathering of psychologists in London, even if the subject was not recognized at the APA meeting in Worcester.

Reactions and the Realities

And yet, the impression Professor Sidgwick received was, as it turned out, more than a little over-optimistic. Nothing really important for parapsychology seems to have come of this day of recognition— nothing at least as far as the next twenty years of psychological history indicate on either side of the Atlantic. There were no recorded efforts of attempts by psychologists, even in Britain, to follow up the high recognition given the subject of psychical research in London. Brilliantly as the light of tolerant interest had shone for those three resplendent days, it seems in retrospect to have been a flash in the pan. Even in later international congresses, there was no further recognition.

Let us look for an explanation. Professor Sidgwick was a philosopher and did not represent British psychology. There is no indication that the psychologists of Britain were as much affected even as those in the U.S. by the psychical research movement—at least during the first twenty years under review. Their names do not appear in the reports of publications of the SPR of London, and neither do those of the psychologists from the Continent. The fact is, however, that there were other university scholars who did pursue psychical research on both sides of the Atlantic during these years; and this suggests that psychology, as a new field, was not prepared to handle these difficult borderline claims.

This reserve seems, on the whole, reasonable enough. Psychology was having a hard time making its own way in the universities in the shadow of better established branches of science. Psychologists needed to work with something that could be nicely measured under controllable conditions and would give results that could be readily reproduced from one laboratory to another. One sees from Stanley Hall's account of Wundt's academic difficulties and his own memory of how much his first laboratory had been on trial at Johns Hopkins that the new science was quite on the defensive. The individual psychologist, like the psychology profession as a whole, was seeking acceptance. He needed to choose his ground with care and confine himself to research material that was manageable.

The case material of psychical research represented by the Census of Hallucinations was not, as everyone can agree, the type to impress experimental psychologists. The parapsychologist himself does not claim for such case material sufficient reliability to warrant final conclusions, valuable and even essential though it is in its rightful place and use. But even the experiments that had been conducted in psychical research for a decade or more before 1892 would also have presented difficulties for the academic psychologist. Professor Charles Richet's experiments with his hypnotized subject, Léonie, will suitably illustrate the point. Richet had been testing Léonie for clairvoyant ability (ESP of concealed, objective targets). The targets used were playing cards, each one enclosed in an opaque envelope, and the rate of success shown by the subject's guesses was evaluated by means of the mathematics of probability. The methods were in principle generally commendable and the results significant. But when Richet was invited to demonstrate Léonie in England and attempted to do so, she failed in that country to reproduce the impressive results she had given in Paris. Whatever Léonie's capacity actually was, it turned out to be more elusive than Richet had supposed. The ability being tested did not lend itself to the easy demonstration which a new academic science in the competitive university world would have required at the time.

The type of handicap illustrated by Richet's case was by no means all that psychical research had to contend with. Such claims as that of clairvoyance were identified with strange cults (e.g., spiritualism) which were difficult to take seriously, even apart from academic restraint. Clairvoyance was an ability claimed by the spiritualist medium; investigation of the former was associated with the latter. Accordingly, while a physicist like Sir William Barrett, a psychiatrist like Pierre Janet, or a philosopher like Sidgwick could openly take part in such investigations, the university psychologist at the turn of the century, trying to walk the straight and narrow path of his new science, felt much less free to wander off into this occult hinterland.

A backward glance over this first period reveals one point that seems especially worth making: The relations between psychology in the universities and the parapsychology of the societies for psychical research were fairly normal. There were some criticisms by psychologists, but there were defenders, too, much as between any two branches of inquiry. There was no great display of philosophical antagonism and rejection. One gets the impression that if parapsychology had been ready with easily reproduced test demonstrations of any single one of its phenomena, the entrée into academic psychology would have met with no serious opposition from any quarter. The professional minds were still rather widely open; no fixed and firm lines of the image of psychology had yet been drawn. The abilities under study in psychical research, however, were not such as to lend themselves to an easy approach. Only a few of the more independent men of the period, such as James and McDougall (who were perhaps less academically oriented than most psychologists, in any case) could see far enough ahead to reserve in their charts of human nature a place, at that stage, for such elusive phenomena.

HOPE IN UPHEAVAL: 1912–1931

Psychology of the Period

The second twenty years of APA history roughly represent another stage in the history of psychology, and a different type of period for psychical research as well. It was a time of considerable change and upheaval in American psychology, what with the Watsonian rebellion, the landing of McDougall at Harvard Yard, the phenomenal rise of psychotechnologies and specializations, and the infiltration of new European schools and movements in psychology. All these developments made for a disturbance of ideas and a babel of new jargons that broke up the relative complacency of the first two decades of the APA. Under such abnormal conditions things could happen to the academic departments of psychology that would earlier have been unthinkable.

Psychical Research Gains Admittance

It was then that psychical research began to penetrate psychology departments, and it did so in quite a number of universities, here and abroad. Coover conducted experiments in telepathy and clairvoyance at Stanford; Munsterberg, Troland, and Estabrooks did telepathy tests at Harvard, as did Stratton at California and Titchener at Cornell; Heymans and Brugmans did likewise at Groningen. There were others as well—over a dozen of the best-known names could be rounded up—so that by the end of the period, in 1931, one might hopefully (and with much more reason than Sidgwick had had forty years earlier) have expected that parapsychology was at last successfully invading the academic departments of psychology. The test results obtained were good enough for that period to justify continued interest. More than half of the reported studies gave adequately significant evidence of one or the other of the two types of ESP ability investigated. Most of them had to do with the guessing of playing cards or other target objects the results of which were relatively easy to evaluate by familiar, acceptable mathematical methods. The test conditions were, on the whole, as good and as well guarded as the experimental psychology of the time was prepared to make them.

And yet, as it turned out, something was seriously wrong, individually and in general. The ESP invasion of the already well-established departments of psychology was definitely not a success. There was no adequate continuity about any single one of these separate investigations. It is true, Coover had a laboratory for psychical research and continued, even after 1931, to give lip-service courses with that name, but he was effectively through with the subject after publishing his results in 1917. In fact, in his report it looks as if he deliberately hid the acceptable (by present standards) significance of his findings under a camouflage of statistical obscurity. (He is known to have been under great pressure.) At Harvard, Troland did not obtain significant results; but both Munsterberg and Estabrooks did. The latter offered very strong evidence (much stronger, as later analysis showed, than he himself realized), but he failed to get confirmatory results later, at another institution, when he turned the experiment over to an assistant. Brugmans too gave up psychical research when his subject seemingly lost his ability. These are some of the individual examples of the widespread failure to continue with the ESP research efforts in this twenty-year period in which psychology opened up for a time to the claims of psychical research.

Insuperable Difficulties Encountered

Obviously, psychology, with its greater security, was at least a little more open than before to the investigation of the problems of psychical research, but the latter branch of inquiry was still not ready for the new opportunities offered. It is true some good work was done in these undertakings; some minor advances in method were made. For example, in the tests allowing telepathy, different rooms were used (e.g., by Brugmans and Estabrooks) for the sender looking at a card and the receiver attempting to identify it. Unselected volunteer subjects were used by Estabrooks; Coover used his psychology classes. But the idea of recognizing the psychological peculiarities of the ability under test had not come sufficiently into focus. ESP was still lumped off with the other mental abilities being tested; that is to say, it was treated as something always readily available and only waiting to be caught by the simple administration of a test. Had the capacity actually been comparable, let us say, to memory or learning, parapsychology would presumably have remained in the psychology departments of the university world where it had already gained these openings. But ESP was not so easily handled. The timing was premature.

Also, unfortunately, considerable extramural pressure was exerted to induce acceptance of psychical research. The issue was in some cases forced upon a psychology department by popular interest in the claims of spiritualism. Such influence was felt in several ways. In the American universities money for research was a factor. Wealthy people interested in spiritualism made gifts to Stanford, Harvard, Clark, Pennsylvania, and other institutions to encourage psychical research. The interest of the public was very strong, and persons of prestige and influence in some cases publicly espoused the spiritualist cause. The societies for psychical research organized lay interest in the claims and helped to bring more attention to the problem than the methods, the available research workers, and their capabilities could sustain.

The outcome is more understandable today than it was then. The great project of proving the existence of "life after death" seemed compellingly simple to the lay mind as well as to many scholars; and the question was, of course, incomparably important. The same science that lauded Darwin for helping to solve the mystery of the origin of man could not easily be excused from looking at evidence on the question of his post-mortem destiny—especially when persons like James, Hyslop, and McDougall in psychology and men of like stature in other sciences were willing to concede that it was at least worthy of study.

Besides, it seemed then that it should be easy to do telepathy tests in the psychology laboratory. Telepathy was a key concept, equally so for those who favored as for those who opposed the hypothesis of spirit communication through mediums. The very concept of spirit contact assumed a basis of telepathic exchange; it was merely telepathy with the dead instead of the living. Even those who were attempting to refute the claims of the spiritists clung to the counterhypothesis that the medium could be obtaining her information by telepathic exchange with living persons instead of the discarnate. Telepathic ability was therefore of central importance to both sides of this issue, which was itself one of the great intellectual questions of the period.

But all the pressure and support of public interest, even though reinforced with financial help, were not enough to make up for the difficulties I have mentioned as inherent in the research itself. Again, just as in the preceding period, the academic culture of the day was evidently still tolerant enough to permit these ventures into psychical research; there was still no significant display of philosophical bias against it. But tolerance, though certainly advantageous, was not enough by itself. Research has to succeed if it is to sustain interest, encourage workers, and receive support and approval. When it is too difficult for successful exploration, the problems, however important, fall into neglect. We can see better today that parapsychology was awaiting a combination of special conditions that the period of the first forty years of APA history plainly failed to provide. In the light of present understanding it is hard to see any way in which it could have succeeded during this period in holding a place in the academic world, either in psychology or, for that matter, in any other department of science. It was simply not ready for the demands of the academic arena.

EXCLUSION BY CONSOLIDATION: 1932–1951

The third section of APA history was a more settled period of psychology in America than the preceding one, a time marked by rapid growth in numbers as well as increased diversification of research and more widely extended application. It was, also, of course, the period that included World War II, from which came the heavy involvement of psychological services as it reached into broad areas of human life and action. Debate over schools of psychology declined, and a more open-minded interest in new developments was shown. It was a comparatively good time to introduce parapsychology, provided a strong and dependable case could be made for it.

Parapsychology at Duke University

This third score of years of APA history covers the main part of the development of parapsychology at Duke. Already in the fall of 1927 McDougall had moved there from Harvard, and there, too, my wife and I had gone, intending to work under him for a time. What followed then in North Carolina has been reported elsewhere and needs to be outlined here only inasfar as it relates to the interaction of parapsychology with psychology. This does call, however, for a brief tracing of the development of parapsychology during this period when it so closely centered in and around the Department of Psychology at Duke.

In 1926, Professor McDougall, in his Clark University address entitled "Psychical Research as a University Study," had urged that this subject be encouraged within the universities. The fact that this attitude was also shared by the founding president of Duke, Dr. William Preston Few, made that institution an unusually favorable center for such study. In addition to this, the very newness of the University, as well as the already liberal tradition which the school had inherited from Trinity College, gave an air of intellectual freedom and adventure that was exceptional. Both in and out of the Department of Psychology, which I was invited to join, the fullest co-operation was given to the work attempted in the field of psychical research, and this persisted undiminished throughout the seven years of preparation leading up to the first publication of results.

The situation changed, however, in 1934 as soon as the results were published. The first report was my monograph, *Extrasensory Perception*, describing the first six years of initial experimentation. The main point reached in this modest, obscurely published volume was the conclusion that extrasensory perception had been found in some carefully controlled experimental tests (along with many more freely exploratory series). The conditions used in the better tests of clairvoyance were regarded as the more conclusive part of the findings. The card-guessing techniques which were the basis of the tests were not in themselves novel, and the mathematics of probability applied to the results was standard procedure. The various types of precautions that had been taken against sensory cues, such as the use of wooden screens and opaque envelopes and, in some experiments, separate rooms and different buildings, emphasized progressive safeguarding on that problem and by now are more or less familiar.

There were, however, some features that were, at the time, a little more unusual; for example, the introduction of a two-experimenter plan which gave the additional assurance of essentially "double-blind" accuracy. Also, the standards of acceptable significance of the results were above those used in other sciences. The main difference between the Duke results and all that had preceded them was their rather steady six-year continuity and also the impression the work gave of being a vigorous, on-going program of university psychical research. The world, the university, and the psychology profession had not had to consider the like hitherto. An impact such as parapsychology had never made before was now being experienced.

A still further sign of the permanence of this intrusion was given when, in 1937, the *Journal of Parapsychology* was established. The *Journal* soon became the main educational instrument of the field and in the course of time took on some features that improved its role. One of the first of these was the Board of Review, appointed in 1938 and composed of nine critical American psychologists who were willing to read and evaluate all papers before publication. Following that unwieldy and short-lived plan, came the appointment of one, and later two, competent mathematicians to the staff for the prepublication screening of all statistical papers. In these and other ways, a systematic effort was being made not only to advance the study of ESP on sound lines, but also to meet each challenge to its reliability as it arose.

New research developments, of course, reinforced the early work by adding more evidence and advancing it to stronger positions. For example, reports of precognition tests began to appear in 1938 and they completely removed what had been a major issue in the debate over clairvoyance testing: the counterhypothesis of sensory cues. In the new experiments, ESP was found to operate as well on a target order that was not merely hidden from view but which did not even exist anywhere at the time of the test.

Then there appeared, in 1940, the book *Extrasensory Perception After Sixty Years,* a volume that rounded up all the experimental evidence of ESP to date, along with all the criticisms thus far recorded. For this book the seven leading critics of parapsychology among the psychologists were asked to contribute their critiques on the material assembled. Only three of the seven accepted the invitation. Their criticisms were answered in the book. From that time on, open criticism of parapsychological research dropped off almost completely and the research was able to move ahead with greater freedom. So firm was the internal security of the Duke center and such the stability of the research methods and findings that the program did not waver; there was even some continuing progress.

Principal Findings

As a matter of fact, the actual findings of this research period at Duke and elsewhere were substantial, although only the broader lines can be indicated here. First, parapsychology began to take definite shape as a field and to assume outlines of an organized whole. The loosely connected types of phenomena that were being studied began to show lawful interrelation and even a degree of unity. An acceptable definition was found for parapsychology as well as a clearly distinguishable boundary. One by one the major claims which had been based originally only upon spontaneous human experiences were subjected to laboratory test and experimentally verified. Independent confirmations, both in and out of the Duke center, followed in the course of this period.

Simplest to handle experimentally was the hypothesis of clairvoyance; it was naturally the first type of ESP to be investigated because it was the easiest to be adequately established and confirmed. Telepathy was the type most familiar to the public, but this hypothesis required much greater complication of experimental design than clairvoyance. With two subjects to control, the precautions had to be very much more elaborate. In fact, a telepathy test was so complicated that a proper experiment had never before been carried out. The first distinctive test of telepathy—that is, one that excluded other types of ESP—came with the Duke work of this period.

Next in line for attack was the claim of precognition, or ESP of the future. The original tests have since gone through many stages of advancement and have reached a level of methodological control unsurpassed in any division of behavioral study. This advantage, along with the ready convenience of the techniques, has made it the most extensively used psi research method in the field today.

Last of all the types was PK (psychokinesis), or "the direct action of mind on matter," as Charcot originally defined it. This claim lent itself to easy laboratory testing through the use of dice-throwing techniques which yielded results so objectively conclusive that the Laboratory in 1945 published an invitation to any qualified scientific committee to examine the evidence for themselves. The mere fact that the invitation is still unaccepted is a sufficient rebuke to the critics.

Still more important than the findings in each area were the relationships between them, i.e., the impression of lawfulness which the results gave and which extended from one research to another as a broader picture emerged. After a time, certain general characteristics of the psi process stood out, the most revealing of all being the subjects' lack of conscious control over all the types of psi ability. This observation meant that it occurred unconsciously, a fact which accounted for its elusive nature. After that discovery, it seemed an important step just to be able to measure effectively and quantitatively a genuinely unconscious mental process. It was new methodological ground even for psychology.

Again, it was surprising to find psi ability to be widespread, most probably even a specific human capacity instead of being confined to a few rare individuals as had been the popular belief. Likewise, the observation that psi was not linked with illness or abnormality was another advance.

Most significant of all, however, at this stage of our culture, was the cumulative evidence that psi communication simply does not show any of those physical relations to the target common to sensorimotor exchange. The case for precognition more definitely sealed the evidence of this fact which had accrued from the other branches of the research. Thus there appeared for the first time in history a sharp experimental challenge to the pervading belief (a sort of intuitive conviction) that man is entirely physical.

Difficulties and Developments

Confirmation of such a new finding as psi was of course crucial to its survival. Even before 1892, however, it was known that psi-testing was difficult. It was still not easy in the 1930's and 1940's. Some of those even at Duke who attempted to get results were unable to do so, while others under the same conditions and with the same subjects were significantly successful. The general tendency at first was to treat the capacity like any other ability, but such an approach almost invariably failed to produce anything but chance results for certain experimenters. In order to manifest psi, most subjects had to be motivated, put at ease, allowed to concentrate, and to be given helpful, suggestive, and sometimes challenging instructions. The subject-experimenter relationship was found to be important.

Gradually, however, enough discerning and qualified workers (including some psychologists) undertook the experiments to supply a marginally adequate basis of confirmation for the work initiated at

Duke. In some of these cases, even a higher rate of scoring than that of the Duke work was produced, and some advances were made also on the side of methodology. After a time, the original idea that specially gifted subjects were necessary for significant research was modified and played down. The use of such subjects did favor the production of high scoring rates, but it greatly confined the research to the few experimenters who were fortunate enough to find the rare individual. For a number of additional reasons, the research at Duke turned early to the use of all volunteers available and to reliance upon lower rates of scoring from a larger number of subjects. This procedure paid off comparatively well; at the same time a few individual experimenters continued to look for exceptionally high scorers, while one or two others even attempted to produce them through training. . . .

What counted most was that psi research was continuing fairly steadily and even showing some progress. Centered at Duke, a sustained and forthright effort was being made to keep psi research going, to meet the criticisms, and to develop methods that others could follow. There were many independent repetitions, not only in the U.S.A. but in Western Europe as well. Gardner Murphy, already well oriented in his own independent interest, began ESP work at Columbia and later supported Gertrude Schmeidler in her work at the College of the City of New York. Lucien Warner at New York University, Dorothy Martin and Frances Stribic at Colorado, Hans Bender at Bonn, Whately Carington and S. G. Soal in Britain, along with many others, confirmed the case for ESP, adding new independent findings of their own in so doing.

Reactions of Psychologists

What responses were the psychologists making to these findings? When the monograph *Extrasensory Perception* appeared in 1934, the profession showed a lively interest. While some psychologists were justifiably annoyed by the sensationalism given to the findings by popular writers (over whom no control could be exercised), there was for the most part little about which to complain. It is true, a few old-timers such as Joseph Jastrow and McKeen Cattell, who had (with some good reason) been critical of psychical research now and then in their own writings, registered scepticism of the new work, but only in vague generalities. Even the foremost behaviorists, whose view perhaps most definitely clashed with the findings of parapsychology, took a fair, if not friendly, interest. Karl Lashley told me that he once sat up all night guessing cards. Even John B. Watson expressed an interest in a copy of the book, *"ESP-60."* Hunter actually initiated some experiments at

Clark, in which he and his wife took part. Knight Dunlap told me he went through five hundred packs of ESP test cards himself. The point is not whether any of these people convinced themselves or were satisfied by the evidence that ESP occurs, but that they were not so close-minded they would not look or listen.

Also, a number of surveys were made (notably by Lucien Warner and C. C. Clark) as to psychologists' opinions of ESP; and while very few psychologists were found ready to accept the findings, the percentages were overwhelmingly positive on the question of whether the field was a legitimate one for science. Eighty-seven per cent were affirmative in the first survey. Even at the three universities (Stanford, Harvard, and Clark) where there was still unused money for psychical research, and where one might expect to find special reluctance to acknowledge the subject, there were psychologists who paid some attention to the ESP work. E. G. Boring once told me he had considered inviting me to Harvard for a year to conduct my researches there, and at least two psychologists from Stanford served for a time on the Board of Review that helped in the criticism of papers before publication in the *Journal of Parapsychology*. Even though they may all have expected to help me discover the errors they suspected I had fallen into, this was not un-friendly co-operation.

This did not mean, however, that parapsychology was at all settled in the field of psychology at this time. The 1934 and later publications did bring many criticisms, rather gentle and objective at first, and later more vigorous in tone. The statistics were assailed for a while, but in 1937 there came the well-known release, by the President of the American Institute for Mathematical Statistics at the meeting of their Institute, endorsing the statistics. That statement more or less ended the attacks on methods of evaluation. The next year, the APA held a round table at its Columbus meeting. Three psychologists criticized the methods, and three parapsychologists defended them. The huge crowd that filled the auditorium that day represented a large part of the psychology profession as it was in 1938.

And yet, a dozen years later, as this period approached its close, it was evident that none of those hundreds of psychologists had returned to his university and set up the continuing research program in ESP which their massed attendance and response at the symposium might have led one to expect. There were a few colleges where psi research was being pursued by psychologists, the most outstanding being City College, New York, where Murphy himself was chairman of the psychology department. Here and there was a biologist, a physicist, or a psychiatrist doing something on psi, but the departments of psychology on the university level in the U.S.A. were almost as bare of parapsychology in 1951 as when the period began.

Even at Duke, by the time the period closed, the Laboratory no longer had any connection with the Department of Psychology. As far back as 1934, immediately following the publication of the monograph, it became evident that the unexpected spontaneous notoriety the work at once received was not a healthy outcome for the department. My own natural reaction was to isolate the psi researches from the rest of the department; and with Professor McDougall's approval, I asked for a different name to identify my area of work. And so began the Parapsychology Laboratory at Duke. Over the years the distance tended to widen between the Department and the Laboratory, and in 1950 I resigned my professorship, which was by then the only remaining bond with the department of Psychology. From then on until my formal retirement from the University (in 1965), parapsychology at Duke was entirely independent of psychology.

But even as we in parapsychology took up our separate status on the Duke campus, no one thought in 1950 that McDougall's dream of parapsychology as an integrated part of psychology was an illusion. The thought would have been, rather, that in due time, given the strengthening of the findings of parapsychology that is normally to be expected, psychology would be prepared to welcome the addition of psi research. As the saying went, the "para" was thought to be only a temporary "prefixation." Many more psychologists were interested in parapsychology than ever before, even if only a few were doing research. It stood to reason that our findings had to belong eventually to a properly inclusive psychology of man.

Analysis of the Third Period

What, then, was delaying that stage? First, there was the same old trouble of psi research, that it was much more difficult than work in other areas of psychology. Even in 1950, it was still hard to say just how a researcher could be certain he could get significant test results. There were still individuals, some of them mature, well-trained psychologists, who just did not succeed. (As a result they often became very critical of the successful work of others.)

But meanwhile an important development had taken place in the field of psychology itself. Its rapid growth as an established academic department naturally developed increased confidence in what "good psychology" really was. Any body of academic scientific workers naturally wants prestige, respectability, and the general approval of other groups. One of the ways to obtain these rewards is to avoid open interest in such far-out claims as psi communication. This is easier to do if they are also hard to verify, and much easier still if, at the same time, the results challenge existing boundaries to knowledge—in short, are a bit revolutionary. While this conservatism has many good advantages for a professional field, it places a degree of restraint on the membership as the organization grows in power and influence. The individual who wants approval, advancement, and status tends to keep in line. There were many psychologists in this period who would admit of a private interest; some, too, who did worthwhile research they chose not to publish. But while this restraint was strongest with psychologists, it was by no means confined to them. It seems a normal enough professional group response.

But even while this restrictive influence was growing with the very success of the professional organizations, the unrelenting progress of psi research increased the pressure on academic psychology. The persistence and vigor of the work in parapsychology now had to be reckoned with, all the more with every year and with the growing confirmation it continued to receive from new workers and from other centers as time passed. Moreover, along with intelligent lay interest in the research, there came an active and widespread development of enthusiasm among students which seemed to promise a long-continuing interest in the subject.

In reaction to this development, the university departments became increasingly inattentive to the claims of the psi field. After all, they could no longer intelligently criticize the real case for psi, and yet they could not accept it either, because (as D. O. Hebb well said) ESP could not be accounted for by physics and physiology. To such a situation the response of indifference and silence was a natural consequence.[1]

Finally the aggravating sensationalism which went on unabated was a factor in generating this studied coolness to the work with psi. Many said as much. Parapsychology now belonged far too much to the entertainer, the popular writer, the comic-strip artist, and even to Broadway. This overpopularization troubled even most of those working in parapsychology itself, but there was little they could do to restrain it. It did

---

1. Hebb wrote as follows in the *Journal of Personality*, *20* (1951), 45: "Personally, I do not accept ESP for a moment, because it does not make sense. My external criteria, both of physics and of physiology, say that ESP is not a fact. . . . My own rejection of [Rhine's] views is—in the literal sense—prejudice." —Ed.

make the research more of a target for critical attack, as if the research workers were themselves to blame for the amount of publicity.

Thus it was that, as the period ended, there was more uncertainty concerning the relation of parapsychology to the general field than there had been twenty years before. In spite of all the progress that had been made in psi research, it would have been a worse time to try to start a new research center in any university department of psychology in the U.S.A. than it had been to make the beginning at Duke a quarter of a century earlier. . . .

11

Henry Margenau

(1901–   )

What is the relation of parapsychology to physics or, for that matter, to all of the rest of science? If the phenomena of parapsychology involve the unexplained transfer of informational bits through space and the movement of physical objects by an unknown force, the scientific understanding of these effects must somehow connect them with physical reality.

What are the accepted rules of the game that the sought-for connection must obey? Are there any strange phenomena at the frontier of physics that might point in the direction of a connection? These two important questions are answered for us by Yale professor, Henry Margenau, a physicist-philosopher of distinction.

Surprising as it may seem to a layman, the rules of theory building are largely unknown by practicing scientists, although long familiar to philosophers of science. In established fields this does not matter because the requirements of a good theory are unconsciously met by the leaders. But in what T. S. Kuhn calls a "preparadigm" field of science, there are no leaders, and foolish theories abound.

So it has been in parapsychology for nearly a century—and will continue to be unless would-be theory builders take time to familiarize themselves with the epistemological principles of scientific method. These are set forth briefly in the paper that follows.

Margenau's answer to the second question is likewise frequently misunderstood by those hoping to explain psi phenomena. His evaluation can be summed up very simply: For parapsychology, the phenomena of modern physics are inspirational but not explanatory.

The following essay has been adapted from a lecture given by Dr. Margenau to a forum sponsored by the American Society for Psychical Research in 1965 and published in the Journal of that society (60, 214-228).

ESP AND MODERN PHYSICS
(1965)

by Henry Margenau

The Framework of Science

As I look upon many of your researches in paranormal psychology and ESP, I am reminded of the state of affairs in physics some seventy years ago when scientists had first learned about the phenomenon of radioactivity. People might have gone around with Geiger counters or similar devices. They would have found them clicking here and there and everywhere—but just a little bit. On this evidence physicists surely could have tried to convince their colleagues that this was a real effect, that there was indeed something important in the idea of radioactivity—the emission of charged particles which was not understood by anyone at the time.

However, in those days physicists did not content themselves collecting samples and measuring them promiscuously. They did not go from one place to another making statistical studies of the intensity of this effect. Instead, they succeeded in finding circumstances under which the phenomenon became enhanced and became controllable. In other words, they were very specific, and by being specific, persistent, and judicious in their selection of experimental conditions they transcended the need for statistical arguments and probability estimates of validity; they uncovered clear evidence of the existence of the effect. My point is simply this: in order to study these obscure things, you must practice selectivity and concentrate your attention upon instances where positive results are incontrovertible and, of course, demonstrably free of fraud. I believe that as long as you go around making statistical studies everywhere and on everybody, you are not likely to be convincing for a long time to come.[1]

---

1. At the present time, 13 years later, I would add a caveat to the foregoing paragraph. We have learned in the meantime that there are important areas of science in which all significant evidence is statistical, in which results are not uniquely predictable, in which probabilities are the only decisive observations in terms of which a theory, an effect, can be verified. This observation weakens the import of the preceeding remarks and justifies the use of statistics in a fundamental way. —H. M.

Now the second thing you need, I believe, is theory. No amount of empirical evidence, no mere collection of facts, will convince all scientists of the veracity and the significance of your reports. You must provide some sort of model; you must advance bold constructs—constructs connected within a texture of rationality—in terms of which ESP can be theoretically understood. The remainder of my talk will center about possibilities of constructing such vehicles of understanding.

In order to put these problems in their proper context, let me say a few words about a matter which may at first seem irrelevant here, a few words about the competence and the limitations of science in general. Science is more than a mere collection of facts, a catalogue of observations. Observations alone, facts alone, lack the cohesion, the logical consistency, which every science demands. Science is a style of inquiry; it is a peculiar way of organizing human experience which integrates and thereby confers lucidity, clarity, and cohesion upon our immediate sense impressions and upon our observations. Every kind of human experience, or fact, is at first vague, meaningless, incoherent. Because of this, the scientist finds it necessary to set up or construct, vis-à-vis every given set of unorganized experiences, a model, originally invented by the human mind, which stands somehow in correspondence with the facts themselves. These constructs are not introduced arbitrarily without rhyme or reason. They are subjected by the scientist to certain requirements, called metaphysical requirements.[2] Among them are the following:

1. They must be fertile in a logical sense; that is to say, they must make a difference to what you are observing or explaining. An idea such as the Berkeleyan God who causes every event in the world by merely thinking about it, the theory according to which every happening in the world is a thought in the mind of God, provides no fertile scientific explanation because it cannot be tested effectively; it does not furnish any way of understanding or of checking. All scientific constructs must satisfy the "principle of logical fertility"; they must make a difference to your pursuits.

2. They must be extensible. Science rejects them if they merely illuminate a very small part of your immediate experience, only a few of the facts you wish to explain. Useful scientific ideas must have a fairly inclusive reach.

---

2. A more extensive account may be found in the author's *The Nature of Physical Reality*. New York: McGraw Hill, 1950.

3. They must be richly interconnected among themselves, aside from their reference to facts. By virtue of this pervasive relationship, the ideas of science permit themselves to be controlled by general principles which are not directly suggested by the scientific enterprise itself. It is not allowable for a scientist to employ an idea in terms of which he can explain one or two observations while the idea does not set itself into some logical relation with anything else. Large internal coherence between constructs of explanation must be sought, although it is not always achieved.

4. There must be simplicity. A scientific theory must be formulated in terms, or in mathematical equations, which are in some sense simple. To be explicit, invariance with respect to transformations is the present version of simplicity in physical science.

5. There must be a certain elegance ruling the manipulations of the scientific constructs which serve as explanations of the obscure facts.

6. The principle of causality comes into play here too, but this is a rather technical philosophic matter which hardly needs to be discussed in the present context.

These, then, are the metaphysical requirements of every science. Notice that the list does not contain one which was held to be important and clinching in the sciences of the last century, namely, the requirement of detailed pictorability. The models used in modern science, the constructs of explanation, do not have to be couched in terms of *visual* concepts. We no longer explain the atom in terms of a group of electrons moving mechanically around a nucleus, each electron having a certain trajectory and occupying a definite point in space at a specified time. The electrons of today do not have paths any longer. Their motions are not visualizable at all, and this for various reasons like the following:

Electrons are far smaller than a wave length of light and hence they have no color. Their position cannot be ascertained by the usual kind of physical experiment, which involves the reflection of electromagnetic or other kinds of signals from the entities themselves. Such procedures would fail simply because the entities are too small. Trying to find out where an electron is would be very much like trying to find out the position of a ping-pong ball by shooting cannon balls at it. No, in a very fundamental sense these entities have lost the facile attributes of localizability in space and time. We operate in terms of probabilities, and these probabilities may be the irreducible determinants of natural happenings. What I am saying here is that the requirements upon the constructs in terms of which we now explain the physical world have become exceedingly elusive and abstract.

So much for the *metaphysical* requirements. There is also the well-known *empirical* requirement of *verifiability*, of experimental or observational confirmation.

I sometimes find it useful to present the pursuits of science, its methodology, by means of a graphical analog. Imagine with me all the obscure facts, all the unconnected observations, these contingencies which do not explain themselves, as being mapped on a certain plane, the "protocol" plane of human experience. From that plane we can go by means of rules of correspondence into the domain of theory, where you manipulate logically fertile constructs. After passing into that domain, you can now calculate, you can now reason. Reasoning amounts to an ideal movement among, to a transformation of, the constructs of explanation. Such a procedure, which is essentially that performed by the theoretical scientist, leads to a certain place within the field of constructs where you can again use a rule of correspondence (operational definition) which permits you to return to the protocol plane of experience, to "Nature" if you please. This picture, together with a more detailed exposition of the scientific method, can be found in the book already mentioned (footnote 2).

Now, that latter transition is a prediction. The empirical requirement of verification insists that a circuit from a certain point in the plane of protocol observations into the domain of theory and back again to observation shall be successful. In other words, you must be able, as outlined elsewhere, to predict, not on the basis of some a priori kinds of concepts, but to predict on the basis of having previously injected into the scientific theory a material bit of knowledge at some other place in our diagram.

Forgive me for being so technical in my discourse. I shall soon try to be much more specific and concrete, but I thought it well at the beginning to say a few things about the workings of scientific theories in general.

There is one further point of rather general import which I must not leave unmentioned. Old-style science, the physical science of the last century, believed that its fundamental premises were secure and not subject to question or to change. To be sure, scientists spoke of postulates, of axioms. These included the basic principles of arithmetic (the postulates concerning natural numbers), the basic principles of geometry (the postulates of Euclid), the basic principles of physical science (the law of conservtion of energy, momentum, etc.). These were Truths, with a capital T, firmly embedded in human knowledge, truths which had to be accepted by every sane mind, truths which carried within themselves the affidavits of their validity. Now this attitude has changed. The modern scientist has learned that even his postulates are held on trial. The whole business of science is in a flux: science is a progressive, self-corrective, dynamic enterprise which subjects itself, in response to the ever-present threat of falsification, to repeated changes and revisions of its fundamental tenets. To put it bluntly, science no longer contains absolute truths.

We have begun to doubt such fundamental propositions as the principle of the conservation of energy, the principle of causality, and many other commitments which were held to be unshakeable and firm in the past. And this has, I think, an interesting bearing upon your own pursuits, for it means that the old distinction between the natural and the supernatural has become spurious. That distinction rested upon a dogmatism, a scientific dogmatism, which supposed that everything in the way of fundamental facts and basic matters was known and that there was an obvious distinction between what was possible and what was not possible. Today we know that there are many phenomena on the fringe, at the periphery of present-day science, which are not yet understood, which are still obscure, but which will nevertheless be encompassed by the scientific method and by scientific understanding in the future.

An analogy which does not appeal to me as a description of science is that of the picture puzzle, the pursuit of finding facts, then putting them together and somehow discovering a pattern in them, a pattern whose completion closes and solves the scientific problem. This analogy is incorrect because you cannot resolve a scientific problem in any manner that is ultimate.

I like to think of science as a crystal which grows within an amorphous matrix of liquid experience. This amorphous matrix—unorganized, interesting because of its caprice, the chicanery of chance which it embodies—is most important in our lives. But somehow our minds are disposed to organize this material, and the organization is very much like the growth of a crystal within its liquid environment. Nobody can tell where the crystal is going to grow. Starting unpredictably from some small seed, it stretches out a long arm in one direction, or it proceeds in a broad front along another. But whatever it does, it changes the amorphous liquid into a pattern, a lattice, which makes prediction possible, which confers order upon the constituents of the matrix and understanding upon those who perceive it. Now this process of crystal growth is not self-limiting—if the vessel permitted it, the crystal would grow forever. And yet it would never exhaust all the infinite supply of liquid. The crystal of science will go on growing forever. And since the number of facts, these immediate experiences in the protocol plane of which I spoke, is practically infinite, one sees no limit at all to the growth of science and there will probably never be a time at which all the liquid, unorganized, and therefore occult matrix of human experience will have become crystallized into a rigid scientific pattern. . . .

THE LAWS OF PHYSICS

Let me now recall to you briefly the laws of physics in their most general features; for there may be a lesson in them for psychical researchers.

First of all, there is the principle of conservation of energy. This is an all-pervasive law which is partly being read from nature, partly being injected into nature. It is not merely a generalization of empirical fact because whenever we find something which violates the principle, we are tempted to invent a new form of energy. Let this be acknowledged. Helmholtz "proved" the principle of conservation of energy in the 1850's, but his proof involved the assumption that there exists a new kind of energy previously unknown, namely, potential energy. Only by introducing this as an additional concept was he able to prove the law. The addition was proper because the concept proved fruitful; it satisfied all the metaphysical requirements.

Today, the principle of conservation of energy is thought to hold in nearly all domains. However, it is not valid without exception. At the forefront of current physical research, in the fields of quantum theory and elementary particle physics, the principle of conservation of energy is frequently breached because we find it necessary to invoke the existence of "virtual processes." Virtual processes do not conserve energy. They follow no ordinary law, but are confined to extremely short durations. For a very short time, every physical process can proceed in ways which defy the laws of nature known today, always hiding itself under the cloak of the principle of uncertainty, to be sure. The point I am making is that when any physical process first starts, it sends out "feelers" in all directions, feelers in which time may be reversed, normal rules are violated, and unexpected things may happen. These virtual processes then die out and after a certain time matters settle down again in obedience to the principle of conservation of energy. The term "virtual" is not synonymous with "unreal," for these processes cannot be ignored without falsifying the scientific prediction of actual events.

A great deal is made about the fact that physical processes decline in intensity with an increase in distance. This appears indeed as a worthwhile field of experimentation. It is quite true that most physical processes follow an attenuating law of some sort. However, it should also be recalled that not all interactions obey an inverse square law—in fact, almost none do. Only interactions between physical points follow an inverse square law, and strictly speaking there are no physical points. An electric field in front of a charged plane of infinite extent shows no attenuation at all. It would be as strong at a distant star as it is right in front of the plane. There are "resonance forces" encompassed in modern quantum theory, which may possibly have interesting applications in biology and in psychology and which decrease very slowly with distance. . . .

Theoretical physicists today invoke a principle known as the "exclusion principle"; it was discovered by Pauli. The exclusion principle is responsible for most of the organizing actions that occur in nature. We actually speak of "cooperative effects." All of these are brought about by the so-called Pauli principle, which is simply a principle of symmetry, a formal mathematical characteristic of the equations which in the end regulate phenomena in nature. Almost miraculously it calls into being what we call exchange forces, the forces which bind atoms into molecules and molecules into crystals. It is responsible for the fact that iron can be magnetized, that matter cannot be squeezed together into an arbitrarily small volume. The impenetrability of matter, its very stability, can be directly traced to the Pauli exclusion principle. Now, this principle has no dynamic aspect to it at all. It acts like a force although it is not a force. We cannot speak of it as doing anything by mechanical action. No, it is a very general and elusive thing; a mathematical symmetry imposed upon the basic equations of nature producing what appears like a dynamic effect.

Toward the end of the last century the view arose that all interactions involved material objects. This is no longer held to be true. We know now that there are fields which are wholly non-material. The quantum mechanical interactions of physical psi fields which play an important role in the theory of measurement—interestingly and perhaps amusingly, the physicist's psi (the square root of a probability) has a certain abstractness and vagueness of interpretation in common with the parapsychologist's psi—these interactions are wholly non material, yet they are described by the most important and the most basic equations of present-day quantum mechanics. These equations say nothing about masses moving; they regulate the behavior of very abstract fields, certainly in many cases non-material fields, often as tenuous as the square root of a probability.

Finally, there has emerged in these studies the view that there can be no instantaneous action at a distance, that there must be causality of a specific kind. This means that there can be no causal connection between two events at different points in space if they are further apart than the distance which light could travel within the time interval between the two events. Such is one meaning of causality in modern physics. It imposes a real limitation upon what can actually happen in the world. Yet, if you assume the correctness of that principle (and there are few who doubt it), you will not get any effective limitations upon what you report as being the case in your studies of ESP and other paranormal occurrences. For the restrictions imposed by causality involve events so far apart in space or so close together in time that they would hardly come under your observation with the techniques presently available. I am saying that the principle of causality as it is now conceived by the physicist is almost without significance for paranormal effects.[3]

The foregoing remarks were meant to show that physics, indeed all so-called exact sciences, are not closed books, that they contain many unresolved problems which are not entirely without analogy, and perhaps even of some relevance, for the worker in psychical research. They also suggest that current physics is different from the science of the last century and that some of its ideas are as difficult to grasp as those of parapsychology.

THE PHENOMENA OF PARAPSYCHOLOGY

Now, let me speak very briefly about a few present possibilities which are sometimes invoked for explaining clairvoyance. Here, I fear, my conclusions will be somewhat discouraging. In quantum mechanics one meets an effect which is called the "tunnel effect." It implies that if you set up an obstacle between two bodies which would normally stand in physical communication via electromagnetic signals, through the passage of photons, electrons, or other kinds of particles (the situation is perfectly general) you cannot with rigor exclude all possible transmission of effects, all communication. To be sure, in classical physics, if a particle coming from one body and going to another does not have enough energy to surmount the obstacle or barrier, it simply cannot get through. According to quantum mechanics, this is no longer true. If a lot of particles—a lot of photons, electrons, neutrons, or whatnot—are

---

3. However, I think Dr. Margenau would agree that precognition is a prima facie violation of both the physicist's and the layman's ideas of causality. —Ed.

emitted by an object, some *will* get through under practically all conditions. In other words, complete screening is no longer possible. Now, I am not suggesting that you can explain clairvoyance by the transmission of a few photons from the distant event to the person who perceives it clairvoyantly. Nevertheless, there is perhaps something here to be thought of a little further. But I see no great promise in this direction. . . .

A few words remain to be said about precognition, a field which seems rife with conjectures of a quasi-physical sort. Unfortunately, I know of no physical theory available at present which can be drawn upon to explain temporally prior knowledge of coming events—except again through an analysis, perhaps unconscious or supraconscious, of pre-existing causal clues. Two hypotheses have been invoked most frequently to account for inverted knowledge of a causal sequence. One is Feynman's theory of time reversal. It is alleged to permit time to flow backwards, since it assigns meaning to trajectories of electrons in which the time-axis is reversed. These are, in fact, normal paths of anti-particles, positrons in this instance, on which the latter travel forward in time.

The time concept has been greatly distorted by philosophers who fail to distinguish between time as a conscious, protocol experience, the "stream vector of consciousness," and time as a theoretical construct. No physical theory is qualified—by virtue of the methodology outlined earlier—to say anything about the structure of subjective time. Physics deals with measured, objective time, which means the construct. This, however, is connected with the stream of consciousness by rules of correspondence which must conform to immediate experience. To put the matter simply, even if constructed time flows backwards, as in the case of the normal motion of a positron, the relation between constructed time and consciously experienced time *must* be such, and is meant to be such, as to leave conscious time flowing forward. I have dealt with this and other related matters elsewhere.[4] This does not rule out such radical reinterpretations as precognition might require. The point is that contemporary physics provides no example of it.

Another instance I have seen cited focuses on the circumstances that quantum electrodynamics features Feynman diagrams in which the effect precedes the cause. A nucleus is supposed to explode before the missile reaches it. But the correct interpretation of these diagrams rec-

---

4. Henry Margenau, "Can Time Flow Backwards?" *Philosophy of Science,* Vol. 21, 1954, pp. 79-92.

ognizes no causal connection in these cases: the nucleus *happens* to explode with a certain (very small) probability spontaneously before the missile arrives, and a causal sequence is simulated by the fact that the emitted positron *later* collides with an electron passing near the nucleus in an act of mutual annihilation.

An artifact occasionally invoked to explain precognition is to make time multidimensional. This allows genuine backward passage of time, which might permit positive intervals in one time direction to become negative ("effect before cause") in another. In principle, this represents a valid scheme, and I know of no criticism that will rule it out as a scientific procedure. If it is to be acceptable, however, a completely new metric of space-time needs to be developed, a metric which will account not only for the facts to be explained, but also for the known laws of physics which can be fully understood without it. Remember the principle of extensibility!

I have probed physics for suggestions it can offer toward a solution of the sort of problems you seem to encounter. The positive results, I fear, are meager and disappointing, though perhaps worth inspection. But why, I should now like to ask, is it necessary to import into any new discipline all the approved concepts of an older science in its contemporary stage of development? Physics did not adhere slavishly to the Greek rationalistic formulations that preceded it; it was forced to create its own specific constructs, even to the point of denying the basic geometry of Euclid. Lo and behold, these were later shown to be compatible with, and often generalizations of, earlier more primitive notions.

Hence I should think that you need not be discouraged by the lack of suitability of physical ideas, or ideas strictly based on present-day physics, for your purposes. If your facts are clear, reproducible, and beyond the vagaries of chance, then I see no reason why you must heed the objections of unimaginative colleagues in the physical sciences.

The parapsychologist, I think, is not likely to find theories which will illuminate his area of interest already prepared by physicists. He must strike out on his own and probably reason in bolder terms than present-day physics suggests. The only bridle upon his speculations is occasioned by the need for empirical verification and by those clearly recognizable metaphysical principles which control all of science. The concepts of parapsychology may well turn out to be at first completely different from the concepts of contemporary physics.

12

J. G. Pratt

(1910–1979)

After receiving a doctoral degree in animal learning in 1936, J. G. Pratt devoted his professional life to parapsychology, first at the Parapsychology Laboratory at Duke University and later in the Psychiatry Department at the University of Virginia, from whence he retired in 1976. His contributions as experimenter, journal editor, author, and traveling investigator are too extensive to list.

With Dr. Pratt's approval the paper presented here was adapted from a lecture of the same title delivered by him at the First South African Conference on Parapsychology in Johannesburg on October 12-14, 1973, and later published in the Journal of the American Society for Psychical Research *(68, 133-155).*

In this lecture Dr. Pratt discusses several topics of importance: the long road to theory, the relation of parapsychology to physics, possible limits to experimental repeatability, the extent of present knowledge of psi, and spontaneity as a factor in the experimental situation.

SOME NOTES FOR THE FUTURE EINSTEIN OF PARAPSYCHOLOGY
(1973)

by J. G. Pratt

A quotation from R. H. Thouless (1969) appropriately sets the stage for the ideas to be presented in this paper. In the following paragraphs he not only aptly characterizes the progress of parapsychology thus far in relation to T. S. Kuhn's study (1962) of how science advances, but he also describes clearly the essential role to be played by the future Einstein for our field.

> The demonstration of the reality of ESP, of precognition, and of psychokinesis is a demonstration of the presence of a series of anomalies. These are plainly occurrences not expected by the psychologist working in the field of normal psychological research. . . . If the history of science is a reliable guide in this matter, we should expect them to be rejected until a new explanatory system is put forward which will accommodate them; it is not to be expected that rejection will be overcome merely by the accumulation of stronger evidence in favor of their reality.
>
> It would, however, be a misunderstanding of the implications of Kuhn's ideas to infer that our task now is to think out a new paradigm. It is not thus that scientific revolutions have taken place in the past. The call is rather to more detailed and more precise research. As we know more about the psi phenomena and as our knowledge becomes more exact, the shape of the future paradigm will gradually become clear. That is likely, I think, to be a long time ahead, since the difficulties of the research are much greater than any in the physical sciences. Then an individual like Darwin, Newton, or Einstein will put forward a new explanatory system in terms of which the phenomena of psi will not merely be explained, but will be shown to be such as we should have expected. If Kuhn is right, this individual is likely to be young or new to the field. Many of us are neither, and we are likely to be even less so when the time is ripe for such a paradigm change. We had better not be tempted to picture ourselves as the potential Einsteins of parapsychology, but rather as workers who have the job of preparing his way by finding out more about the field for which he will ultimately have to produce the theoretical explanation (Thouless, 1969, p. 290).

In my view, Thouless correctly places the Einstein for parapsychology far in the future, and he sees parapsychologists today as forerunners who can prepare the way through "more detailed and more precise research." It is obvious that *research*, in the context of his remarks, involves more than merely sorting and labeling facts gathered through field observations and laboratory experiments. Even during the preparatory stages the field needs theories in terms of which the investigations can be organized and directed toward specific objectives.

The need for theories, even if they are limited in scope, has not gone unrecognized. K. R. Rao (1966) devotes a chapter to characterizing briefly and evaluating a score of theoretical contributions advanced to account for different aspects of the findings. No theory has yet been adequately confirmed by later experimental tests, nor has any been accepted in the field because of its logical consistency and strength.

The theories surveyed by Rao were offered some years ago, most of them dating from the first six decades of this century. The past ten years have been marked by an absence of new theories about psi. There is widespread agreement among research workers in the field that the need for new basic insights is a paramount one and that acceptance of the findings of parapsychology by other scientists will not occur until a theory is available that "makes sense" of psi phenomena. But the lack of theory-building activity during the past decade may reflect a general feeling that further halfway measures would serve no useful purpose.

This paper is not offered as one to end the theory famine. As the wording of the title and the opening quotation from Thouless both imply, the value of the ideas to be set forth must be judged in terms of later developments in the field.

How Does Parapsychology Relate to Physics?

One of the continuous debates in parapsychology is on the relation between parapsychology and physics. Does psi belong among those aspects of the universe that are the direct concern of physicists, or does it fall outside the range of natural events encompassed by physics? Some parapsychologists insist on an affirmative answer to the former question, on the ground that physicists recognize no outer boundaries to their field. According to this view, physics is *the* all-encompassing science, and the many other recognized branches of science, such as astronomy, biology, geology, physiology, and psychology, are only subdivisions made for the convenience of dealing with different areas of natural phenomena that require special methods and techniques of investigation. But to the degree that new knowledge is gained and progress is made toward a better scientific understanding, the results (they say) can properly be counted as adding to the dominion of physics.

A more meaningful approach is to take account of what physicists who have publicly taken a stand on parapsychology have said about the relation between the two fields. One who has chosen to make a career in the field is R. A. McConnell. His first scientific publication in parapsychology was on the question whether psi phenomena are physical or nonphysical. His conclusion: "To label these newly discovered activities as *non-physical* seems legitimate, but to call them *psycho-physical* would be more appropriate" (McConnell, 1947, p. 117). I do not know whether McConnell would still express the matter in just this way after nearly a quarter-century of working in the field, but there is no indication that he has changed his opinion.

Another physicist who has been active in ESP research and who has made important contributions to the literature is J. H. Rush. He also devoted his first scientific publication in the field to the question of how psi phenomena are related to the known physical universe. In summarizing his views he states:

> . . . it must be acknowledged that no known process of energy-transfer has suggested even a plausible explanation of such phenomena. Past experience lends weight to the probability that we have come upon a "mutation" in scientific discovery, an experience as novel as the intimations of the first lodestone or bit of electrified amber—no extra-physical agency, to be sure, but one so far removed beyond present outposts that its relation to recognized phenomena is not yet discernible (Rush, 1943, p. 49).

This quotation does not place parapsychological phenomena outside of physics, but it acknowledges complete inability to foresee how thay can be integrated with scientific knowledge as it then existed in that field.

F. Karger of the Max Planck Institute for Plasma Physics and G. Zicha, a teacher of physics in a technical high school in Munich, stated as a result of their findings in the Rosenheim poltergeist case that

> Physics . . . is now confronted with a completely new situation in view of . . . the inexplicable nature of the phenomena. This is because it has mostly been assumed in the natural sciences that the known physical laws are also valid for describing man so that no new interaction mechanisms need be postulated. It seems, however, as if the psychokinetic phenomena observed here and elsewhere will make it necessary to introduce a fifth kind of interaction. Since the phenomena only occur in connection with a certain person, *physics* is presented with the unforeseen possibility of making *basic* physical discoveries by investigating *man*. This is the reason why these phenomena are of such interest to physics. It is certain, moreover, that clarification of these phenomena will, in turn, have repercussions on our knowledge of man's being (Karger and Zicha, 1968, pp. 386-387).

It is not clear whether Karger and Zicha regard the PK effects as basically physical in nature, but it is obvious that they (like McConnell and Rush two decades earlier) think that the findings cannot be explained in terms of present-day science and that PK research will have far-reaching influence on both physics and psychology.

Only two professional physicists who have not actually worked in parapsychology have explicitly stated their views on the relationship between the two fields. Pasqual Jordan (1951) expressed strong agreement with the view of J. B. Rhine that psi phenomena are not physical. Henry Margenau warned psi research workers against looking to physics for their answers: "The parapsychologist, I think, is not likely to find theories which will illuminate his area of interest already prepared by physicists. He must strike out on his own and probably reason in bolder terms than present-day physics suggests" (Margenau, 1966, p. 277).

In spite of the limited encouragement that parapsychologists have had from physicists, some scholars who were trained along other lines (principally mathematics) have made themselves thoroughly at home with the concepts of nuclear physics and quantum theory and have written about the relevance for parapsychology of recent developments on the frontier of physics. The most vigorous and imaginative advocate of possibilities of finding a physical basis for psi was H. A. C. Dobbs (1965, 1967). His untimely death, according to the views stated by C. D. Broad (1970) in an obituary expressing strong appreciation for Dobbs's work, cut short theoretical contributions of great importance for the field. On the other hand, C. T. K. Chari (1972) finds inadequate all efforts to interpret psi phenomena in terms of quantum physics.

A recent article by J. H. M. Whiteman (1973) goes far toward the goal of breaking this impasse by putting the relationship between physics and parapsychology in a new light. He points out that the scientific model of "one-level determinism" is implicit in the scientific approaches in the life sciences, including parapsychology. Thus many scientists are still clinging to the concept of a mechanistic universe that was dominant in pre-relativity physics but that has now been overthrown by the developments of quantum theory. He reviews the evidence which has led physicists to reject strict determinism, but he does not see in the findings of nuclear physics the answers that the parapsychologist is seeking.

Rather, Whiteman suggests that the recent revolutionary changes in physics provide a model for the further changes in scientific thought needed to integrate psi phenomena with the rest of science. Physics had to break free from the limiting paradigms of the Newtonian era to achieve a level of conceptualization adequate for dealing with sub-atomic events. A comparable advance seems to be required to move beyond both of those areas of impersonal events into a third level of conceptualization capable of dealing with psi phenomena. Those new concepts, when they have been achieved, will not be mere imitations of familiar scientific laws drawn from already developed paradigms; rather, they will be principles that are uniquely applicable to the facts to which they apply. They will not, in other words, equate psi phenomena with events that have already been explored and explained in physics. They will make psi phenomena understandable in their own right and also harmonize them with other natural phenomena in the universe. No one will then ask: What is the relation between parapsychology and physics? We will have the answer.

REPEATABILITY AND SCIENTIFIC REALITY

Over the years many parapsychologists have hoped to develop an experiment that anyone could perform and get a reliable demonstration of psi. For some, the highest priority in the research has been the development of a test that yields a repeatable result. They say that parapsychology either should not or will not be accepted as a branch of science until this goal has been reached. Outspoken critics of psi re-search base their strongest objections to the evidence that has been offered for the reality of the phenomena upon the fact that new evidence cannot be produced upon demand. The situation invites a reexamination of the concept of the repeatable result in science and some further thought to its relevance for parapsychology in particular.

The first point to be made is that science is not based only upon the repeatable *experiment*. Many of the sciences are based upon systematic observations rather than upon designed experiments. In such areas of study as geology, archaeology, and paleontology the basic findings do not lend themselves to controlled demonstrations of effects, yet there is no reason to doubt that sound scientific discoveries have been made.

Next, surely everyone would agree that the repeatable experiment, when it is possible, is the most effective means yet found for the ad-vancement of knowledge. But there are two requirements that must be satisfied before this scientific tool can be used: (*a*) The phenomena to be studied must lend themselves to experimental study. (*b*) It is neces-sary to know the conditions that influence an effect and to be able to control them in the experimental situation. Deficiencies of either knowledge or skill may cause experiments to fail.

The conception of the repeatable experiment as the keystone of science first emerged in classical physics. This was a natural result of the fact that the effects encountered lent themselves to demonstration and direct observation under conditions that could be fully and clearly specified. Later, when efforts were made to extend the experimental method to biology and the various subdivisions of the life sciences, the factors involved were so complex that it was no longer possible to control all of them. It became necessary, instead, to single out one variable or a small number of them that seemed to be relevant and to vary the conditions systematically in the effort to find if they really did influence the effect under investigation. In such statistically evaluated experiments there were always possible factors that were not individually controlled but were lumped together under the rubric of "chance."

The notion of the invariably repeatable experiment as an essential requirement for science was necessarily set aside in research involving statistical procedures giving results that could only be evaluated in terms of probabilities. The possibility that an experiment dependent upon statistical assessment of the results may fail even though the hypothesis is a valid one is an inescapable uncertainty in the method. Consequently there are large sections of science in which we require *general*, but not *invariable*, repeatability of results even when the highest degree of competence is shown in planning and carrying out the research.

The idea of repeatable experiments as the most essential feature of scientific method arose during a time when the prevailing paradigm called for a completely predictable universe. The assumed model was what Whiteman (1973) calls a one-level naturalism in which every event was considered to be part of a mechanistic universe. To a degree the experimental method in science is inextricably intertwined with this paradigm, since an experiment is essentially an effort to set up a submechanism within the universal mechanism for the purpose of arriving at new deterministic statements about cause and effect relationships. It attempts, in other words, to locate events within a time-space framework.

The controlled experiment in parapsychology is borrowed from this same scientific tradition and thus shares its basic assumptions and limitations. We know that many—perhaps most—research workers in parapsychology and other scholars who have grappled with the enigmas of the field consider that psi is not bound by space and time. Is it not surprising, therefore, that we seem so strongly committed to a scientific approach that basically assumes that we will ultimately be able to describe psi events in deterministic terms? When we consider how little there is to show for a century of efforts to discover scientific laws (in the meaning of that term in classical physics) that govern parapsychological phenomena, we may be well advised to pause and ask whether we have been correctly interpreting nature's direction signs.

Perhaps we should drastically shift our emphasis and no longer insist upon achieving strict predictability and repeatability in parapsychology. This is not to say that we should abandon the concept of lawfulnes in the field. In fact, the *absence* of strict repeatability may be as fundamental for psi, and therefore just as much a "law," as its *presence* is, for example, in astronomical events. We may, I think, move closer to the heart of our phenomena if we take as fundamental what we may call the law of *recurrence*. The genuine psi phenomenon is, along with its other defining characteristics, one that happens, intermittently and unpredictably, again and again. Thus persistence and inevitability may have a position in the realm of psi events comparable to predictability and repeatability in classical physics.

OPINIONS AS TO WHAT WE NOW KNOW

Investigators in our field seem to be strangely divided among themselves as regards where the field now stands. On the one hand there are the optimists who express general satisfaction about how far we have come. Both Rao (1966) and Thouless (1972), for example, express themselves in recent books surveying the field in terms that place them in this category, and I think that readers of my new book (Pratt, 1973) will agree that I belong there also. On the other hand there are pessimists who emphasize how little we know. In a strict sense of the word, both are right. We do know a lot more than we did a hundred years ago, and even much more than we did fifty years ago, when the first permanent university laboratory for parapsychology was still only a dream in the mind of William McDougall. But we still do not have a way of viewing the findings that makes sense of the whole collection of psi phenomena, and this fact is enough to make us acutely aware of how far we still are from an adequate understanding of psi.

Gertrude Schmeidler, for example, was reported (Rhine, 1973, p. 137) as having told a NASA group in March, 1973, that we know little about psi phenomena except that ESP and PK occur. Yet when she presented her presidential address at the 1971 convention of the Parapsychological Association (Schmeidler, 1971b) she seemed confident that a number of basic principles have been discovered regarding psi processes. While her address chiefly gave her own opinions on a number of scientific issues in the field, she also used the occasion to have those who were present register their own views. The results (Schmeidler, 1971a) showed that an overwhelming majority agreed that ESP is firmly established and that it occurs in relation to physical situations (clairvoyance), subjective states (telepathy), and even when the "stimulus" is a noninferential future event (precognition). Strong agreement was also expressed that PK occurs.

Opinions registered on other statements covering broad areas of knowledge about psi showed a striking consensus regarding where we stand. The ESP stimulus is a relational or "meaning" situation rather than an object or situation defined in absolute terms, and the information ESP provides is partial rather than all-or-none. The systematic errors that occur in psi tests (incomplete or distorted representation of the target, displacement, decline effects, psi-missing, consistent missing, and the like) provide usable information about process. ESP occurs also in animal species other than man. Psi is a general ability rather than one limited to a few individuals.

It is informative, also, to note the degree of agreement the Schmeidler questionnaire showed regarding what we do not yet know about psi. ESP of past events (retrocognition) and any form of personal survival of death are both not proved—in each instance there are great methodological difficulties facing crucial research. It has not been clearly established that ESP and PK are unitary in nature. Nor is it now known whether psi can be either shielded or augmented by physical means. "The physiological locus or process of ESP input and PK output are unknown." There was strong agreement that the occurrence of ESP or PK in plants has not been established.

On the positive side once more, two questions encompassing a number of lines of research found agreement that negative attitudes, withdrawal, and the like are associated with low ESP scores, while belief, interest, enthusiasm, and the like are conducive to high scoring.

Schmeidler's sampling of parapsychologists' opinions was taken in the informal setting of a lecture and she made no efforts to conceal her own opinions. Her report cannot, therefore, be taken as a scientific manifesto regarding where the field stands. Nevertheless, it reveals a consensus about what has and what has not been achieved as regards a number of the major problems of the field.

Do Experimental and Experiential Psi Differ?

Why are we not further along after nearly a century of organized effort? When we look at the rate of progress in other areas of science, how can we explain the fact that parapsychology has not already had its Einstein? One reason frequently given is that psi phenomena are more complex and they therefore raise more difficult problems than those that scientists in other areas encounter. Without disagreeing with this judgment, I suggest that much of the trouble may lie in the investigators. We may be hampered or even defeated in the research due to our trying to force concepts upon psi occurrences that simply do not apply to the phenomena. Most research workers in the field have expected to deal successfully with the problems of parapsychology by building upon the scientific achievements made in other branches of science. This was a reasonable first expectation and one that needed to be tested. If we have advanced more slowly than it seems we should have done, perhaps it is time to ask whether this may mean that we chose the wrong road.

Rao (1973), in a recent biographical statement, confessed to a change in his thinking that seems to be relevant to what I am trying to say here. He says that he is torn between his loyalty to strictly-controlled experiments in parapsychology and the need he sees for an experiential approach. He suggests that the experimental approach has failed to come to grips with the fundamental issues of parapsychology, and closer attention to the psi processes as found in real-life situations may provide insights that laboratory tests cannot equal.

This idea of two kinds of psi, one that happens spontaneously in everyday life and another that can be detected in more attentuated form in controlled experiments, should not go unchallenged. Perhaps what we are able to capture in our designed psi tests is just as closely related to the psi experiences of everyday life as the electrical sparks produced in the physics laboratory are to the lightning flash of the electrical storm. But if we are to bridge the gap between spontaneous and laboratory psi, which one is likely to prove to be more fundamental? Do spontaneous occurrences provide the key for the understanding of psi-on-demand in the test situation, or will experimental findings eventually explain the daily-life occurrences?

Perhaps we have been misinterpreting the experimental results as controlled psi demonstrations and as therefore occupying a stronger scientific position than the spontaneous material. I propose that we should try reversing the relationship. Instead of assuming that our test results are a superior product because they represent psi on demand, perhaps we should think of them as spontaneous sparks of psi that occur in the framework of the test but that are otherwise just as unpredictable and spontaneous as psi experiences of daily life. Throughout the history of parapsychological research we have largely neglected in the test findings the feature that we have given the predominant place when referring to real-life psi occurrences, their spontaneity. It is as if we have shunned the concept of spontaneity in our laboratory work because it would make psi investigators seem less scientific than other branches of research. To illustrate this point, I checked the index references in the volumes of the *Journal of Parapsychology*. Surprisingly few mentions are found of *spontaneity* as a factor in psi occurrences, but there are many citations of *spontaneous cases*. Even when spontaneity has been considered, it was usually referred to as a characteristic of the *subject* rather than as an aspect of the psi response. In one instance, for example, J. L. Moreno (1948) suggested in a letter to the editor a comparison of results of group tests of ESP and the spontaneity of the subjects as measured in other tests of that personality characteristic. The only explicit study of spontaneity in relation to ESP performance is that by W. B. Scherer (1948), but it is difficult to decide whether the experimenter thought of the spontaneity as a characteristic of the subject or of the psi process.

Some persons may think that this distinction is a mere quibble, but I suggest there may be more to it than that. It is one thing to say that a subject who exhibits a large degree of spontaneity generally is more likely to demonstrate psi than one who does not, and quite another thing to say that a person may under certain conditions make a response that is basically spontaneous in nature and one that under the circumstances can only be interpreted as a psi occurrence. The former formulation emphasizes the spontaneity as a characteristic of the *person*, whereas the latter clearly assigns it to the *psi event*.

SPONTANEITY OF PSI IN THE FORCED-CHOICE TEST

In a thorough study of subjective factors affecting success in planned ESP tests, Rhea White (1964) compared the "old" and the "new" methods used by subjects in responding to targets presented in experiments. By the "old method" she referred to the subjective steps that the percipient went through in preparing for the response that was eventually made to the concealed target. Her description is based upon explicit statements that she gleaned from the research reports in which strong emphasis was placed on the method. She found a surprising amount of agreement among the subjects regarding the steps of subjective preparation that gave the most successful results.

We should note that the method was one which emphasized the individual trials and the quality of the results rather than accumulating a large number of trials in which a high rate of success might be sacrificed. This general approach was perhaps encouraged by the fact that targets were used that had a low probability of scoring purely chance hits. The old method generally characterized research done from 1882 until about 1940 (though the decade of the thirties may be considered as a transitional period).

In contrast, the "new" method is the one that has been used predominantly in ESP testing during recent decades. Its main feature is that the subject is asked to make a large number of responses to targets selected from a much more limited range of possibilities. The most frequently used range has been five, as with the familiar ESP symbols, though a fifty-fifty choice situation has also been used extensively (e.g., Stepanek's choices between white and green and Harribance's responses to the sex of persons depicted in a random order of photographs). The new method of rapid-fire guessing with little or no attention given to the subjective procedure of making contact with the targets predominated from around 1940 onward.

Near the beginning of her article White anticipates what she will later present in detail in the following paragraphs given under the subtitle "Description of the Method":

> It has already been stressed that in the earlier period of investigation a good deal of attention was paid to the way in which the percipient responded to the target. A major development growing out of this emphasis is the somewhat ritualistic technique used for obtaining the correct response. Most of the remainder of this paper will be devoted to a detailed study of this method and a consideration of the advisability of using it, or an adaptation of it, in future experiments.

> This method is divided into several steps, each of which is described together with relevant passages from the original reports. The steps are (1) Relaxation, (2) Engaging the Conscious Mind, (2A) The Demand, (3) The Waiting, the Tension, and the Release, and (4) The Way the Response Enters Consciousness.

> This separation into steps has been made mainly for convenience in presenting the material and to facilitate discussion. As nearly as possible, the separation was made along the lines suggested by the material itself. Other separations may be possible. In any case, it would be unwise to consider any division as hard and fast, for the essence of the method being considered (paradoxically enough, since it is quite deliberate) is to allow the freest response possible to well up in some form of spontaneous expression from the deeper levels of the percipient's mind.

> It may be well to mention here that although the steps in this method are *conscious*, i.e., deliberate, the aim is to produce a spontaneous and *un-*

conscious response, i.e., one not initiated by the conscious mind. By the very nature of the situation, the percipient begins with conscious knowledge of his aim, which is to discern the target by nonsensory and (apparently) unconscious means. In addition to remembering his aim, the percipient is forced by the situation to remind himself that at the moment he does *not* know what the target is, nor will he be able to discover it by any "normal" (sensory and rational) means. This throws him back upon the deeper, non-rational resources of his being.

With the information available to consciousness at that moment, then, the percipient is aware that the only course open to him is pure guessing. Thus far, this approach corresponds to what takes place both in the more recent experiments and the older ones. But in both cases there must be something more than mere *guessing* involved, since the results obtained are not of a chance nature. In much of the modern ESP testing, however, the subject is, so far as he knows, merely "guessing." But the earlier work may have carried the process a step or two further, at least in regard to the percipient's conscious awareness of what was happening. (The actual dynamics at an unconscious level may be the same in both cases.)

As will be seen in the pages to come, one of the purposes of this method is to take the "guesswork" out of the ESP response at the conscious level. Apparently the correct response exists at an unconscious level. By making the contents of the unconscious conscious, much of the guesswork can be eliminated. The main task confronting the conscious mind, then, is to *recognize* the correct response if and when it comes to the conscious level; a second task may be to school itself to *wait* for this response. (It is at this point that many of the modern "guessers" respond, willy-nilly, by indicating the first thing that comes to mind.) (White, 1964, p. 27-28).

The White article was widely heralded among parapsychologists as a contribution of major importance. It was primarily an appeal to research workers to give attention once more in ESP tests to the method that earlier investigators and subjects had used with apparently outstanding success.

A decade has gone by since the White study was published, and there has been no explicit indication in the literature that her plea has been heeded. There is discernible, however, a turning to methods other than the use of the standard ESP symbols, some of them involving the use of unrestricted targets in free-response test. It is reasonable to suppose, therefore, that the White article had an indirect influence upon the research of the past decade, even if not the direct one of inspiring renewed use of the old method of responding to ESP targets.

Several times in her paper White characterizes the "old" method as one with the objective of permitting the subject to bring to the conscious level a spontaneous response to the target. The modern method is described as one of willy-nilly, rapid-fire responses to targets. The subject says the first thing that comes to mind. White decries the modern method chiefly because it gives such a marginal level of success. Considering the period that was included in the study (the two decades of the forties and fifties insofar as the new method was concerned), this evaluation is understandable, since the only exceptions to marginal scoring were in the work with high-scoring ESP subjects in England. But those subjects also gave rapid-fire responses, and this fact is enough to raise the question whether the White analysis of the situation really does justice to the psi process in forced-choice tests with rapid calling. This question is further emphasized by the fact that during the decade since the White study was completed further cases of outstanding ESP performance have been investigated with methods involving rapid responses to targets, Stepanek and Harribance being the most notable examples.

The apparent contradiction in this picture of the situation is removed, I suggest, if we get away from the point of view which identifies the statistical unit of the "trial" in the modern ESP test with the psychological unit of response of the subject. The manner in which the test is conducted as well as the results themselves seem to force us to entertain the view that the subject is not actually calling the individual targets but is responding instead to the run (or sequence of targets) *as a whole*.

The remarkable fact is that in this situation the responses are found to be related to the sequence of targets in many different ways that cannot reasonably be attributed to mere chance coincidence. Because of the manner in which the test is designed and presented to the subject, the investigator looks first at the relation between each call and the target occupying the same position in the sequence. But we have known for a long time that merely counting the number of direct hits does not give a complete picture of the ESP process within the run. We have found a great number of other nonrandom effects, starting with variations in the frequency of hits in relation to the target positions within the sequence, displacement hits on targets coming sooner or later in the sequence than the calls, consistent wrong associations between calls and targets, psi-missing in general, displacement in those areas of the run where the subject failed to score direct hits, and many other forms of extrachance relationship. Taken as a whole—to the extent that we are aware of these intertwined trends—the findings present a picture of a broad spectrum of effects.

The view presented here is that the controlled quantitive ESP test is not one in which the subject gives a rigorously controlled performance. Within the framework of the test, ESP is not something that the subject *does* and over which he has conscious control. Rather, it is something that *happens* to the subject. In the same manner as the spontaneous parapsychical experience of everyday life intrudes upon the person's consciousness, so the ESP suceesses of the card-calling test spontaneously happen to the subject. The real miracle and the great good fortune of the experimenter is the fact that such an ESP test works at all. But it does, and—at its best—very well indeed!

REFERENCES

Broad, C. D. H. A. C. Dobbs [Obituary]. *Journal of the Society for Psychical Research*, 1970, *45*, 392–396.
Chari, C. T. K. Precognition, probability, and quantum mechanics. *Journal of the American Society for Psychical Research*, 1972, *66*, 193–207.
Dobbs, H. A. C. Time and ESP. *Proceedings of the Society for Psychical Research*, 1965, *54*, 249–361.
Dobbs, H. A. C. The feasibility of a physical theory of ESP. In J. R. Smythies (Ed.), *Science and ESP*. New York: Humanities Press, 1967. Pp. 225–254.
Jordan, P. Reflections on parapsychology, psychoanalysis, and atomic physics. *Journal of Parapsychology*, 1951, *15*, 278–281.
Karger, F., and Zicha, G. Physical investigation of psychokinetic phenomena in Rosenheim, Germany, 1967. *Papers Presented for the Eleventh Annual Convention of the Parapsychological Association*. Freiburg i. Br., Germany: Institut für Grenzgebiete der Psychologie und Psychohygiene, 1968.
Kuhn, T. S. *The Structure of Scientific Revolutions*. Chicago: University of Chicago Press, 1962.
McConnell, R. A. Physical or non-physical? *Journal of Parapsychology*, 1947, *11*, 111–117.
Margenau, H. ESP in the framework of modern science. *Journal of the American Society for Psychical Research*, 1966, *60*, 214—228.
Moreno, J. L. Letter. *Journal of Parapsychology*, 1948, *12*, 303.
Pratt, J. G. *ESP Research Today: A Study of Developments in Parapsychology Since 1960*. Metuchen, New Jersey: Scarecrow Press, 1973.
Rao, K. R. *Experimental Parapsychology*. Springfield, Illinois: Charles C. Thomas, 1966.
Rao, K. R. An autobiographical note. *Parapsychology Review*, 1973, *4*, 13–15.
Rhine, J. B. News and comments. *Journal of Parapsychology*, 1973, *37*, 137–150.
Rush, J. H. Some considerations as to a physical basis of ESP. *Journal of Parapsychology*, 1943, *7*, 44–49.
Scherer, W. B. Spontaneity as a factor in ESP. *Journal of Parapsychology*, 1948, *12*, 126–147.
Schmeidler, G. R. Parapsychologists' opinions about parapsychology, 1971. *Journal of Parapsychology*, 1971, *35*, 208–218. (a)
Schmeidler, G. R. Respice, adspice, prospice. *Proceedings of the Parapsychological Association*, 1971, *8*, 117–145. (b)
Thouless, R. H. Parapsychology during the last quarter of a century. *Journal of Parapsychology*. 1969, *33*, 283–299.

Thouless, R. H. *From Anecdote to Experiment in Psychical Research.* London and Boston: Routledge & Kegan Paul, 1972.

White, R. A. A comparison of old and new methods of response to targets in ESP experiments. *Journal of the American Society for Psychical Research*, 1964, *58*, 21–56.

Whiteman, J. H. M. Quantum theory and parapsychology. *Journal of the American Society for Psychical Research*, 1973, *66*, 341–360.

13

Charles Honorton

(1946–   )

A longer version of this paper was presented at the 1978 National Meeting of the American Association for the Advancement of Science at Washington, D.C., by Charles Honorton, a leader of the new generation of experimental parapsychologists. In it he argues that the mind-brain problem of classical philosophy is the central concern of parapsychology.

Reminding us that present knowledge of the brain provides no plausible model of how physical relations between man and his environment are transformed into conscious experience, Honorton gently ridicules the common supposition of scientists that the interaction between mind and brain is one-way. He discusses the challenges to the understanding of psychophysical interaction that are posed by recent findings on the specificity of biofeedback control and on the curative power of the placebo, as well as by the long-unsolved riddle of the role of the observer in determining a quantum-mechanical state.

We are given a description of the automated testing of the hypothesis that mind can influence external physical states using the Helmut Schmidt paradigm—a biofeedback experiment in which the information loop has no physical closure—and a summary of the results of 54 such experiments now in the literature of parapsychology.

Honorton ends with a description of current parapsychological attempts to investigate a neurophysiological hypothesis of the human will that was proposed by Sir John Eccles in 1953. The investigative method involves the correlation of ESP success and the electroencephalographic signals. In the words of Honorton, "We have begun to forge an empirical approach to one of the most profound and ancient of mysteries—the nature of mind and its relationship to the physical world."

PARAPSYCHOLOGY AND THE MIND-BODY PROBLEM
(1978)

by CHARLES HONORTON

The questions we ask of nature have a determining influence on the answers we receive. Both questions and answers are embedded in an underlying system of implicit assumptions through which we negotiate our agreed-upon consensual reality. These assumptive frameworks are fundamental because they define the boundaries of experience; what can and cannot happen; what can and cannot be known; and how we know what we know. We are seldom consciously aware of our implicit assumptions until they have been challenged or clearly violated.

CONSCIOUS MIND VIS-A-VIS BIOLOGICAL BRAIN

As scientists, one of our tacit assumptions is that the process of observation is passive and one-way: our experimental observations are not directly influenced by our act of observation. Once we have formulated the hypothesis, developed an appropriate methodology, and are ready to collect data, we step out of the picture and allow nature to reveal its properties; within, that is, the constraints we have imposed upon it.

The assumptions we make about the process of observation are rooted in even more fundamental assumptions concerning the nature of psychophysical interaction, i.e., the nature of mind and its relationship to the physical world. Consider the assumption of "one-way" traffic between brain states and conscious states: mental states are *always* effects and never *causes* of brain states. Consciousness is apparently some kind of alchemical transmutation of brain activity. Mind "emerges" through complex physical interactions but has no reciprocal power to influence physical states. Obviously, if mind cannot influence its own brain, then it is most unlikely to influence anything else.

That mind and brain are intimately interconnected, we cannot doubt, but there is increasing reason for scepticism over the validity of the assumption that the "traffic" between them is only "one-way." Neurophysiologists such as Eccles (4) and Penfield (16) have been among the first to admit that our present knowledge of the brain and nervous system provides no final solution to the mind-body problem. We have not found a cortical locus for goal-directed action, nor is there even a *plausible* model describing how physical interactions could be transformed into conscious experiences. Although our measuring devices may simply still be too crude, the low level and frequently contradictory correlations between brain states and experiential states (9) does not suggest a psychophysical isomorphism.

In a recent lecture at the New York Academy of Sciences, Eccles provided this commentary:

> Common to all is the assertion that "mind" does not act on the brain. All human actions including the most subtle, such as artistic and imaginative expressions, are behaviors . . . that will be fully explicable by the operations of the neuronal machinery of the brain when neuronal science has accomplished its program. At this millenary time we are promised that the so-called mind-brain problem will be dissolved in a completely materialistic solution. This is what [Sir Karl] Popper aptly derides as "promissory materialism" (5).

Philosopher of science Popper and neurophysiologist Eccles have recently collaborated on a book (17) in which they argue that all varieties of materialistic monism are not only untenable, but also contrary to evolutionary theory: "If mind is *completely ineffective* in bringing about changes in the operation of the brain and so in causing action," Eccles says, "then there is no biological reason why such an impotent 'mind' should occur in the first place and why it should be preserved and developed in the processes of natural selection" (5).

SCIENTIFIC PUZZLES SUGGESTING THAT THE MIND HAS POWER

The challenge of developing more satisfactory *empirical* approaches to the problem of psychophysical interaction is beginning to emerge as an interdisciplinary enterprise, and is attracting the physicist no less than the psychologist, the engineer, and the physiologist. It has, of course, always been of interest to the philosopher.

Take the case of biofeedback: biofeedback is the union of biomedical engineering, neurophysiology, psychology, and cybernetics. As a consequence of this union, consummated only a decade ago, we now know that ordinary human subjects can learn to voluntarily control a wide variety of normally involuntary physiological functions, including skin temperature, brain waves, and even the activity of a single cell, merely by observing peripheral feedback displays which monitor these functions (1,2,3,13,14). Biofeedback training is characterized as "goal-directed," and appears to be most effective when the subject does not actively "strive" or "exert effort," but rather assumes an attitude of *passive attention*, allowing the process to occur spontaneously.

Biofeedback clearly raises more questions than it answers. One of the most challenging problems posed by this phenomenon concerns the specificity of control: how does the subject selectively identify, isolate, and control one of perhaps several hundred motor units that are within the pickup of the electrodes? The mechanisms underlying biofeedback are presently unknown, but we can no longer doubt that it works.

Equally perplexing problems arise in other areas of psychosomatic research. Consider the curative power of the placebo. Placebos are pharmacologically inert substances, and yet they can have marked physiological effects, e.g., to heal tissue damage. The placebo treatment of warts, for example, by painting them with a brightly colored but inert dye and telling the patient that the wart will be gone with the dye wears off, "is as effective as any other form of treatment, including surgical excision" (6). In a well-known study of patients hospitalized with bleeding peptic ulcer (22), 70% showed "excellent results lasting over a period of one year" when the doctor gave them an injection of distilled water and assured them that it was a new medical cure. A control group who received the same injection from a nurse with information that it was an experimental medication of unknown effectiveness showed a remission rate of only 25%.

These and many similar findings in a number of areas raise a crucial question as to how far mental influence may extend on physical systems. The possibility that mind can directly influence physical states external to its own nervous system has been raised by physical theorists such as Henry Margenau, Eugene Wigner, and other specialists in the quantum theory of measurement. After enunciating the principle of epistemological feedback, i.e., the "participation of the observer in the act and outcome of a measurement," Prof. Margenau described real and potential ways in which the observing physicist may interact with and possibly influence the physical system he wishes to measure (11). These range from mundane considerations of the physicist's choice of method, to the speculative and highly provocative possibility that the physicist, through his act of observation, may directly influence the outcome of a measurement through, e.g., the selection of a value permitted by the probability distribution of the physical state.

As Prof. Margenau indicated, any attempt to bring this speculative possibility into empirical focus, so that it can be tested, constitutes the formulation of what is by definition a parapsychological hypothesis:

that mind can directly interact with and influence external physical states.

LABORATORY EXPERIMENTS IN WHICH
MIND AFFECTS ELECTRONIC ROULETTE WHEELS

There are many ways we could set up an experiment to test this hypothesis. One way is to flip a coin. We know that under normal circumstances, a coin will land "heads" and "tails" with approximately equal frequency, such that Prob(heads) = Prob(tails) = ½. We can easily calculate the probability, or "chance likelihood," of obtaining any given distribution of heads/tails from a set number of trials. So we could flip the coin and have our subject/observer consciously "wish" for heads to come up more frequently than tails; or, to eliminate any systematic bias in the coin, we might alternate "wishing" for heads on some trials and "wishing" for tails on other trials. We could also run a parallel control experiment in which there is no effort to mentally influence the distribution of heads/tails.

In actual practice, quantum mechanical random event generators have been used to provide a more rigorous basis for experiments on direct observer influence (19). These devices use fundamentally random natural processes such as radioactive decay or thermal noise in semiconductors to provide an electronic analog of "coin-flipping." In a typical device of this sort, an electron emitted by Sr-90 decay triggers a Geiger counter and thereby registers whether the momentary position of a high-speed binary counter corresponds to "heads" or "tails." These devices can randomly generate the equivalent of 1, 10, or even 1000 "coin-flips" per second, while at the same time automatically recording the total number of events generated and their "heads"/"tails" distribution.

An observer/subject can monitor the current physical state of the random generator through a feedback signal which occurs whenever the device is in, say the "heads" state, and with no (or different) feedback, when it is in the "tails" state. The feedback display may be a digital readout, a visible light or audible tone, or a computer graphics display which changes as a function of the momentary physical state of the random generator. From this point on, the experiment is similar to a biofeedback experiment: the subject/observer's task is to observe the feedback display and attempt to mentally "bias" the normally random output of the device according to preset experimental instructions. The experiment differs from biofeedback, of course, in that there is no direct physical connection between the observer and the physical state to which he is given feedback.

The first experiments of this type were reported in 1970 by the physicist Helmut Schmidt (20). The feedback display was a circle of nine lamps which lit one at a time progressively in the clockwise or counterclockwise direction, depending on which of the two states was randomly generated on successive trials. The 15 subject/observers in this experiment completed more than 30,000 individual trials. Schmidt also ran extensive control trials without subjects attempting to influence the output of the random generator. While these random control trials conformed closely to the expected chance distribution, the experimental trials with subjects deviated significantly (p less than 0.001) from the expected chance values.

Since the publication of Schmidt's first experiment in 1970, 54 experiments of this type have been reported by investigators in seven different laboratories. Of these experiments, 35 were successful at the 5% criterion level and none showed significant departures from chance in associated control tests, i.e., without intended influence. Thus, these random generator studies of observer influence appear to show a substantial level of replicability.

Many of these studies go beyond mere replication of the observer effect to examine a variety of physical, physiological, and psychological variables associated with its occurrence. I will now briefly summarize some of the more important secondary findings.

THE MIND DISPLAYS SMALL-SCALE OMNISCIENCE

These effects, like those studied in biofeedback, appear to be goal-directed. The observer's task is to increase the frequency of a feedback signal. He need not know or be concerned with what is "inside the box," i.e., the internal mechanism of the random generator, in order to influence its output. This is evident from studies in which key physical parameters of the device have been systematically varied. [For example,] in two experiments the feedback display observed by the subject was, without his knowledge, switched between an internally simple and an internally complex random generator, with no difference in the subjects' apparent ability to influence the outcome (12).

Several studies in our laboratory bear this out from a slightly different angle: our random generator automatically alternates the definition of the target ("heads"/"tails") one microsecond prior to each trial. We originally incorporated this feature as a precaution, to cancel out any possible side bias in the output of the device. Indeed, it serves this function admirably: in 7 million control trials (without intended influence) we observed a total excess of 37 "heads" (mean observed = 50.00053%, where mean expected = 50.0%).

Some of our experimental work has centered on the role of feedback in guiding observer effects. In several experiments (8,26), subject/observers received tone feedback over headphones while relaxing in a room adjacent to the random generator. The subjects' task was to keep the tone ON as much as possible. Unknown to the subjects, the feedback tone was sometimes given for a performance rate of 70% or higher over the last 10 trials, and sometimes for a rate of 30% or less. The subjects' goal was to keep the tone ON and they did so regardless of the feedback contingency. The fact that in these experiments the target was defined one microsecond in advance of each trial would seem to preclude any mechanistic "push-pull" interpretation of these effects, since this operation is approximately three orders of magnitude faster than human nervous system functioning, which operates on the order of milliseconds. If this apparent goal-directedness is real and not merely the result of our ignorance of an underlying mechanism, we may be forced to ask: to what extent are we discovering nature's properties and to what extent are we participating in their creation? This brings us, of necessity to an examination of the role of the experimenter.

Do the Experimenter's Wishes Affect His Findings?

Parapsychological experimenter effects have been the subject of five review articles during the past two years (10, 15, 23, 24, 25). By the late 1930s, parapsychologists had somewhat reluctantly come to recognize the crucial role of the experimenter in eliciting significant ESP effects. Different experimenters, using the same method, and sometimes even working in the same experiment (18), obtained different results. The difference could not be attributed to differences in precautions or in the execution of the experimental protocol. It seemed to reflect the quality of the interpersonal interaction between experimenters and subjects. Experimenters who made an effort to help their subjects feel comfortable and relaxed in the experimental setting generally were more successful than those who got right down to business.

My colleagues and I explored this effect systematically in an ESP experiment with automated testing and recording (7). Each of 36 volunteer subjects completed an ESP test after interacting with an experimenter. For half of the subjects, the experimenter was friendly, warm, and supportive. For the remaining subjects, the experimenter acted cool and aloof. Subjects in the friendly experimenter-interaction group scored significantly higher in the ESP test than those who were in the negative interaction group.

More recently, an ESP experiment based on R. Rosenthal's expectancy model was conducted at State University of New York at Stony Brook (21). Some of the experimenters were led to expect that the experimental procedure would show strong positive ESP performance, while other experimenters were "informed" that the procedure was associated with negative ESP scores. Appropriate precautions were taken in the preparation, administration, and scoring of the ESP data. It was found that the subjects' ESP scores significantly reflected the differential expectancies of the primary experimenters.

But the problem goes deeper: there seems to be a fundamental uncertainty involved in parapsychological measurement. If, e.g., in the random generator studies, we accept the hypothesis of direct observer influence, there is no conclusive way to isolate the source of the effect to the presumptive subject. The experimenter is also there as an observer and must be assumed to be at least as interested in the outcome of the experiment as is the subject.

Discussing the random generator work, I repeatedly emphasized that consistently chance outcomes have been obtained in control conditions, without intended influence. But if observers can mentally interact with the random generator so as to influence the values of experimental measurements, how can we rule out the possibility of such influence on the outcome of control measurements? The answer (at least for the present) is that we cannot. While the control condition is not free of possible observer influence, such influence would presumably be motivated to *conform* to the expected distribution, *not*—as is the goal of the experimental condition—to *deviate* from chance expectation. Thus, the control condition continues to serve its primary function as a conditional contrast or difference measure.

The problem remains, however, that we cannot conclusively isolate these effects to specific individuals. There may, perhaps, be at least one way out of this dilemma. If we entertain as a working hypothesis, the existence of mind as a fundamental form of interaction, on a par with gravitation, electromagnetic, and nuclear interaction, then we could conceive of mental states as diffusely distributed in and around the brain. From this standpoint, it would be basically inappropriate to attempt to isolate the source of mind influence to any specific organism or individual. Whatever evidence of mind influence might be detected and measured, via random generator or some other device, would derive from a substratum in which both experimenter and subject were mutually participating. Perhaps we have here a view of epistemological feedback in the "raw."

HOW DOES THE MIND COMMUNICATE WITH THE BRAIN?

In this connection, finally, I will mention one other area that has opened up as a consequence of biofeedback and random generator studies. This is stimulated by the speculations of Eccles on the mind-brain interaction. He suggests (4) that the brain is a *detector* rather than the *generator* of mind, and suggests that weak "mind influence" could modify the pattern of discharge of hundreds of thousands of neurons "as a result of an 'influence' that initially caused the discharge of merely one neuron. . . ."

> Thus, the neurophysiological hypothesis is that the "will" modifies the spatio-temporal activity of the neuronal network by exerting . . . "fields of influence" that become effective through this unique detector function of the active cerebral cortex.
> It will be objected that the essence of the hypothesis is that mind produces changes in the matter-energy system of the brain and hence must be itself in that system. . . . But this deduction is merely based on the present hypotheses of physics. Since these postulated "mind influences" have not been detected by any existing physical instrument, they have necessarily been neglected in constructing the hypotheses of physics.

Eccles advanced this primarily as a plausibility argument in 1953, before the advent of biofeedback and quantum-mechanical random generators. On the hypothesis that the random generator work represents the physical detection and measurement of "mind influence," work in progress in several parapsychology laboratories seeks to put some empirical "meat" on the speculative "bones" of Eccles' plausibility argument.

One example must suffice to illustrate some of the current directions in this research. Preliminary studies are underway to see if random-generator effects correlate with conscious control of brainwaves. Feedback is provided only when the subject produces brainwaves of a certain frequency. The subject's brainwave feedback serves to trigger the random generator so that it is possible to assess departures from randomness in the device in relation to the subject's success or failure in producing the desired brainwaves. Eccles's neurophysiological hypothesis leads us to predict that significant departures from randomness will occur in conjunction with the subject's "willful" production of the desired brainwaves.

Whether the outcome of this and similar experiments is positive or negative, they will have important implications for the empirical resolution of the mind-body problem. Speaking for myself, I would make no stronger claim for the relevance of parapsychological research than this: for the first time in the history of science, we have begun to forge an empirical approach to one of the most profound and ancient of mysteries, and nature of mind and its relationship to the physical world. We have no answers, but we have begun to develop methods that will enable us to ask some different kinds of questions.

References

1. Basmajian, J. V. *Science*, 1972, *176*, 603–609.
2. Brown, B. *Stress and the art of biofeedback*. New York: Harper & Row, 1977.
3. Budzynski, T. H., Stoyva, J. M., Adler, C. S., & Mullaney, D. J. *Psychosomatic Medicine*, 1973, *35*, 484–496.
4. Eccles, J. C. *The neurophysiological basis of mind*. Oxford University Press, 1953.
5. Eccles, J. C. *Annals of the New York Academy of Sciences*, 1977, *299*, 161–179.
6. Frank, J. D. *Persuasion and healing*. Baltimore: The Johns Hopkins Press, 1961.
7. Honorton, C., Ramsey, M., & Cabibbo, C. *Journal of the American Society for Psychical Research*, 1975, *69*, 135–149.
8. Honorton, C. pp. 95–96 in J. D. Morris, W. G. Roll, & R. L. Morris (Eds.), *Research in Parapsychology—1976*. Metuchen, NJ: Scarecrow Press, 1977.
9. Johnson, L. C. *Psychophysiology*, 1970, *6*, 501–516.
10. Kennedy, J. E., & Taddonio, J. L. *Journal of Parapsychology*, 1976, *40*, 1–33.
11. Margenau, H. *Effects of an observer on measurements in quantum mechanics*. Paper presented at the National Meeting of the American Association for the Advancement of Science, February 17, 1978, at Washington, DC.
12. Matas, F., & Pantas, L. *Proceedings of the Parapsychological Association*, 1971, *8*, 12–13.
13. McDonagh, J. M., & McGinnis, M. *Proceedings 81st Annual Convention American Psychological Association*, 1973, *8*, 547–548.
14. Nowlis, D. P., & Kamiya, J. *Psychophysiology*, 1970, *6*, 476–484.
15. Parker, A. *Parapsychology Review*, 1974, *5*(2), 21–27.
16. Penfield, W. *The mystery of the mind*. Princeton University Press, 1976.
17. Popper, K., & Eccles, J. C. *The self and its brain*. Heidelberg: Springer-Verlag, 1977.
18. Pratt, J. G., & Price, M. M. *Journal of Parapsychology*, 1938, 2, 84–94.
19. Schmidt, H. *Journal of Applied Physics*, 1970, *41*, 462–468.
20. Schmidt, H. *Journal of Parapsychology*, 1970, *34*, 175–181.
21. Taddonio, J. L. *Journal of Parapsychology*, 1976, *40*, 107–114.
22. Volgyesi, F. A. *British Journal of Medical Hypnotism*, 1954, *5*, 8.
23. White, R. A. *Journal of the American Society for Psychical Research*, 1976, *70*, 133–166.
24. White, R. A. *Journal of the American Society for Psychical Research*, 1976, *70*, 333–369.
25. White, R. A. Pp. 273–301 in B. B. Wolman (Ed.), *Handbook of parapsychology*. New York: Van Nostrand Reinhold, 1977.
26. Winnett, R., & Honorton, C. Pp. 97–98 in J. D. Morris, W. G. Roll, & R. L. Morris (Eds.), *Research in Parapsychology—1976*. Metuchen, NJ: Scarecrow Press, 1977.

14

Ray Hyman

(1928–   )

Parapsychologists are people who have encountered psi phenomena, either directly in themselves or friends, or indirectly through the printed word, and who as a consequence have given these phenomena continuing thoughtful attention. In most cases, sooner or later, they have become convinced of the reality of at least some of the phenomena and have thereafter publicly favored the advancement of parapsychology as a science.

Professor Ray Hyman is a rare kind of parapsychologist. He is deeply interested in this field, but he has never, so far as I can discover, admitted to any degree of belief in its phenomena. He is a psychologist at Oregon State University with research interests in perception and cognition. His role in parapsychology, as he describes it, is that of responsible critic of the field.

In the present essay he examines the practical consequences of the intolerance of orthodox science toward strange phenomena, including those of parapsychology. This paper was presented at the History and Philosophy of Science Section at the Annual Meeting of the American Association for the Advancement of Science at San Francisco in January 1980 and was subsequently published in the Zetetic Scholar (1980, No. 6, 31–39). It is reprinted here in its entirety by permission of the author.

PATHOLOGICAL SCIENCE: TOWARDS A PROPER DIAGNOSIS AND REMEDY
(1980)

by RAY HYMAN

How would you react to the following situation:

A competent and respected colleague reports to you that he held a seance in his own home. During the course of the seance, one of the sitters asked if the medium could materialize a sunflower. Following this request, a sunflower, six feet high, fell upon the table. Your colleague produces affidavits from witnesses, each of whom is a respected and honorable man. He insists that both the house and the medium were carefully examined prior to the seance and that all precautions were taken to prevent trickery. Furthermore, he concludes that the only explanation is that the medium somehow had access to a new force, one that he refers to as a "psychic force."

Take a moment to consider what your response might be. Remember that this colleague is one who has earned a reputation as a competent and successful scientist in his chosen field. He is still doing acceptable science within this field. But now he insists that as a result of the seance just described, as well as a number of others which he conducted under carefully controlled conditions, he has obtained many phenomena that cannot be accounted for by currently accepted scientific principles.

Such a situation actually occurred to scientists during the Victorian era in England. Alfred Russel Wallace, the cofounder of the theory of evolution by natural selection, shocked his scientific colleagues in 1869 when he made public his conversion to spiritualism. Up until that time, his scientific colleagues had taken it for granted that he shared the same materialistic and naturalistic outlook that they had. In addition to shocked disbelief, Wallace's colleagues responded in a number of confused ways—with embarrassment, with attempts to ignore it, with open hostility, with attacks on his character, with refusals to listen to his arguments or view his evidence, with misrepresentations of his claims, and with a variety of other reactions which could hardly be called rational, dispassionate or scientific.

PATHOLOGICAL SCIENCE

Wallace's bizarre claim and the confused reaction of his scientific colleagues is a good illustration of what I am calling "pathological science." I have borrowed this term from a talk that Irving Langmuir, late Nobel Laureate, gave at the General Electric Company back in December, 1953 (Langmuir, 1968). Langmuir defined "Pathological science" as "the science of things that aren't so." His examples dealt mainly with claims of mysterious radiations or forces such as N-Rays, Mitogenetic Radiation and the like. I would add to his examples such cases as Martian Canals, the non-existing planet Vulcan, Gall's faculties, as well as Wallace's "psychic force." I would also broaden his definition to include cases in which scientists have wrongly insisted something wasn't so. For example, meteorites, the impossibility of heavier-than-air flying machines, Semmelweiss's childbed fever, and many cases of missed discoveries. We should also include cases of data massage, unconscious plagiarism, deliberate cheating, and a variety of mixed cases.

The distinctive characteristics of these examples, as I see them, are the following:

1. a scientist of acknowledged competence and accomplishments
2. surprises his colleagues by claiming the existence of a phenomenon or relationship that is considered to be bizarre or even impossible by currently accepted principles
3. the scientific establishment either ignores or attacks with hostility this bizarre claim
4. the deviant scientist, along with a few deviant supporters, sticks resolutely to his guns in the face of attacks and indifference
5. the bizarre claim is considered to be discredited in the eyes of the scientific community
6. the claim is banished from further consideration in scientific literature, textbooks and education.

THE PROBLEM POSED BY PATHOLOGICAL SCIENCE

Wallace's scientific colleagues, for the most part, could not believe that a six-foot sunflower could be materialized out of thin air by a psychic force. I suspect that most of you cannot believe this either. But this poses a problem for Wallace's friends and colleagues who respect him as an honest and outstanding scientist. They could not accuse him of being an incompetent scientist; nor of being dishonest.

How should scientists respond to such a bizarre claim from one of their own trusted and distinguished members? Whatever the answer, one would like to say that the response should be consistent with rationality, objectivity, fair play, integrity—in short, with accepted scientific principles. Unfortunately, scientists are not trained nor given models about how to behave under such circumstances. The reactions, understandably if regretfully, are typically confused, ambivalent, erratic, and emotional. The reaction in these cases of pathological science appears to be more one of panic than of considered critical analysis.

If there is truly "pathology" in these cases, the pathology seems to be exhibited as much in the reaction of the scientific community as it is in the claims of the offending scientist. The gut reaction of the scientific orthodoxy is to discredit the offending claim by any means possible—ad hominem attacks, censorship, innuendo, misrepresentation, etc. This panic reaction usually does succeed in discrediting the bizarre claim. It becomes completely cut off from the main body of scientific lores and future generations of scientists have little opportunity to become exposed and possibly contaminated by it. But the manner of the discrediting and the results, I will argue, have consequences for the future of science that may not be worth the price.

THE REACTION TO A. R. WALLACE'S CLAIMS

As I have already indicated, the response by the scientific community to Wallace's psychic claims was confused, erratic, inconsistent, and often emotional. Some, like Darwin, merely tried to avoid any public reference to the matter. Others dismissed it out of hand without actually trying to account for the specific evidence and arguments put forth by Wallace. The most dedicated critic—one who seemed to act as the "hit man" for the rest of the scientific community—was the physiologist William B. Carpenter. His basic position can be summarized by his own words:

> I have no other 'theory' to support, than that of the constancy of the well-ascertained Laws of Nature; and my contention is, that where apparent departures from them take place through Human instrumentality, we are justified in assuming in the first instance either *fraudulent* description or unintentional *self*-deception, or both combined,—until the absence of either shall have been proved by every conceivable test that the sagacity of skeptical experts can devise. (Carpenter, 1877).

In addition to assuming fraud or self-deception, Carpenter also attacked claims on the grounds that the scientist making the claim was incompetent and had earned his reputation by being specialized just for one specific narrow field of science.

Carpenter saw the psychic and spiritualistic claims as part of an "epidemic delusion" and saw his mission in these terms:

> I have no other motive than a desire to do what I can to save from this new form of Epidemic Delusion some who are in danger of being smitten by its poison, and to afford to such as desire to keep themselves clear from it, a justification for their 'common-sense' rejection of testimony pressed upon them by friends whose honesty they would not for a moment call into question. (Carpenter, 1877).

Thus, Carpenter had no hopes of saving those such as Wallace and Crookes who were already "smitten by its poison." Instead, he was crusading to save those not yet contaminated. This might account for why Carpenter did not feel it necessary to look closely at the exact nature of the evidence and claims put forth by Wallace and Crookes. His task was to attack the epidemic by any means available. He was not concerned with the specific arguments and evidence being put forth. Rather, he wanted to make sure that those who might be tempted to listen, would not. His job was to frighten them away from temptation by any means possible.

And it is just in this sort of reaction that I see a serious problem for the continued viability of science.

THE NEGATIVE CONSEQUENCES OF INAPPROPRIATE REACTIONS

It may both be understandable and almost inevitable that the reaction of the scientific critics to heretical hypotheses are emotional, irrational, and irrelevant to the specific arguments put forth. But whatever the reasons for such reactions, I believe that they have negative consequences for the conduct of science. The sorts of tactics employed by the establishment's "hit men" against the offending claims—blocking access to regular communication outlets, ad hominem attacks, misrepresentation of claims, dismissal on a priori grounds—do succeed in a way. They serve to "discredit" the deviant hypothesis. And once it is so tainted, then the establishment scientists feel relieved and ignore it.

But "discrediting" is not the same as disproving. As it turns out, often only through hindsight, most of discredited hypotheses deserved their fate. And perhaps the militant crusaders such as Carpenter can take comfort in the fact that their emotional and often irrational put downs of pathological sciences saved both contemporary and future generations of scientists from becoming smitten by the poison of wrongheaded heresies.

But the nature of the discrediting and some of its aftermaths may actually foster the very "evils" the crusaders were hoping to banish from science. Let me briefly elaborate upon this point.

First, let us consider the effect of the discrediting procedure upon the proponents of the "pathological" claim. Biographers and historians have written about how his defense of embarrassing causes harmed Wallace's subsequent fame. The main effect during his lifetime, however, was a forced compartmentalization of Wallace's orthodox biology and his unorthodox psychical inquiries into separate worlds. His scientific colleagues continued to accept and respect his orthodox contributions while they simultaneously tried to ignore his unorthodoxies. As a result, Wallace had to live in two separate worlds. When he did regular biology, he could talk, correspond, and publish within the world of established science. When he talked or wrote about his investigations of mediums, he could do so only in an entirely different world of individuals who were outcasts or non-entities with respect to the scientific establishments.

The same was even more strikingly so for Wallace's contemporary, William Crookes. Crookes tried to conduct laboratory research on psychic phenomena produced by mediums. He not only was bitterly attacked for this, but all his attempts to get his work read at scientific meetings or published in scientific journals were ruthlessly blocked. He finally gave up trying to get a hearing for these unorthodox views among his scientific colleagues and published his findings in spiritualist magazines. At the same time, however, he continued his purely orthodox chemical and physical experiments which were not only completely accepted by the scientific establishment, but which eventually won for him just about all the honors possible for a scientist of his period, including knighthood (Palfreman, 1976).

This enforced compartmentalization, in fact, seems to be true for most of the other cases of pathological science.

Consider what this compartmentalization accomplishes. It isolates the deviant scientist and his claims from further debate and interaction with orthodox science. He is restricted in his further consideration of his position to discussions and exchanges with individuals who already believe in and support his claim. In addition, most of these individuals have neither the training nor aptitude for rigorous scientific evaluation. Thus, the deviant scientist has no further incentive to refine, improve, or correct loopholes in his position. This further entrenches him in his belief that his initial claims were correct.

But even when the deviant scientist was in the process of being discredited by establishment spokesmen, the ineptness and irrelevancies of the criticism further strengthened him in his belief. For the proponent and his few supporters within the scientific establishment could see that the criticisms were based on misrepresentations, irrelevancies, character assassination, plausibility arguments and that they failed to deal with the actual substance and specific arguments put forth. Such inept criticism, far from forcing the deviant scientist to re-examine his evidence and arguments, strengthened him in his belief that he was being treated unjustly and unscientifically. It further strengthened him in his conviction that he must be right.

But such inept discrediting procedures, in my opinion, have an even worse impact upon the conduct of science itself. By discrediting the offending hypothesis, the critics succeed in getting further consideration of it banned within the scientific community. This, indeed, might have the intended effect of saving the uncommitted scientists from becoming contaminated. But at what cost?

By banishing the failures of otherwise accomplished scientists, we prevent from consideration the learning of any lessons from them. Future scientists not only do not learn why and how such failures occurred, they do not even learn that they *did* occur. If they read about Wallace at all it is in connection with the theory of natural selection or Wallace's line. They do not read about his defense of psychic phenomena, phrenology, or his attacks on vaccination. If they come across discussions of Sir William Crookes, it is in connection with his discovery of thallium, his work with the cathode ray tube, and his invention of the radiometer. They are kept ignorant of his claims to have discovered a psychic force that enabled the medium Home to float or that allowed Florence Cook to materialize full-bodied spirits out of thin air. Similarly, they do not read about Newton's commitment to alchemical pursuits or Sir Oliver Lodge's studies of survival, etc.

Is it any wonder then, that several scientists today endorse as genuine psychic feats the conjuring antics of Uri Geller? Or that others claim scientific evidence for the ability of certain individuals to project thoughts upon camera film? Or that still other competent scientists argue tht we can cure cancer with large doses of vitamins?

If we keep future generations of scientists ignorant of the follies of some of their most accomplished ancestors, how can we hope to prevent repetitions of these very same follies? How can we learn lessons from examples that are banished from further consideration?

When I talk about cases of pathological science such as that of Wallace, I often get two related responses from scientists in the audience. One is that Wallace's situation occurred 100 years ago. But it could not happen today, because we know more today and science has become more sophisticated. The other response is to the effect that Wallace (or whatever example I happen to be using) is a special case and that most scientists could not get trapped into such an error. Both these responses seem to me to beautifully illustrate what Zimbardo, and his co-authors call "the illusion of personal invulnerability" (Zimbardo, *et al.*, 1977). They both are a way of saying it cannot happen to me.

In fact, it not only can happen today, but appears to be happening with increasing frequency. Paradoxically, this very attitude that it cannot happen to "us" or to "me," contributes to the vulnerability of scientists to such pathologies. And the fact that the discrediting procedure keeps scientists unaware of the many failures by otherwise recognized scientists further contributes to this illusion of scientific and personal invulnerability. The scientist, as part of his education, only hears about the successes of his great predecessors. The illusion is enhanced that science is much more a series of successes than is actually the case. By banishing the many and outstanding failures to a skeleton closet, both the scientists and the laymen become victims of the myth of scientific invulnerability and continue along a path of false security.

Another counterproductive aspect of this discrediting procedure is that sometimes otherwise promising students of science do go back and check upon the circumstances of the supposed debunking of a bizarre claim. They sometimes become antiscientific or cynical about the objectivity and rationality of science when they see how the establishment has reacted in putting down a heresy.

I could list other counterproductive consequences of the typical reaction of the scientific establishment to suspected heresies among their ranks. But I probably have suggested enough to at least raise questions in your mind about the advisability of continuing to condone such tactics just because they seem to be effective in keeping us from having to cope with uncomfortable embarrassments.

The Benefits of a More Appropriate Response

At this point, let me recapitulate my main points and forestall any misunderstandings that might arise. Maybe I can do this best by putting my message into a more positive format.

First, I want to make it clear that I am not defending unorthodoxy as such. Nor do I believe that most claims of pathological science deserve serious consideration in themselves. I do not believe, for example, that Wallace's claims about a psychic force have any chance of being true.

Second, I fully appreciate that it is very difficult and demanding to develop an effective and rational response to such bizarre hypotheses. I myself know how demanding and difficult this can be from my experiences in trying to be a responsible critic of parapsychological research.

Nevertheless, I strongly urge the scientific community to bring the pathologies out of the closet and to openly work towards developing a more appropriate and rational response. The fact that such pathologies have occurred and continue to occur should be taken as a sign that all is not well. At the very least, there are germs that can potentially contaminate much that will be done under the name of science. The very fact that these pathologies are committed by otherwise competent scientists means that the response to them should be sober and scientific.

We need to keep the great failures as well as the great successes constantly before us. Not just as reminders of our own vulnerability, but as the first step towards comparing and contrasting them in the hopes of finding out just what it was, if anything, that lead the very same scientist, such as Wallace, to recognized success in one instance and ignominious failure in another. At the very least, we can hope that such a step will prevent us from repeating identical mistakes in the future. At best, it might help us discover what it is about scientific thinking and procedures that leads to success and what it is that can produce failure. Or, as some historians and philosophers of science seem to be implying, it may teach us that any system for discovering truth has built-in limitations.

Furthermore, by insisting upon proper criticism and fair play in any critiques of heretical claims, we may move closer to a proper diagnosis of what actually went wrong. We focus on the claims and the evidence and this forces the deviant scientist to respond with further replications, refinements, controls, etc. At the same time, it forces the critic to not only show that the proponent is wrong, but in what ways he went wrong. This could lead to better understanding about how trained scientists can be trapped into defending false systems.

Conclusion

If "pathologies" do exist in the sense that some of our best scientists defend bizarre positions, then like all sicknesses, they are a symptom of something. Something is wrong and requires remedy. We cannot discover what is wrong by bad diagnoses—by failing to acknowledge the disease exists, by preventing others from learning about it, or by isolating the disease from the main body of science. Good science requires good and effective criticism. Bad and irrational criticism, even when the object is bizarre or outrageous, benefits no one. In the short run it "discredits" the object of the attack; in the long run, however, it "discredits" science itself.

REFERENCES

Carpenter, W. B. *Mesmerism, Spiritualism, &c.* New York: D. Appleton & Co., 1877.

George, W. *Biologist Philosopher: A Study of the Life and Writings of Alfred Russel Wallace.* London: Abelard-Schuman, 1964.

Langmuir, I. *Pathological Science.* Schenectady, N.Y.: General Electric Technical Information Series, No. 68–C–035 (April, 1968).

Palfreman, J., "William Crookes: Spiritualism and Science," *Ethics in Science and Medicine, 3,* (1976), 211–227.

Wallace, A. R. *On Miracles and Modern Spiritualism: Three Essays.* London: James Burns, 1875.

Zimbardo, P. G., Ebbesen, E. B., & Maslach, C. *Influencing Attitudes and Changing Behavior.* (Second edition). Reading, Mass.: Addison-Wesley, 1977.

15

Robert G. Jahn

(1930–   )

Some of the chapters in this book are by pure scientists who after many years came to the conclusion that psi phenomena do occur. The present chapter differs in two ways: (1) It is written by an engineering physicist concerned with practical applications of science. (2) After several years familiarity with the literature of parapsychology he is not fully convinced that psi phenomena occur.

In this respect he is in good company. Close to one third of the members of the Parapsychological Association have some degree of doubt as to the reality of ESP. (See McConnell and Clark, "Training, Belief, and Mental Conflict Within the Parapsychological Association," appended to this book).

The opinion of an engineer is especially to be valued on a question of new scientific truth. When a scientist asks, "What do we know?" he tends to emphasize the theoretical harmony of supposed experimental facts and to reject those that seem incongruous. The engineer begins at the other end. "How dependable are the empirical observations? The theory could be wrong."

Because there is no accepted theoretical explanation for psi, scientists are hard to interest in this topic. Engineers are more open-minded, but not necessarily easier to convince—or at least, such has been my experience.

The present brief survey of the field of parapsychology was presented by Dean Robert G. Jahn of Princeton University at the New Horizons in Science Seventeenth Annual Briefing, sponsored by the Council for the Advancement of Science Writing, Inc., Palo Alto, California, on November 8, 1979. It has since been published in the Zetetic Scholar (1980, No. 6, 5-16). It is reprinted here in its entirety by permission of the author.

NEW DIMENSIONS OR OLD DELUSIONS?
(1979)

by Robert G. Jahn

INTRODUCTION

No field of scholarly endeavor has proven more frustrating, nor has been more abused and misunderstood, than the study of psychic phenomena. Dealing as it does as much with impressionistic and aesthetic evidence as with analytical substance, and carrying by its nature strongly personal and numenistic overtones, it has been incessantly prostituted by charlatans, lunatics, and sensationalists, categorically rejected by most of the scientific establishment, and widely misunderstood by the public at large. The purpose of this presentation is to review some of the history, nomenclature, and contemporary serious effort in this area; to discuss whether, once the overburden of illegitimate activity and irresponsible criticism is removed, there is sufficient residue of valid evidence to justify continued research; and, if so, to suggest how this research might best be styled, facilitated, and evaluated.

At the risk of some immodesty, it is probably worthwhile to set my remarks in the context of a bit of the personal history which leads me to this task. My formal training is that of an engineer and applied physicist, and the bulk of my research has concerned a sequence of topics in the broad domain of the aerospace sciences: fluid mechanics, ionized gases, plasmadynamics, and most recently, electric propulsion. My appointments have been primarily in the academic sector, at Lehigh, Caltech, and Princeton, where for the past eight and one-half years I have been Dean of the School of Engineering and Applied Science. This school, which currently enrolls 850 of the university's 4400 undergraduates, features a substantial amount of independent work in its curriculum, and it was in that context three years ago that I was requested by one of our very best students to supervise a project in psychic phenomena. More specifically, this young lady proposed to bring her talents and background in electrical engineering and computer science to bear on a study of controlled, low-level psychokinesis. Although I had no previous experience, professional or personal, with such topics, for a variety of pedagogical reasons I agreed, and together we mapped a tentative scholarly path, involving a literature search, visits to appropriate laboratories and professional meetings, and the design, construction, and operation of simple experiments. My initial oversight role in this project led to a degree of personal involvement in it, and then to a growing intellectual bemusement, to the extent that by the time this student graduated, I was persuaded that this was a legitimate field for a high technologist to study. It is in that spirit I have continued to consider the problem and in that tone I speak to you today.

To proceed with the effort, I obtained the appropriate approval from my university, assembled a small staff, and secured the requisite funding from a few private sources. I should emphasize that my fractional involvement with this program is quite minor in comparison to my other responsibilities, and that the work is still very preliminary and tentative, but it provides the base of cognizance for my broader remarks on the field.

I confess that I shall make these remarks with some trepidation, borne of previous unpleasant experiences. For example, an earlier lighthearted article in the Princeton alumni magazine,[1] in which I attempted to share some of our experiences in this field with the university community at large, brought an intensity and breadth of reaction for which I was totally unprepared, ranging from irresponsible and categorical condemnation on one extreme, to equally irrational messianic accolades on the other. Rather than precipitating further such distracting outbursts, I have largely avoided opportunities for public presentation, a guideline I am setting aside on this occasion only because I believe that this audience can have an unusually significant effect on the development of the field by the manner in which it chooses to represent it to its respective constituencies. It is my request that you treat this as a tutorial presentation, hopefully contributing to your cognizance of, and attitude toward psychic research, rather than as any claim of specific individual achievement therein.

HISTORY

To get on with the matter in terms of a brief historical background, I would remind you that whereas human interest in psychic phenomena is at least as old as recorded history, clearly displayed in the cave drawings of ancient man, in varied activities of the early Greek, Roman, and Oriental civilizations, in the Bible, and in medieval and renaissance art

---

1. Jahn, Robert G. Psychic process, energy transfer, and things that go bump in the night. *Princeton Alumni Weekly*, 1978, *79* (7), S1–S12.

and literature, systematic scholarly search for understanding of these phenomena is just one century old. It was in 1882 that the Society for Psychical Research was founded in London, providing the first professional forum for presentation of controlled experiments in telepathy and clairvoyance. The American counterpart, ASPR, was formed three years later, with William James as one of its leaders. The most familiar and substantial academic effort in this country was initiated at Duke University in the 1930's, when J. B. Rhine and Louisa Rhine established a parapsychology laboratory and began publication of the *Journal of Parapsychology*. A second professional organization called the Parapsychological Association was formed in this country in 1957, and in 1969 was recognized as an affiliate by the American Association for the Advancement of Science.

Over this first 100 years of scholarly effort, the field has attracted a significant number of eminent scholars from established fields. The SPR alone has numbered among its presidents three Nobel laureates, ten Fellows of the Royal Society, one Prime Minister, and a substantial list of physicists and philosophers, including Henry Sidgwick, William James, Frederic W. H. Myers, Lord Rayleigh, Edmund Gurney, Sir William Crookes, Sir William Barrett, Henri Bergson, Gardner Murphy, and G. N. M. Tyrrell.

At the present time, there are five English language publications covering this field,[2] supplemented by numerous less formal magazines and countless books of widely varying quality and relevance. Research activity is reported from over twenty U.S. universities and colleges and many foreign institutions, but in most cases it is of very small scale. There are very few credible academic programs of study, although some fifty M.A. and Ph.D. theses have been accepted on psychic topics at reputable universities over the past forty years. Some ten research institutes and private corporations in the United States have also authorized publications and reports in the field. The extent of Eastern Bloc effort and of classified research in this country are matters of considerable speculation on which I cannot comment with authority.

In many respects the present status and growth pattern of this field resemble those of the natural sciences in their earliest days, or perhaps even more those of the incubation of classical psychology, in terms of

---

2. *Journal of the Society for Psychical Research, Journal of Parapsychology, Journal of the American Society for Psychical Research, European Journal of Parapsychology, Research in Parapsychology* (formerly, *Proceedings of the Parapsychological Association*).

the absence of replicable basic experiments and useful theoretical models, and low level of financial support and internal professional coordination, and the low credibility in the academic establishment and public sectors.

NOMENCLATURE

For purposes of constructing a concise catalogue, I shall define psychic phenomena to include all processes of information and/or energy exchange which involve animate consciousness in a manner not presently explicable in terms of known science. By psychic research, I shall imply any scholarly study of such phenomena employing scientific methodology, as opposed to any dogmatic, ritualistic, or theological approaches. With this definition, the field may be roughly divided into two major categories: (1) extrasensory perception (ESP), which includes such information transfer processes as telepathy (perception of another's thoughts or emotions), clairvoyance (perception of hidden objects or events), precognition (perception of future events), and various animal ESP indications (homing, trailing, group consciousness, etc.); and (2) psychokinesis, which subsumes a variety of effects wherein energy is transferred to a physical system, either in controlled or spontaneous effort, and over a wide range of energy levels. (A few types of psychic process, such as survival/reincarnation, psychic healing, out-of-body experiences, etc., while not fitting these categories quite so neatly, actually involve aspects of both at a more fundamental level.) Note that in this subdivision, the field conforms to the two major thrusts of present-day science and high technology, i.e., the extraction, the processing, transmission, and storage of information, and of energy.

STATUS

In my opinion, a comprehensive, objective survey of the scholarly research into psychic phenomena over the past one hundred years would support the following conclusion: some of the results are suggestive, some even provocative; none is fully convincing in the traditional scientific sense. Obviously, more extreme opinions have been voiced on either side of this position. On the one side, there are zealots who claim the case has been made, by their own experiments or others; I cannot claim that for my own work, or for any other I have seen. On the other side, there are critics who reject the field categorically for an assortment of reasons, including instances of outright fraud; naiveté of method, such as sensory cueing of subjects, application of improper statistics, or other theoretical incompetence; failure of replicability, evasiveness of the phenomena under close scrutiny, and sensitivity of results to the observer, all of which violate the scientific method; and the vague conviction that since nothing totally convincing has been demonstrated during this century of study, the domain must be fundamentally invalid.

In my view, all of these criticisms are justified to some extent, but in some cases they have been overworked. This field, by the nature of its phenomena and its inherent numenistic overtones is immensely vulnerable to fraudulent exploitation and naive gullibility, and such have indeed occurred to a distressing degree. Yet, it seems shortsighted and irresponsible to tar all sincere and scholarly work with this brush. To my knowledge, there have been no totally replicable experiments yet performed; what yield there has been has been anecdotal, or at best, statistical. It should be noted, however, that numerous areas of modern science percolate contentedly on lower statistical yield than is offered by some of the better psychic studies. The sensitivity of psychic experiments to the particular observer could indeed by indicative of fraud or delusion; but it could also be an important clue to the role of human consciousness in such processes. The frustrating evasiveness of the phenomena to more precise and refined experimental techniques is perhaps the most damning criticism from a scientific standpoint; yet even this may offer a legitimate indication of a basic characteristic of the processes: e.g., just as great art, great music, or great creative thought in general may be stifled or sterilized by excessive analysis or constraint, so psychic interactions may be intrinsically casual and free-flowing, rather than deliberate. Finally, the complaint that enough effort has already been squandered on this psychic goose-chase should be moderated by the recent availability of far more precise instrumentation, and far more powerful theoretical tools and data handling methods than have heretofore been deployed.

On balance, then, categorical rejection seems to me equally as untenable as blind acceptance. Rather, I prefer at attitude which first strips away the illegitimate and sloppy work, and then submits the remainder to close individual scrutiny. This done, one finds a few—to be sure, a very few—experiments which provide sufficiently provocative anecdotal evidence to justify further serious and systematic study. From my engineering point of view, I am most interested in three such categories of study: (1) the so-called "remote perception" work of a number of laboratories, notably SRI,[3] Mundelein College,[4] and our own, which

---

3. Puthoff, H. and Targ, R. A. A perceptual channel for information transfer over kilometer distances: Historical perspective and recent research. *Proceedings of the Institute of Electrical and Electronics Engineers*, 1976, *64*, 329–354.

has provided an adequately large data base, of sufficiently high yield, to allow quantification and parametric correlations of the inexplicable results; (2) certain experiments in controlled, low-level psychokinesis, such as performed by physicists at the Mind Science Foundation in San Antonio,[5] at Birkbeck College, University of London,[6] and in our laboratory among others, which have the advantage of focusing on quantifiable physical systems, wherein the departures from classical behavior can be made more explicit; and (3) the rare and spectacular poltergeist events, or so-called recurrent spontaneous psychokinesis (RSPK), which in the magnitude of their effects, and in the demonstrated correlations with neurologically extraordinary adolescents,[7] seem to offer rich, yet largely unutilized opportunities for insight.

This list is not exhaustive; other commentators might prefer the extensive series of "ganzfeld" or sensory deprivation studies of free response clairvoyance and telepathy as pioneered at Maimonides Hospital[8] and replicated at other laboratories[9]; the systematic and conservative reincarnation studies at the University of Virginia[10]; the modern psycho-physiological studies at Duke University[11]; the personality correlates originally studied at CUNY[12]; or a few other deliberate programs elsewhere.[13]

4. Dunne, B. J. and Bisaha, J. P. Precognitive remote viewing in the Chicago area. *Journal of Parapsychology*, 1979, *43*, 17-30.

5. Schmidt, H. A PK test with electronic equipment. *Journal of Parapsychology*, 1970, *34*, 175–181.

6. Hasted, J. B. Paranormal metal bending. In *The Iceland Papers*. A. Puharich, ed. Amherst, Wisconsin: Essentia Research Associates, 1979.

7. Roll, W. G. *The Poltergeist*. New York: New American Library, 1972.

8. Honorton, C. Psi and internal attention states: Information retrieval in ganzfeld. In *Psi and States of Awareness*, Shapin, B. and Coly, L., eds., New York: Parapsychology Foundation, Inc., 1978.

9. Sondow, N. Effects of associations and feedback on psi in the ganzfeld. *Journal of the American Society for Psychical Research*, 1979, *73*, 123–150.

10. Stevenson, I. *Twenty Cases Suggestive of Reincarnation*. Virginia: University Press of Virginia, 1974.

11. Kelly, E. F., Kanthamani, H., Child, I. L., and Young, F. W. On the relation between visual and ESP confusion structures in an exceptional ESP subject. *Journal of the American Society for Psychical Research*, 1975, *69*, 1–31.

12. Schmeidler, G. R. and McConnell, R. A. *ESP and Personality Patterns*. Westport, Conn.: Greenwood Press, 1958/1973.

13. Wolman, B. B., ed. *Handbook of Parapsychology,* Van Nostrand Reinhold Co., 1977.

New Experiments

Since even the best extant research has been tediously slow to yield convincing results, if a new round of experiments is to be considered it seems important to reexamine *ab initio*, the criteria, topic selection, and philosophical attitude that should prevail. For example, given the preceding pattern of incomplete satisfaction of the normal requisites for scientific credibility, what is the healthiest attitude toward data collection and assessment in this field? Should one reject out-of-hand all results that do not rigidly conform to the normal tenets of replicability and insensitivity to observer? Should one waive those requirements and attempt to theorize and deduce solely on the basis of anecdotal phenomenology? Or is there a useful intermediate position which, while retaining full rigor in the experimental design, controls, protocol, and analysis, and still striving for some degree of reproducibility in the observations, tolerates imperfect replicability as possibly indicative of as yet unidentified parameters, or of an intrinsically statistical nature of the phenomena, or even of a basic flaw or incompleteness in the established physical models?

Whatever the attitude, it seems clear at this primitive stage of understanding that the specific experiments selected should be as clearly posed and conceptually simple as possible, with a minimum of reasonable alternative interpretations of any positive results. In addition, they should lend themselves logistically to rigorous, tightly controlled experimentation, and demonstrate sufficient positive yield to permit accumulation of a significant data base and its subsequent correlation with variable experimental conditions. Given these attributes, it would also seem best to focus on those studies which seem to have the greatest significance in terms of basic understanding of the phenomenology, contradiction of established scientific models, and ultimate practical application.

In all of the zeal for scientific rigor, there may be some risk of over-sterilizing the experimentation. If the phenomena derive to any significant degree from conscious or subconscious processes of the human mind, it is important that such not be ignored or inhibited in the design and operation of the experiments. More specifically, it is probably essential to include the insights, interpretations, and intuitions of those who have dealt most effectively in such processes, including not only the academics and professional observers, but most particularly those who have demonstrated creative capabilities in the generation of the phenomena. It is quite possible that the difference between a sterile experiment and an effective one of equal rigor lies in the more aesthetic aspects of its ambience and feedback than in the elegance of its instrumentation, and those aesthetic aspects need to be well-tuned to the human subjects who are asked to function as components of the experimental system.

On the basis of this sort of logic, our own program at Princeton has selected two classes of experiments for its principal foci.[1] The major portion of the program revolves about a number of table-top experiments in controlled, low-level psychokinesis, using relatively simple physical systems—mechanical, optical, thermal, electrical, atomic, etc.—each of which involves a specific element or process that is vulnerable to disturbance, and which signifies such disturbance by a relatively large change in some feedback display for the subject. So, for example, our interferometer can indicate a disturbance of one of its optical plates of less than one-millionth of a centimeter by a perceptible change in an attractive pattern of luminous concentric circular fringes displayed before the subject. Using this display much like a biofeedback indicator, that subject can then experiment with his own conscious or subconscious strategies for achieving the desired disturbance of the system. Other experiments monitor the deviations in temperature of thermistors to one-thousandth of a degree with a progressive pattern of small colored lights; the variations in electrical noise from a solid-state diode interface with an illuminated digital display; or the development of the statistical deflections of 10,000 marbles cascading through an array of obstructing pins by direct visual and photographic observation.

It is far too early to claim any definitive results from these experiments. On numerous occasions we have seen effects that to the best of our understanding and control of the prevailing conditions are classically inexplicable, but these effects vary from experiment to experiment, from subject to subject, and alas, from day to day. Whether substantial increase in our data base will sort any of this out remains to be seen.

The minor portion of our program addresses certain aspects of the "remote perception" problem mentioned earlier. In this type of study, the subject attempts to perceive aspects of a randomly selected target scene in which a colleague in the experiment, termed the agent, is immersed at a given time. Typically the percipient records his impressions of the target on tape, by sketch, or by notes, which then are rank-ordered against a pool of alternative targets by independent judges. Our particular effort has been to replace the necessarily subjective human judging process which is inherently vulnerable to personal biases and interpretations, by a more analytical method for evaluation of the degree of information transfer in such perception efforts. Briefly, the strategy involves coding of both the targets and perceptions in terms of some thirty binary descriptors, e.g., outside/inside; dark/light; noisy/quiet; motion/none; water/none; etc., and allowing a variety of scoring and ranking algorithms for the purpose of deriving quantitative indices of the quality and quantity of the information transfer.

Again it is too early to make firm claims, but this method clearly holds promise of reducing the ambiguity in interpretation of this class of experiment, which has shown some of the highest yields of any controlled psychic studies. It should be added that our particular experiments have dealt primarily with the precognitive mode of remote perception, wherein the percipient completes his report substantially before the target site is selected. We find the yield to be at least as high as for similar experiments peformed in "real time," and we prefer this mode for two reasons. First, the logical impossibility of the task is heightened, forcing the subjects to abandon various unproductive strategies for the perception of the target and to rely more completely on "paranormal" mental process. Second, the contradiction with established physical conception of space/time is more stark, hence potentially more generally illuminating.

THEORY

Next to the evasiveness of the phenomena under controlled experimentation, the second greatest frustration in the study of psychic processes has been the absence of viable theoretical models with which to begin the traditional dialogue between theory and experiment on which all scientific progress eventually depends. Early hypotheses tended to presume wavelike propagation of psychic effects, usually in the electromagnetic modes, but their logic was vague, and a number of experimental results have raised serious doubts that such models are tenable. Only quite recently, with the attention of a significant number of theoretical physicists drawn anew to this task, have broader and more elegant representations been attempted which hold higher hope of accommodating the diverse and bizarre phenomena characteristic of this field.

Attempts at theoretical explication can proceed from any of several levels of presumption as to the fundamentality of the effects observed. For example, one may presume that:

a) the effects observed are illusory (e.g., artifacts of poor experimentation);

b) the effects can be assigned to known physical processes,

associated with, but not deliberately precipitated by the subject (e.g., heat transfer, vibration, aerochemistry, etc.);

c) the effects are precipitated by the subject, but involve only known physical and physiological processes (e.g., electromagnetic radiation from brain circuitry or intercardial potentials);

d) the effects are precipitated by the subject, but can be accommodated within existing physical formalism only after identification of heretofore unrecognized modes of energy/information transfer;

e) the effects cannot be handled within existing physical formalism (e.g., the fundamental laws need further generalization, perhaps similar to the evolution of classical mechanics into special and general relativity);

f) the effects, although observable under controlled conditions, cannot be handled within a scientific paradigm (e.g., they are intrinsically irreplicable). Obviously the subtlety of the model required, and the breadth of its significance increase markedly as one proceeds through this hierarchy of possibilities.

Extant theories of psychic phenomena tend to cluster into four or five broad groups which can only be described here in the most superficial terms. As mentioned, the first serious models dealt in terms of electromagnetic waves, usually in the very low frequency bands,[14] some versions of which proposed modulation of the earth's magnetic field, or of prevalent electrostatic fields of the ambient environment. Other types of geophysical waves have since been considered, such as geoseismic waves, infrasonic waves, and barometric fluctuations,[15] but all of these now seem to be fundamentally inadequate to deal with certain classes of psychic phenomena, most particularly precognition.

More recent efforts have involved applications of the formalisms of various other categories of physical mechanics, for example:

a) statistical mechanics and statistical thermodynamics, whereby the subtle interplay of the thermodynamic concept of entropy with information theory is allowed to take on a broader implication in terms of the role of human consciousness in influencing random processes[16];

---

14. Ryzl, M. A model for parapsychological communication. *Journal of Parapsychology*, 1966, *30*, 18–30.

15. Persinger, M. A. Geophysical models for parapsychological experiences. *Psychoenergetic Systems*, 1975, *1*.

16. Puthoff, H. and Targ, R. Physics, entropy, and psychokinesis. Chapter in *Quantum Physics and Parapsychology*, L. Oteri, ed. New York: Parapsychological Foundation, 1975.

   b) hyperspace theories, whereby the basic laws of physics are re-cast and re-solved in more than the four coordinates of normal experience (3 space, 1 time), and the consequent new terms are applied to the representation of paranormal effects[17];

   c) quantum mechanics, whose inherently probabilistic approach lends itself to representation of phenomena that depart significantly from strictly deterministic sequences of cause and effect, and wherein the interaction of the observer with the observed physical system is explicitly acknowledged[18,19,20];

   d) holographic inversions, whereby all of reality is regarded as deployed in an infinite syllabus of amplitude/frequency information, and the brain is hypothesized to function as a Fourier transform device to provide the familiar space/time localized imagery.[21]

Although none of these has yet produced anything approaching a comprehensive theoretical model, each probably has something to contribute to our conceptualization of the phenomenological processes addressed. For example, their application in various forms to the anecdotal experimental evidence assembled to date leads me to speculate that the following rather unconventional possibilities may be worthy of more detailed examination:

   1) The phenomena may be inherently statistical, rather than directly causal, and we may be observing them "on the margin," i.e., the observed phenomena may represent marginal changes from normal behavior, on a very grand scale, and with fluctuation times which tax human observational capability.

   2) Human consciousness may have an information-ordering capability that can be projected into an external system as well as received from it.

   17. Rauscher, E. A. Some physical models potentially applicable to remote reception. In *The Iceland Papers*, A. Puharich, ed. Amherst, Wisconsin: Essentia Research Associates, 1979.

   18. Oteri, L. ed. *Quantum Physics and Parapsychology*. New York: Parapsychology Foundation, 1975.

   19. Whiteman, J. H. M. Quantum theory and parapsychology. *Journal of the American Society for Psychical Research*, 1973, *67*, 341–360.

   20. Walker, E. H. Consciousness and quantum theory. Chapter in *Psychic Exploration*, E. D. Mitchell, ed. New York: Putnam, 1974.

   21. Pribram, K. H. A progress report on the scientific understanding of paranormal phenomena. In *Brain/Mind and Parapsychology:* Proc. of an International Conference held in Montreal, Canada, August 1978, Shapin, B. and Coly, L., eds., New York: Parapsychology Foundation, Inc., 1979; and G. Globus, et al., eds. *Consciousness and the Brain*. New York: Plenum, 1976.

3) Quantum mechanics may be more than a system of physical mechanics; it may be a fundamental statement about human consciousness and perception processes, and the empirical pillars of this formalism, such as the uncertainty principle, the exclusion principle, the indistinguishability principle, and the wave/particle dualities may be more laws of consciousness than laws of nature.

4) Psychic processes may be inherently holistic, and thus the ultimate model may need to integrate both the scientific and the aesthetic aspects in order to identify the sources of the phenomena. That is, psychic processes may be manifestations of the intersection of the analytical scientific world with the creative aesthetic, and thus, to represent them effectively, it may be necessary to balance insights of both perspectives, without sacrificing the integrity of either.

Clearly, any of these intuitions would have to be developed in far more philosophical and analytical detail before a trenchant theoretical model could emerge, but at this primitive stage it is probably healthy to consider a few such radical possibilities, along with more prosaic explications.

CONCLUSION

Let us close by returning to the basic questions which undeniably underlie our attention to this topic. Namely, are psychic phenomena real; and, if so, should they be studied? The latter question begs a sequence of others, i.e., can such phenomena be studied systematically; would the knowledge derived from such study be significant; would that knowledge be useful; etc.? The honest response to all of these is that at present we simply do not know. The jury is still out—or more accurately, it has not even left yet; adequate evidence has not yet been presented to it. At this phase, therefore, everyone should be entitled to his own informal and considered opinions on such questions, and should be equally entitled to the tolerance of others toward those opinions.

But to the much broader, and indeed even more significant question: "do we have the right to inquire?", as a scientist and an academic I must make much firmer response, and if need be, defense. The fundamental requisites of scientific methodology: dispassionate rigor, humility in the face of observations, limitation on extrapolation of results, and openness of mind apply to any sincere scholarly endeavor, including psychic research. When these criteria are met, the results should be heard openly and fairly.

And these criteria are equally appropriate to the process of criticism. When they are honored, that criticism can play a healthy and constructive role. But when the criticism lacks any of these; when it is tainted by categorical rejection, guilt by association, or sloppy logic, it should be at least as suspect as the object of its attack.

I have spoken to you thus not as an advocate of psychic phenomena as valid science, but as an advocate of the right—indeed the obligation—of science to inquire into this field, with the same diligence, patience, integrity, openness, and tolerance—in both its study and in its criticism—that have characterized its noblest achievements of the past.

As recorders, transmitters, and interpreters of such activities for the public benefit, you have the same right, and—if you will permit me—the same obligation, to maintain that same high tone.

16

R. A. McConnell

(1914–   )

It is an understatement to say that the acceptance of para-psychological phenomena is less than universal. As for any field of science, acceptance is important because it determines how much research support will be given by society and, hence, how fast our knowledge will grow.

What do we mean by acceptance? Acceptance by whom? By the populace? By working scientists? By the leaders of science? By the intellectual elite who determine economic policy? The last, of course, is the group that counts, but they take their cues from the scientists.

*Acceptance of what? Acceptance of the reality of one or more psi phenomena? In the light of the material presented in this book, would it be reasonable to hope for the acceptance of the **possibility** of these phenomena?*

Why are psi phenomena not accepted by the leaders of science? What reasons do they give? What prejudices do they hide?

Parapsychologists have enjoyed a martyr's role for the past century. Are they seriously interested in overcoming the doubts of their academic colleagues? What are the parapsychologists' rationalizations for not taking a more aggressive stand? What are their unconscious reasons for timidity?

*In the sociohistorical bibliography appended to this volume, I have gathered background information on various aspects of the problem of the acceptance of psi. From that bibliography, I have selected for presentation a 1977 paper of my own (*Journal of Parapsychology, 41, *198-214).*

In it, after an analysis of 16 arguments used by sceptical scientists to reject ESP, the existing polarization of scientific opinion is modeled as the resolution of cognitive dissonance between a subjective antecedent probability (SAP) and a subjective counterexplanatory probability (SCEP). A big SAP with a little SCEP inclines to the acceptance of ESP, and vice versa. However, if SAP and SCEP are both small, cognitive dissonance results. Psychological consistency theory predicts that dissonance will be avoided at any cost. Usually, this is done by keeping SCEP large, by invoking whatever plausible counterexplanations of ESP may be most palatable to the anxious sceptic.

In this paper, possible relations of SCEP to SAP are considered for intellectuals vs. nonintellectuals and for laymen vs. scientists. From a statistical survey it appears that even parapsychologists suffer doubt and conflict concerning ESP.

In the course of the analysis that produced this paper, it became apparent how the supremacy and specialization of science have contributed to present-day cultural nihilism among academic intellectuals. This is explained under "Levels of SAP." There may be other ways in which a study of orthodoxy's rejection of ESP could cast light upon sociological puzzles of some importance.

THE RESOLUTION OF CONFLICTING BELIEFS ABOUT THE ESP EVIDENCE
(1977)

by R. A. McCONNELL

Most scientists have not given serious attention to the possibility of extrasensory perception. Among those few who have examined the evidence with care, there are some vigorous sceptics. However, it is usually difficult to get such persons to specify in detail why they find the evidence unconvincing.

In the pursuit of intellectual rapprochement I have gathered a list of 16 ostensibly good reasons for rejecting the best available evidence for ESP. The individual sceptic is unlikely to employ all of these counterexplanations. Generally, he will use one or two to discount the bulk of the ESP evidence, reserving several others for special cases, while neglecting the remainder as inapplicable or even illogical. Nevertheless, each of these arguments, except possibly the last, has been offered by competent scientists upon various occasions in recent history.

THE POLARIZATION OF SCIENTISTS' ATTITUDES

Those who have examined and rejected the evidence for ESP are not likely to be uncertain concerning the value of further experimentation in this field. Their attitudes usually vary over the narrow range extending from: "Parapsychological research is a waste of time" to "Parap-

---

Author's Note: Some of the ideas of this paper were anticipated by Henry Sidgwick, the first president of the Society for Psychical Research, in his addresses to that society on July 17, 1882; December 9, 1882; July 18, 1883; May 28, 1884; and May 10, 1889.

In this paper I begin with the tacit assumption that opposition by scientists to ESP always has an ostensibly rational basis. The reader should be warned that this may be an over-simplification.

This paper was offered in its present form to *Science*, the journal of the American Association for the Advancement of Science. The comment of one referee is given here in full:

"I find this a hard paper to judge. I have no familiarity with the literature dealing with ESP. At the same time I have an initial sense that ESP is fraudulent: I am one of those very people about whom McConnell is writing his paper, and who, he very much doubts, will ever open their minds to what he and others are trying to say. After reading his very readable paper I remain unmoved. I am not

sychological research should not be permitted in a university." Among outspoken sceptics it is rare to encounter the position: "The evidence, while not convincing, is good enough to warrant further research."

Contrariwise, those who look carefully at the evidence and initially find it difficult to reject, usually end by accepting the reality of ESP as being highly probable or certain.

This polarization of attitudes among those who have examined the literature is a fact deserving exploration. Considering the potential scientific importance of the purported phenomenon, one would expect, if there were even a modicum of favoring evidence, that there would be many middle-of-the-road sceptics urging that the research be diligently pursued. Such is not the case.

This apparent discontinuity in scientific judgment could mean that opinions, either pro or con, are being biased by emotion. Perhaps some investigating scientists whose objective opinions would naturally fall in the gap, "suggestive but not conclusive," are being moved by irrational considerations to a more firm conclusion in one direction or the other.

ARGUMENTS FOR THE REJECTION OF ESP

In an attempt to understand this situation, I shall begin by listing the reasons for rejection most often given by scientists who have examined the evidence for extrasensory perception and found it to be without merit:

1. "ESP is theoretically impossible."
2. "ESP is contrary both to common sense and to practical experi-

---

now more interested in learning about ESP; I am not less inclined to believe that ESP is fraudulent. Yet, at the same time, I do not wish to say, straight out, do not publish this paper.

"McConnell is trying to show what stands in the way of people's receptivity to research dealing with ESP. He is not, in this paper, essaying a general defense of the genuineness of ESP phenomena; nor giving an account of ESP research. Rather he is offering a contribution, if you will, to the sociology of knowledge (to use Karl Mannheim's famous phrase). He sorts the various assertions opponents make, and comes up with sixteen main types. I believe that mutatis mutandis these sixteen types would be often present in the minds of people opposed to some scientific hypothesis, or to some disputed doctrine in the non-sciences. That is to say, McConnell's method has relevance beyond his own purpose. Herein is the great interest of the paper. But I am still not confident that his method is sophisticated enough, even for his own purposes."

What is not clear in this referee's comment is how a belief that "ESP is fraudulent," reached despite "no familiarity with the literature dealing with ESP," constitutes a proper basis for opposing publication of this paper.

ence in real-life betting situations where, in fact, the laws of chance have been found to govern."

3. "A theoretical explanation must be offered by parapsychologists before the possibility of ESP can be seriously entertained by scientists generally."

4. "A small null-hypothesis probability value appearing in any published ESP experiment may be presumed to represent merely the selection of a chance fluctuation from among many unsuccessful, unreported experiments."

5. "One cannot prove anything by statistics because, in testing the null hypothesis, there is always a finite probability that the experimental result happened solely by chance."

6. "To be proved real, ESP must be more reproducible than it is at present." What is meant is that the degree of repeatability that has been demonstrated by different experimenters, or by the same experimenter in series of experiments with one or more test subjects, is insufficient. What is needed is reproducibility in the presence of sceptics upon demand.

7. "There must be better controls against fraud." Whatever the degree of control used in otherwise convincing experiments, it was not enough. What is desired is successful demonstrations witnessed by ad hoc committees of eminent scientists and specialists qualified to detect dishonesty. Since this requirement would be considered inappropriate if applied to other areas of science, it is sometimes supported by the following argument.

8. "Fraud is a reasonable counterexplanation for any ESP experiment because parapsychology deals with strange abilities that attract emotionally deviant individuals who crave attention or power."

9. "There may have been sensory leakage." Two illustrative forms of this argument are:

(a) "If the experimenter could have had sensory access—however little—to the target material, and if the subject could have had subsequent sensory contact—however limited—with the experimenter, then target information leakage may have occurred."

(b) "Because modern signal-in-noise detection theory has supplanted the concept of sensory threshold, ordinary methods of sensory isolation must now be regarded as inadequate."

10. "There may have been procedural errors (e.g., recording errors, loss of data, selection of the analysis) unless every such possibility was specifically known to have been excluded."

11. "Since no written report can be complete, some unknown crucial

weakness may not have been revealed despite the good intentions of the author.''

12. ''Since most ESP experiments can be shown to have a possible flaw, if there are any experiments without apparent weakness, this may mean merely that their flaws are yet to be found.''

13. ''It is well known that there is always an indefinitely large number of imaginable ordinary mechanisms by which any set of observations can be explained. It can be reasonably assumed that some such mechanism is the true explanation of any supposedly conclusive experimental proof of ESP.''

14. ''A chain is only as strong as its weakest link. If an experiment has a weakness, it should be discarded as evidence for ESP. When one follows this rule, one finds no experiment good enough to stand alone as proof of the reality of the phenomenon.''

15. If an entire ESP experiment (including random target-number generation and data recording) was automated:

(a) ''The equipment could have failed temporarily in the course of the experiment so as to create a spurious ESP effect even if tested and found to be working properly before and after.''

(b) ''The target generator may have had a systematic bias that the empirical tests for randomness were inadequate to discover.''

(c) ''Fraud cannot be ruled out unless the testing was supervised by a committee of competent electrical engineers.''

16. ''Since the prior (Bayesian) probability of ESP being real is infinitesimally small, and since the true probability of accidental success in any one experiment (when spurious nonchance causes are also considered) is surely never much smaller than 0.01 (regardless of how small the calculated chance probability may be), any one experiment cannot perceptibly affect the improbability of ESP.'' This argument extends by its own logic to any finite number of seemingly perfect experiments.

Discussion of the Arguments

Using the above paragraph numbers, I shall comment on each of these arguments against ESP—not in an effort to prove the reality of the phenomenon, but rather to establish the ground rules under which the evidence for it might be considered.

The 16 listed arguments fall into three natural groupings: Nos. 1 and 2 claim that ESP is a priori impossible. Nos. 3 and 4 concern straightforward technical matters upon which agreement in principle should be reached easily. Nos. 5–16 hold that the laboratory evidence is weak in diverse ways. The common theme of the latter arguments is the absence of an absolute proof of ESP by one or more perfect experiments. None of these 16 arguments is devoid of interest. All may have weaknesses, as I shall now attempt to show.

1. The argument that ESP is theoretically impossible is untrue in the following sense. There is no established scientific theory that says ESP is impossible. A theory is inherently incapable of affirming the nonexistence of a phenomenon that lies outside its domain. What is usually meant by those who argue for impossibility is that ESP is contrary to the metaphysical presuppositions of Western science. This, of course, is why ESP is important—if it is real.

2. It cannot be denied that ESP, in the opinion of many reasonable people, is contrary to common sense and to practical experience. But twentieth-century physics, starting with the work of Planck and Einstein, has shown that common sense and practical experience are useless as arbiters of the limits of reality. Tiny, rare, or seemingly trivial experimental anomalies may eventually lead to profound modifications of our understanding of nature.

3. In science, unexplained experience comes first; theoretical understanding, later. If history is a safe guide, after a large group of empirical facts has been gathered, there will always be some ingenious model-builder who can summarize the observations in a useful and elegant fashion.

Statistical Questions

4. The argument that statistical experiments seeming to show ESP are merely selections from an otherwise unpublished population of chance data is too broad as it is stated, but it does raise a useful question concerning the customary criterion levels for rejection of the null hypothesis. In parapsychology, as in all fields of science, unsuccessful experiments are not ordinarily reported in the journals. Before one can interepret a calculated chance probability from a "successful" experiment, one needs at least an upper limit to the number of unreported unsuccessful experiments relating to the same effect.

Such a limit might be established in various ways for the case of parapsychology. For example, in the years 1970–1975 more than 50% of all of the statistically evaluated experimental papers in the *Journal of the American Society for Psychical Research* were authored or co-authored by one of five parapsychologists. (This concentration of scientific productivity is not surprising. See Dennis, 1955, and Bloom, 1963). By informal questioning of each of the five authors I have learned that, on the average, they publish about two out of three of all of their experiments that would be eligible for publication if successful.

For these experimenters I would personally regard a reported probability level of 0.02 as presumptive evidence of a nonchance result and a p value of 0.001 as conservative for this purpose. It is well known that these experimenters frequently report values much smaller than 0.001.

5. It is true but irrelevant that statistical analysis always yields probabilities greater than zero and therefore can never provide logical certainty against chance as an explanation of observational data. Scientific certainty about a particular aspect of nature does not result from isolated, logically compelling proof but from the integration of many related experiences into a coherent pattern—preferably, but not necessarily, with the aid of a formal theory. Statistical method is merely a tool for weighing the experimental odds when dealing with a phenomenon "buried in noise."

Reproducibility of Findings

6. The requirement of unlimited reproducibility may be presumptuous. There has been no revelation from God that all experimental phenomena must be repeatable upon demand. It is the hope and aim of science to get control of system variables so as to improve reproducibility. It is possible that ESP may be real and yet forever beyond dependable control. I once strongly suspected that this was so. Recent research developments have led me to take a more optimistic view.

Of course, the degree of reproducibility at any stage of its investigation will enter into the economic judgment as to whether a supposed phenomenon is worth pursuing. If the argument is cast in these terms, one is tempted to ask: Given the degree of reproducibility already achieved in parapsychology, is the general reluctance of scientists to encourage this research a matter of dollar economics or does it involve the "emotional economy" of the sceptic? The question can just as well be turned around to deal with the enthusiasm of the parapsychologist and his emotional needs.

This kind of question, involving the motivation of scientists, is difficult but not impossible to investigate. By way of encouragement may I discuss my recent re-evaluation of the possibility of rapid progress in parapsychology?

Those who know me may remember that as late as 1965, after nearly 20 years in this field, my stock answer to eager laymen was: "Without doubt, ESP is real. Come back in 200 years. By then we may have some answers as to how it works." Now I am saying that there is a fair chance of a major research breakthrough within two decades. Does this shift of opinion represent a sound judgment of recent events in parapsychology, or does it reflect merely the desperation of an aging aficionado? This is a question the sceptic could evaluate by examining the experimental progress of the last ten years. Similarly, the larger matter of the overall worthwhileness of parapsychological research is not beyond objective consideration.

Fraud

7–8. To call for witnesses on a grand scale to ensure honesty in an experiment is to caricature the scientific process. Broadly viewed, fraud by the subject or by the experimenter are merely two possible experimental flaws whose likelihood must be estimated and then dealt with accordingly.

How likely is fraud? A distinction should be drawn between fraud by subject and fraud by experimenter. Except insofar as the subject is a person of established integrity, controls to prevent intentional sensory leakage, etc., must be a normal part of the experimental protocol. On the other hand, sociologically speaking, the method of science requires for its success that the professional experimenter be presumed honest, although such a presumption may in some instances be unwarranted. Experimental assistants constitute an intermediate case, which the senior experimenter will carefully consider.

Whether the probability of experimenter fraud is higher in parapsychology than in other fields of science is a matter for investigation. I dare say that those of us who are in the field tend to believe that our fellow parapsychologists, to the extent that they have been professionally trained and occupy responsible positions, are neither more nor less likely to engage in conscious scientific fraud than the scientists whom we know from other fields. Elsewhere, I have developed the question of the motivations of scientists as these may relate to the professional honesty of parapsychologists (McConnell, 1975).

Sensory Leakage

9. Since the purpose of an ESP experiment is to investigate a new mode of information transfer, care must be taken to exclude the old, well-known modes that might vitiate the results. In some research, by separating the target information from the responding subject by a large distance, practical certainty can be achieved that there was no unintentional sensory leakage. But to insist, as some sceptics do, that all research be done under conditions of "total isolation" and that any re-

search done under ordinary laboratory conditions is without value, is to dictate research tactics that may be counterproductive for the purpose of learning the nature of ESP.

Scientific technique is not regimented by authority. Research is a catch-as-catch-can art. Each experimenter will use his own judgment and in the course of time will be vindicated or ignored. Meanwhile, for any one of his experiments the possibility of sensory leakage must be evaluated as far as possible and the discovered uncertainties made a part of our assessment. This is not the same as total rejection of an experiment that fails to meet the sceptic's prescription for perfection.

The Need for a Perfect Experiment

10–13. One must agree that in any seemingly successful experiment there may have been an unreported weakness. What should we make of this possibility?

The sceptics who use arguments 10–13 evidently believe that, since no experiment can be proved free of flaws, all ESP experiments are worthless. The missing premise of this syllogism is that "ESP must be proved by one or more logically tight experiments." I believe this premise to be false.

In the earlier discussion of argument 5, I questioned whether attempting a logically rigorous proof of the occurrence of a phenomenon is appropriate in science. The uncertainty of historical facts—including those reported to have happened in the course of an experiment—is a facet of the human condition and must be accepted even by scientists.

In every experiment the possibility of an invalidating flaw must be considered, using all available information. The resulting, overall "engineering judgment" determines the weight to be given to a particular experiment in deciding to what extent the total available evidence for ESP is conclusive for immediate purposes.

14. One must grant the premise that "a chain is no stronger than its weakest link," but it does not follow that an experiment with a real or possible technical weakness is necessarily without evidential value. To demonstrate the limitations of this argument by analogy, one might ask: "How many other chains are supporting the load?"

Automated Experiments

15. In principle, the arguments dealing with the automation of ESP experiments are variants of earlier arguments demanding certainty of

proof. Argument 15a needs no further discussion, but 15b and 15c have new features of some interest.

Even though a random number generator may have been built using a fail-safe design, a cautious experimenter will wish to test large samples of its output by searching for evidence that any one number either comes up more frequently than others or is frequency-dependent upon—and thus partly predictable from—the numbers that precede it.

Because there is an indefinitely large number of possible tests for randomness, the sceptic can always require additional tests (argument 15b) even though he may be unable to say how the nonrandomness that he seeks could have occurred in the given electronic design, or—assuming that it did—how it could have been discovered and used by the subject to achieve the ESP scores that were reported. This problem arises because the sceptic is seeking logical certainty instead of some degree of probable proof.

Argument 15c illustrates the difficulty of overcoming a firmly established disbelief. The two most outspoken ESP sceptics of recent times, G. R. Price (1955) and C. E. M. Hansel (1966), recommended automatic equipment to remedy what they saw as the inadequacies of earlier research. Now that total automation is frequently used, suspicion has shifted from the simple, wholly observable operations of guessing and recording a deck of playing cards to the uncertainties of an exotic "black box."

I have been seriously told that the witnesses to an experiment must include engineering inspectors capable of detecting electronic fraud. This recommendation suggests interesting questions that lie beyond the scope of this paper: To whom is *logical* certainty as to the reality of ESP important, and why is it important to such persons?

SUBJECTIVE COUNTEREXPLANATORY PROBABILITY (SCEP)

16. The final, Bayesian-flavored argument is one I have never explicitly received, but it seems to me to represent a sceptic's best possible response to my discussion of the first 15 arguments. For ease of understanding, I shall paraphrase it more bluntly as follows: "Since ESP is perceived as impossible, no finite amount of evidence pointing to an anomalous sporadic transfer of information will make reasonable the supposition that a new mode of communication has been encountered." So interesting an argument deserves extended consideration.

Most experimental parapsychologists agree that a very small null-hypothesis probability occurring in an experiment is useful to eliminate the selection-of-experiment counterhypothesis but cannot otherwise be taken at face value.

The rule they *unconsciously* follow is that in any one experiment one must add to the calculated chance probability the subjective probabilities of all other possible counterexplanations, such as fraud, equipment failure, the oversights that bedevil us all, and mistakes arising from incompetence. In this way one obtains a total subjective counterexplanatory probability (SCEP). Experimental parapsychologists might estimate this counterexplanatory probability for any supposedly well done experiment to lie somewhere in the range 0.5 to perhaps 0.01, depending upon their knowledge of the experiment and their confidence in the experimenter. For example, a SCEP of 0.1 associated with an ESP experiment would correspond to the subjective belief that the odds are 9 to 1 that the experimental outcome did, in fact, depend on ESP— under the assumption that no other evidence for or against the phenomenon exists.

Only to the extent that two experiments are independent can their ordinary chance probabilities be multiplied. Similarly, to obtain a convincingly small subjective counterexplanatory probability for the existence of any purported experimental phenomenon, its investigation must be carried out by different experimenters, at different laboratories, and with differing procedures.

Evidence from Outside the Laboratory

Direct empirical evidence for a new mode of information transfer need not come only from the laboratory. Spontaneous cases of ESP have a special value as a mirror to nature; for they are undistorted by experimental restrictions. When independently verified and responsibly reported in a scientific or scholarly vehicle, they become a persuasive form of evidence. Although each such case may have a subjective counterexplanatory probability no smaller than perhaps 0.1, large numbers of such incidents, occurring over an extended period of time in various places at all socio-economic levels, and supported by less well verified cases occurring in many countries and at all periods of history, can be joined to yield an extremely small overall probability.

There is another class of evidence that is neither experimental nor spontaneous but that lends itself to scientific scrutiny and should not be ignored. The supposed spirit messages from entranced mediums such as Mrs. Piper and Mrs. Leonard, who were investigated by sceptics for years and never caught in fraud, constitute substantial independent evidence for ESP.

SCEP for the ESP Phenomenon

What finally emerges from study of the history of selected events inside and outside the laboratory is a personal, subjective estimate of the combined probability of all conceived counterexplanations to the hypothesis that an unknown mode of communication was functioning at least somewhere in the collection of events examined. More simply stated, this SCEP is an estimate of an upper limit for the direct-evidence "probability" of the nonoccurrence of ESP in nature.

If one's purpose is to assess the reality of ESP, SCEP cannot be used by itself. It is an estimate based upon *empirical* evidence *directly* bearing upon the ESP hypothesis. Perhaps there is other, contrary evidence. In a logical sense, direct evidence for the universal nonexistence of a phenomenon cannot be obtained. Nevertheless, there may be indirect evidence that, by some train of logic, weighs for or against ESP. Since our evaluative process up to this point has been subjective, it is essential in the cause of truth that any contrary evidence be given appropriate consideration even though it may be of a tenuous character.

SUBJECTIVE ANTECEDENT PROBABILITY (SAP)

Consideration of the indirect evidence bearing on the ESP hypothesis can lead to an estimate of what is sometimes called the "subjective antecedent probability" of the reality of ESP (SAP). This probability is antecedent in the sense that it is usually based upon generalized experience rather than upon ad hoc study.

For an intelligent and well-informed member of our society, the SAP of ESP is likely to be small. To the extent that it is smaller than SCEP, and if the two probabilities are weighted equally, the individual will be inclined to deny the reality of ESP, and vice versa.

The fact that ESP violates the metaphysical presuppositions of Western science and also that it does not appear to be of much importance in everyday life are two powerful considerations for a small SAP. (See the discussion of arguments 1 and 2 above.) Presumably the size of this SAP will depend also upon such things as:

1. The investigator's familiarity with the current factual knowledge (as distinct from theory) in psychology, physics, and biology to which ESP must somehow be joined.

2. His ingenuity in conceiving how ESP might be fitted to that knowledge.

3. His understanding of the history and method of science.

4. His degree of enculturation, respect for authority, and intellectual flexibility.

Other personal attributes probably important in estimating both SCEP and SAP for ESP are intelligence, curiosity, empathy, and a grasp of current and historical social reality.

WHERE BOTH SIDES CAN AGREE

I have tried to present this discussion in a way that will be acceptable to both the ESP sceptic and the believer. I hope that the following summary statements will be agreeable to both: (1) If ESP is real, a consensus among scientists can be expected eventually. (2) The question of the reality of ESP has an immutable answer in nature, so that the controversy constitutes a test of one's grasp of reality. Either the believer or the disbeliever is wrong in his judgment. (3) Without more understanding, we should refrain from interpreting the fact that believers are generally eager for more research while sceptics are usually antagonistic to the entire subject. This could reflect merely the nature of the controversy rather than the merits of the case. (4) The juxtaposition of SCEP and SAP involves emotional elements so that it is perhaps not surprising that there are relatively few midway opinions among those who claim to have studied the evidence.

These last two points of possible agreement will be discussed in later sections after a pause for consideration of the technical nature of SCEP and SAP.

THE BAYESIAN RATIONALE

While the analysis pursued in this paper draws its inspiration and legitimacy from Bayesian method, it is not of that mathematical genre. Bayes's theorem is not used. However, both SCEP and SAP are intuitive or "prior" probabilities in the Bayesian sense. Their final comparison for the purpose of making a net probability judgment of the reality of ESP has the same justification—no more, no less—as their individual intuitive formulation.

Mathematicians today do not limit themselves to the frequency definition of probability but conceive probabilities of occurrence for any set of events subject only to Kolmogorov's axioms. In this paper the events are the occurrence and nonoccurrence of ESP in certain past situations. It is the lesson of Bayesian method that we can assign as event probabilities any consistent values that we please. In the present case we assign fixed nonexplicit values.

In Bayesian method the sole justification for this procedure is post hoc and pragmatic. For example, after the adjustment of industrial production-line parameters on the basis of Bayesian theory, one asks: "Did the assumed prior probability distribtion, as it affected Type I and Type II errors, result in dollars saved?" In the case of our determination of the reality of ESP (which from a methodological standpoint is not an unusual life problem) the post hoc justification will come eventually by having obtained the correct consensus, "yes" or "no," as quickly as possible. This is a matter of no less social importance than efficiency on a production line.

SCEP vs. SAP

Using the concepts of SAP and SCEP, one might develop possibly useful speculations about the nature of belief and disbelief in ESP. As a beginning attempt, I shall consider the SAP of ESP in nonintellectuals vs. intellectuals, and the SCEP of ESP in laymen and in scientists.

By way of review: SCEP, the subjective counterexplanatory probability, is concerned with the direct empirical evidence for ESP; SAP, the subjective antecedent probability of ESP, reflects indirect evidence. SCEP derives presumably from active consideration of the ad hoc evidence; SAP evolves, for the most part, passively and from many areas of experience. The nominal range of these probabilities is from zero, corresponding to impossibility of the hypothesis, to one, or certainty of its truth. The value, one-half, is the point of indifference at which the hypothesis is neither favored nor disfavored.

Levels of SAP

In our society today, there is widespread uncritical belief in ESP. Among nonintellectuals I would place the average SAP of ESP as above 0.5. Elsewhere, I have discussed the nature of popular occultism and its hazard to parapsychology as a science (McConnell, 1973).

Among Western intellectuals, ESP is traditionally regarded as superstition and its SAP is near to zero. Like other beliefs of well-informed people, this one comes from the specialists (in this case, the scientists) to whom the responsibility for determining received public belief has been delegated by society.

As ever larger areas of knowledge are pre-empted by science, the mentally competent members of our society are intellectual prisoners in a sense that they never were in earlier times when the ultimate authority was a philosopher or prophet. Science has established a hegemony that can not be challenged. The thinking elite is bound in allegiance to the twin principles of observation and reason and to the beliefs established thereform by scientific consensus. Moreover, adherence to what is safely orthodox is reinforced by a well-founded fear of the undisciplined thinking evident daily in the press and television. Creative rebellion is possible for scientists within their specialized disciplines, but nihilism is the only escape for the intelligentsia as a whole. In this situation the antecedent probability of ESP remains small among intellectuals because ESP is rejected by our scientific leaders.

SCEP in the Layman

SCEP is not directly determined by the culture but by the individual's consideration of empirical evidence for ESP. Its value as an appraisal of reality is different in the layman and in the scientist. Laymen, regardless of their intellectual ability, are usually not technically qualified to evaluate published reports of ESP, although they will inevitably attempt to do so. The only kind of direct evidence for ESP that might be validly assessed by the layman is any personal experience of the phenomenon by himself or by immediate associates whose credibility he can competently judge.

Thus, for the most part, the values of SCEP of ESP held by laymen are determined indirectly by the subculture and correspond to SAP values, i.e., are determined in our society by the secondary sources of knowledge that laymen accept. The latter range from tabloid newspapers to the *Scientific American*, with television covering the same gamut. The treatment of the subject of ESP by these sources tends to create a gradient of disbelief among laymen with a direction closer to the vector of intelligence than to that of socio-economic status.

ESP Conflict Among Scientists

Only for those scientists who consider themselves competent to judge the direct evidence for ESP is there a likelihood of conflict between SCEP and SAP. For this group, initially, SAP will be small and SCEP nonexistent, resulting in a rejection of ESP. As a scientist hears of experiments purporting to show the phenomenon, he at first ignores them. However, if he attends to the literature of parapsychology, he will generate a SCEP, perhaps initially in the vicinity of 0.5. With continuing study this may drop, leading him into a conflict in which SCEP and SAP point to contradictory conclusions.

In social psychology this kind of internal conflict is dealt with under the heading "consistency theory" and is most colorfully described in terms of "cognitive dissonance" (Festinger, 1957). The mechanisms may be arguable, but the outcome is inevitable: gross intellectual inconsistency cannot be knowingly tolerated. The scientist who has read the ESP literature must either explain away the evidence by arguments such as those I have just reviewed, or he must revise his SAP upwards until the discrepancy reaches a tolerable level. Because of the intuitive and pervasive origins of SAP its modification will be painful, and for some persons, impossible. Thus, cognitive dissonance provides a plausible explanation as to why there are relatively few scientists who say that they are half-convinced by the existing evidence for ESP and are eager to have more research done to settle the matter.

Doubt Among Parapsychologists

The Parapsychological Association, with an international membership of about 240, is the only professional society in its field. Preliminary tabulation from a recent self-report survey, with an 84% response, showed that an estimated 78% of the membership has had academic training *beyond* the bachelor or equivalent level. This is a highly educated group. How have these people reconciled cultural preconceptions with experimental findings on ESP sufficiently to allow a comfortable, public association with the field?

As might be expected, in many of these cases there has been a direct experience with the phenomenon. Of the survey respondents, 77% said that psychic effects observed in themselves or in persons close to them have contributed to their belief in ESP.

More surprising is the statistic that, of the respondents, only 68% are currently wholly free of doubt concerning the reality of ESP. Moreover, upon first exposure to the published evidence for psi phenomena, 48% of the respondents had experienced some degree of conflict with prior beliefs, and for 16% of respondents this conflict is recognized as still unresolved. Even for the highly selected population of parapsychologists, the bondage of the culturally given has been difficult to loose.[1]

Although parapsychologists and other scientists interested in ESP may have examined the evidence piece by piece and may have used arguments, pro and con, and thus may have arrived at a judgment on the phenomenon, I believe it is true that few have assembled their thinking

---

1. A full report of this survey is given as an appendix to this book under the title "Training, Belief, and Mental Conflict Within the Parapsychological Association."

at the intermediate conceptual level of SCEP and SAP. It is my hope that if they do so, they will achieve a self-awareness that will encourage the separation of emotion and reason in dealing with the difficult question of the reality of ESP.

REFERENCES

Bloom, B. S. Report on creativity research by the Examiner's Office of the University of Chicago. Pages 251-264 in C. W. Taylor and F. Barron (Eds.), *Scientific creativity: Its recognition and development*. New York: John Wiley, 1963. (Reprinted, 1975, by Robert E. Krieger Publishing Co.)

Dennis, W. Variations in productivity among creative workers. *Scientific Monthly*, 1955, *80*, 277-278.

Festinger, L. *A theory of cognitive dissonance*. Evanston, Ill.: Row Peterson, 1957.

Hansel, C. E. M. *ESP, a scientific evaluation*. New York: Charles Scribner's Sons, 1966.

McConnell, R. A. Parapsychology and the occult. *Journal of the American Society for Psychical Research*, 1973, *67*, 225-243.

McConnell, R. A. The motivations of parapsychologists and other scientists. *Journal of the Amerian Society for Psychical Research*, 1975, *69*, 273-280.

Price, G. R. Science and the supernatural. *Science*, 1955, *122*, 359-367.

EDITOR'S POSTSCRIPT

Although I have no idea what man's future will be like, I am convinced that if civilization exists a hundred years hence, it will represent a psychological separation from today greater than our distance from ancient Greece. Life a century from now is not simply unknown to us; I believe it is at present inconceivable because we do not have language that would describe it. A major psychological discontinuity is what I see as the most optimistic outcome as interacting curves of growth and depletion produce a multitude of physical and social problems that are unsolvable within the cultures presently existing on earth.

How might we progress toward a sustainable future? The challenge is fundamentally psychological. It seems obvious that we must increase our scientific understanding of man. In this view, all other new knowledge is important only if it advances, or buys time for pursuing, the psychobiological sciences.

From my students I often hear: "Isn't that expecting too much of science?" My answer is this: "Don't we try to solve all of our problems by first understanding them? What is scientific understanding? How does it differ from ordinary understanding?"

The process of understanding is a combination of observation and reasoning. That process becomes "scientific" merely by the addition of one ingredient: discipline. If we say that science cannot solve humanity's problems, we are saying that man cannot help himself.

Perhaps I should explain that I do not belittle human relationships and the fine arts that give life its most precious meanings. I merely say that, while such activities sustain us, they are not guiding us toward the future. What is lacking is an understanding of the mental nature of man.

In my more hopeful moments I like to think that there may be a threshold of psychological understanding, analogous to the threshold of physical knowledge that led to the Industrial Revolution, beyond which all spiritual achievements become increasingly possible.

Past experience shows that only certain kinds of scientific understanding have direct revolutionary consequences. Presumably, what is missing for a psychological revolution is an empirically consistent theory of the essence of man, i.e., of the nature of his consciousness.

In this book I have gathered some significant contributions to a public understanding of how far we have progressed in the search for such a theory. As the reader may infer, I believe that seed facts for a scientific explanation of consciousness have been found in the little known field of parapsychology.

Appendix

TRAINING, BELIEF, AND MENTAL CONFLICT WITHIN THE PARAPSYCHOLOGICAL ASSOCIATION

By R. A. McConnell and T. K. Clark

ABSTRACT: From a 1975 self-report survey and other sources covering 203 or 84% of the Members and Associates of the Parapsychological Association, the following were determined: areas and levels of professional training, year of birth and of first familiarity with the parapsychological literature, prior belief in ESP and mental conflict occurring at the time of study of the literature, the time needed to resolve such conflict, the extent of currently unresolved conflict, the strength and sources of current belief in ESP, the investigatory and publishing activity of the membership over a five-year period, and some characteristics of those who left the organization between 1975 and 1980.

The membership of the Association is drawn from 26 countries with 33% residing outside the U.S.A. Seventy-eight percent of the Members and 56% of the Associates hold doctoral degrees. Seventy-one percent of the Members published something in the journals of parapsychology over the years 1971–1975. Of all respondents in 1975, 75% were still enrolled in 1980. The average age in the sample was 50. The average age at first familiarity with the literature was 22. Forty-eight percent experienced mental conflict when they first became familiar with the literature, and for 16% that conflict remained unresolved when the survey was taken. Thirty-two percent of all respondents still had less than complete conviction as to the reality of ESP. Belief in ESP derived one-third from "experiential" sources (spontaneous psi in self or close acquaintances) and two-thirds from "rational" sources (one's own experiments and the literature).

The statistical findings are illustrated by quotations from respondents whose identities are concealed but whose characteristics are presented in some detail.

INTRODUCTION

Who are the parapsychologists? Where do they come from? What has been their training? As scientists, are they laymen or professionals? What do they believe about the phenomena they investigate? Are they credulous or skeptical? Are they remnants of an earlier, more innocent age or perhaps the flotsam of today's counterculture? How well do living parapsychologists span the gap from pre-World War I Edwardian self-assurance to post-World War II disgruntlement? Can parapsychologists' interest in psychic phenomena be dismissed as adolescent or senile—or perhaps simply naive? Where did they get their beliefs about those phenomena? Are they themselves psychic?

Reprinted from the *Journal of Parapsychology*, *44* (1980), 245-268.

How many so-called parapsychologists are active in the research and how many have only a peripheral interest? Have they—do they— experience any conflict between the twentieth-century idea that man is a gypsy in the universe (as so nobly argued by Monod, 1971) and the possibility that consciousness may someday reveal man as one with nature?

Several years ago we set out to find the answers to these questions. Defining parapsychologists was easy. Belonging to the Parapsychological Association ensures neither competence nor honesty, but it is a good bet that anyone who calls himself a parapsychologist and is not a member of that organization is, in fact, a salesman and not a scientist.

METHOD

The Sample

The population for our study was the membership of the Parapsychological Association as officially listed in January 1975. Our data were gathered in mid-1975 but not analyzed until 1980. The passing of five years has allowed us to measure the stability of membership in the Association and to characterize the members who left the field in that period.

Questionnaires were sent to all 241 Members and Associates. Eleven letters were returned by the post office as undeliverable. No response was received from 27 of the remainder. The nonresponders were 2 U.S.A. and 4 foreign Members, and 14 U.S.A. and 7 foreign Associates. From available knowledge of the nonresponders we infer that the 203 replies received from 84% of the membership of the Association are closely representative of the whole and that our findings can be extrapolated accordingly.

"Membership in 1980" refers to a listing of 1975 respondents in the Association's directory dated 1980 and issued in January of that year. By 1980 the membership had grown to 254 and was drawn from 28 of the United States and from 25 other countries.

Data Reduction

The questions as they appeared in our questionnaire are given in italics at the beginning of the section in which they are discussed.

Missing information, when possible, was obtained or estimated from repeated inquiries, from biographical directories, or from private sources. Uncompleted items show in the tabular totals. All categorizations were done by the senior author with the objective of

Table 1

AREAS OF PRINCIPAL TRAINING

WITHIN THE PARAPSYCHOLOGICAL ASSOCIATION MEMBERSHIP

Area of Training[a]	Number of Parapsychologists With Various Levels of Training			Total
	Bachelor	Master	Doctoral	
†Biological sciences	1	2	9	12
†Chemistry	2	3	2	7
Clergy	0	0	1	1
†Data processing	4	1	0	5
Editing	4	0	0	4
†Engineering	3	1	6	10
Law	1	0	1	2
†Mathematics	1	1	3	5
Medicine (psychiatry)	0	0	19	19
Medicine (other)	0	1	4	5
Parapsychology	3	0	5	8
Philosophy	1	0	10	11
†Physics	1	3	10	14
Psychology (clinical)	2	1	17	20
Psychology (other)	4	6	38	48
Sociology, Anthropology Archeology	1	1	2	4
Other and unidentified	18	2	8	28
Totals	46	22	135	203

Note. This table is based on the 84% of the members who responded. Each member was counted only once. The survey was conducted in 1975.

[a] Areas of training marked † have been grouped as "quantitative" in Tables 3, 4, and 6.

providing maximum information without biasing the picture or appreciably increasing its uncertainty.

Respondents were told they would not be publicly identified. To help conceal the source of a quotation, all references to the gender of the respondents have been given in the male form and most dates have been specified by interval. Possibly identifying details have been presented in one or two cases where the member volunteered permission to use his name.

Activity of Members

To determine the active interest in parapsychology within the membership, we searched the five-year period, 1971-1975, in the following journals: *Journal of Parapsychology, Journal of the American Society for Psychical Research, Journal of the Society for Psychical Research,* and *Research in Parapsychology*—these being the important English-language serials of parapsychology at that time. We classified as "active" those members who produced as authors or co-authors at least one publication. Publications were defined as research reports, theoretical papers, reviews, including book reviews, and monographs. We also included in the active classification, editors and employees of parapsychological organizations.

As an additional classification, we listed as "investigators" all those who in the same period published observations of psi phenomena, whether experimental or spontaneous.

STATISTICAL FINDINGS

Areas of Training

What did/do you do to earn your living (as explicitly as possible); i.e., what is your principal area and level of expertise?

The highest academic degree and the principal area of training of the responding members of the Parapsychological Association as revealed by the above question are presented in Table 1. The noteworthy features of this table are the superior educational level and the professional diversity of the membership.

Among those who responded to this 1975 survey, 66% held a doctoral degree and 11% a master-level degree. The remaining 23%, with few exceptions, held a four-year college degree or its equivalent.

There are uncertainties in our categorizations by area of expertise with which the wording of our question failed to deal. For example, a person may have formally trained in one area and currently be engaged in another. Within the limits of available information, we have been guided by formal training rather than by current activity.

Those who are listed explicitly as parapsychologists are (mainly) four-year college graduates who did not formally complete professional training in any field or are (mostly foreign) members who earned a doctoral degree in parapsychology.

The largest defined category, that of psychologists-other-than-clinical, is heterogeneous in that it includes experimental, educational,

Table 2

PROFESSIONAL TRAINING OF SUBGROUPS WITHIN THE PARAPSYCHOLOGICAL ASSOCIATION AS OF 1975

Membership Training Area	Total %	Members %	Associates %	In U.S.A. %	Elsewhere %	Doctoral %	Subdoctoral %	Active[a] %	Inactive %	1980 member %	Experientialists[b] %	Rationalists[b] %	Doubters[b] %
N =	(203)	(95)	(108)	(136)	(67)	(135)	(68)	(109)	(94)	(153)	(54)	(124)	(62)
Biological sciences	6	10	3	6	6	7	4	5	7	6	2	7	6
Chemistry	3	1	6	3	5	1	7	4	3	3	2	4	5
Engineering	5	5	5	4	6	4	6	4	6	4	5	6	3
Parapsychology	4	7	1	3	6	4	4	7	0	5	4	4	3
Philosophy	5	4	6	4	9	7	2	5	5	5	2	5	7
Physics and mathematics	9	7	11	11	6	10	9	9	10	10	5	11	10
Psychiatry	10	10	9	10	9	14	0	8	11	10	15	6	11
Psychology (clinical)	10	14	6	9	10	13	4	11	9	10	13	10	15
Psychology (other)	24	25	22	25	21	28	15	27	20	24	22	25	24
Other	24	17	31	25	22	12	49	20	29	23	30	22	16

Note. Cell entries are expressed in percent of N, the number of members in that category for whom information was available. All columns total 100%.

[a] For the definition of "active members" see under "Method." The total number of "investigators" was 66. Among Members there were 41 investigators.

[b] For "experientialists," "rationalists," and "doubters" see under "Sources and Degrees of Current Belief."

social, and industrial psychologists, and, at the subdoctoral level, some psychologists whose training involved no research and was never professionally exercised.

Because academic degree information was not explicitly requested, many respondents modestly omitted such data. Where evidence of a higher degree could not be found, the member was assigned to the bachelor degree category.

We have given particular attention to the accuracy of the doctoral degree count. After a case-by-case study of all readily available evidence, we believe that among the U.S.A. members the number of simulated doctorates lies between zero and three. Among the foreign members this figure could rise to perhaps ten, although in most such cases the member occupies an academic position that would normally be filled by a doctoral-degree holder in the U.S.A. These uncertainties arise from several sources, not least of which, in the case of foreign members, is the fact that doctoral degrees in other countries are awarded by academic processes that are substantially different from those in the U.S.A. It is evident that these questions do not affect our conclusion that the membership is predominantly professional and is drawn from a wide range of disciplines.

Professional and Other Categories

To relate professional training to other aspects of membership, we have aggregated training categories so as to eliminate groups smaller than seven. The results appear in Table 2. They show a surprising uniformity in the distribution of member characteristics, including on-going doubt as to the reality of ESP.

Table 2 is to be read by noting the overall percentage strength of any one profession in the Total column and then scanning horizontally to find any column with a markedly higher or lower value. In this way one finds that biological scientists, parapsychologists, and clinical psychologists tend to be full Members of the Parapsychological Association, while chemists and "others" tend to be in the Associate class. As might be expected, psychiatrists, clinical psychologists, and "others" tend to rely heavily on spontaneous psi in self and acquaintances in deciding upon the reality of ESP, i.e., tend to appear in the column labelled "experientialists." Biological scientists, physicists, and philosophers find less assurance from such evidence.

The classifications used for the columns of Table 2, while operationally distinct, are not necessarily independent. In Table 3 we explore this matter in a contingency table. Only three cells show an

Table 3

INTERDEPENDENCE OF MEMBERSHIP CHARACTERISTICS,
PRESENTED AS OBSERVED PERCENTAGE OF THE MEMBERSHIP
OVER THE PROPORTIONALLY EXPECTED PERCENTAGE

		"Member" Class (49%)	U.S.A. Resident (66%)	Doctoral Training (67%)	Quantitative (27%)	Active Members (53%)	1980 Members (76%)
U.S.A. residents	(66%)	30					
		32					
Doctoral training	(67%)	38*	41				
		33	44				
Quantitative training[a]	(27%)	13	19	16			
		13	18	18			
Active members[b]	(53%)	35*	35	37	12		
		26	35	35	14		
Still belong in 1980[c]	(76%)	40	47	53	20	43	
		37	50	51	21	40	
"Experientialists"[d]	(29%)	11	19	20	4	13	19
		14	19	19	8	15	22
"Rationalists"[d]	(67%)	39*	44	45	21	38	53
		33	44	44	18	35	51
"Doubters"[d]	(32%)	14	21	22	9	15	24
		16	21	22	9	17	24

[a] For the definition of "quantitative training" see Table 1.

[b] For the definition of "active members" see under "Method."

[c] The survey was conducted in 1975.

[d] For the definitions of "experientialists," "rationalists," and "doubters" see under "Sources and Degrees of Current Belief."

*$p < .01$, based on a one-degree-of-freedom chi-square with N = 186.

interrelationship significant at the $p = .01$ level: Full members of the Association include a higher percentage of doctorates (78%), of active members (71%), and of "rationalists" (79%) than do Associate members (56%, 35%, and 55%, respectively).

The "rationalists" category will be discussed more fully later. Briefly, "rationalists" are those who have gained conviction concerning the reality of ESP primarily from their own experiments or from the published literature of psychic research rather than from an immediate experience of spontaneous psi.

In Table 3 we offer no comparisons among "experientialists," "rationalists," and "doubters" because these categories are statistically interrelated by reason of their definitions, as will be seen later.

Perhaps the most important feature of Table 3 is the relative independence that it shows among the several methods of categorizing. Because of their independence, these categories should be efficient for exploring the distribution of other membership characteristics in the remainder of this paper.

Member Age and the Psychic Literature

What was the year of your birth? At what age did you first become familiar with the published accounts of spontaneous or experimental psi?

The answers to these questions based upon 200 respondents are presented in Figures 1 and 2. The birth dates of the membership in 1975 spanned more than six decades, ranging from 1891 to 1954, and were rather uniformly distributed in the four decades 1910 to 1949. In

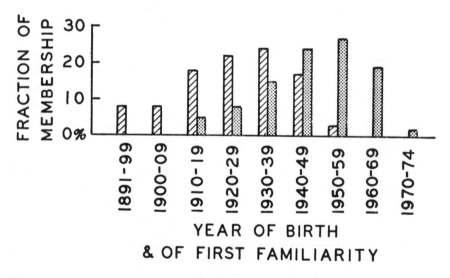

Figure 1.   Year of birth (hatched) bars and of first familiarity with the psychic literature (gray) for members of the Parapsychological Association.

this survey we found roughly 80% of the members to be in their prime years of intellectual activity. We conclude that the organization represents neither the immature nor the aged. Mostly, these are people

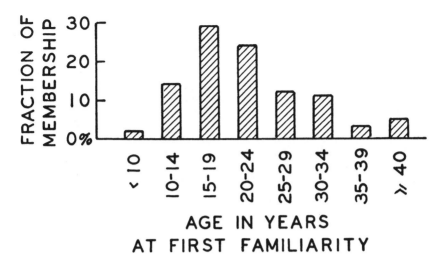

Figure 2.   Age of members at first familiarity with the psychic literature.

whose creative years cover the pre-World War II decade up to the present.

The year of first familiarity with the psychic literature (Figure 1) likewise spans six decades. A substantial fraction (19%) of the members became interested in parapsychology before J. B. Rhine published his first book in 1934. Seventy percent first studied the literature of psi in the three decades 1940–1969.

Figure 2 shows that 69% of the respondents became familiar with the psychic literature before age 25. Bearing in mind that the pool of potential members is large and roughly constant for all ages, we conclude that there is little hope of attracting to the field those who have completed their education and almost none at all of gaining new members among older scientists from other fields.

As shown in Table 4, the average age of the entire membership was 50 in 1975 and the mean age at first familiarity with the literature was 22. The corresponding median values were 49 and 20, respectively.

From this table we find that full Members averaged 8 years older than Associates and that U.S.A. members averaged 6 years younger than those living elsewhere, while the age difference between doctoral and subdoctoral groups was only 3 years. "Doubters," on the average, were 4 years younger than the membership as a whole.

Table 4
AVERAGE AGE IN MEMBERSHIP GROUPS IN 1975
AND AT FIRST FAMILIARITY WITH THE PSYCHIC LITERATURE

	Mean Age in 1975	Mean Age at First Familiarity
Entire membership	50y.	22y.
Full members	54	21
Associates	46	22
U.S.A. Residents	48	21
Reside elsewhere	54	23
Doctoral training	51	21
Subdoctoral training	48	24
Quantitative training[a]	50	23
Nonquantitative training	49	21
Active members[b]	49	21
Inactive members	51	22
Still belonging in 1980	49	21
"Experientialists"[c]	51	22
"Rationalists"[c]	50	22
"Doubters"[c]	46	21

[a] For the definition of "quantitative training" see Table 1.
[b] For the definition of "active members" see under "Method."
[c] For the definitions of "experientialists," "rationalists," and "doubters" see under "Sources and Degrees of Current Belief."

The mean age at first familiarity with the psychic literature varied scarcely at all. Except for those with subdoctoral training, all groups first familiarized themselves with the psychic literature at an age within one year of the grand mean.

Conflict and Prior Belief

Before you first became familiar with the published accounts of spontaneous or experimental psi, what was your prior disbelief/belief in ESP? When you first became familiar with such accounts, did you experience any sense of conflict with your prior beliefs? How long did it take to resolve or dissipate any/all such sense of conflict?

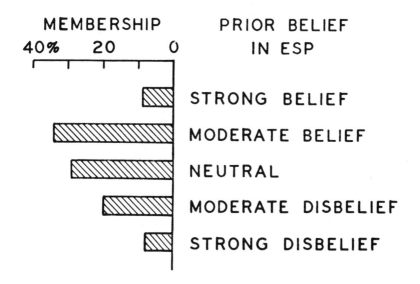

Figure 3. Belief in ESP prior to first familiarity with the psychic literature.

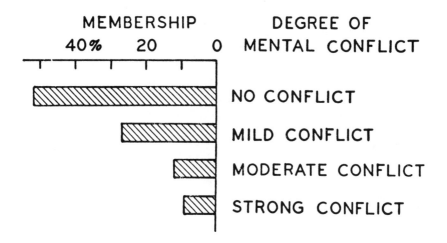

Figure 4. Mental conflict at time of first familiarity with the psychic literature.

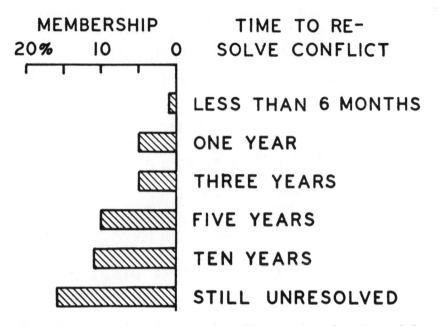

Figure 5. Time to resolve mental conflict experienced at time of first familiarity with the psychic literature, together with the fraction of membership having still-unresolved conflict in 1975.

These three questions are answered in Figures 3, 4, and 5 derived from the responses of 199 members. On the questionnaire the first item was given a seven-point scale, ranging from strong disbelief to strong belief. In our presentation we have combined intermediate degrees of belief and disbelief to give a five-point scale.

These questions had their origin in a broader question: Do Association members suffer mental conflict concerning belief in ESP, and, if so, what light might this cast upon the resistance of orthodox science to parapsychology?

What we would like to have been able to answer is: Among Association members *what* conflicts arise between prior private attitudes toward ESP (derived from self, friends, and milieu) and the published evidence for ESP when first encountered? Our questioning was necessarily more restricted.

What is apparent is that, prior to study of the literature, the membership held a wide range of disbelief/belief in ESP (Figure 3). The fact that 57% of all responding members began without belief, that 48% admit to experiencing conflict when becoming familiar with the literature of the field (Figure 4), and that for 16% this conflict was still unresolved at the time of the survey (Figure 5), suggests that parapsychologists are not all the "easy believers" that their critics tend to assume.

We have found that parapsychologists are a highly educated group. From our study we infer that joining the Parapsychological Association is an intellectual response to encountering either spontaneous psi or the literature of parapsychology. We know that the response of less educated persons to psi is expressed in the indiscriminate beliefs of popular occultism (McConnell & McConnell, 1971). The distinction between these responses should be important to scientists from other fields trying to assess parapsychology.

Sources and Degrees of Current Belief

To what extent did you acquire your first essentially total belief in the reality of ESP from each of the following categories? If you have not yet acquired total belief, this question will describe your present condition. Otherwise, the question applies at the time of your first total belief and Category 5 will be empty.

1. Your own spontaneous experiences.

2. Spontaneous experiences of persons close enough to you to be believed. Include here: (a) the spontaneous experiences of persons whose veracity and judgment you trust because of close personal association, and (b) spontaneous experiences in which you showed no psychic ability yourself but were a first-hand witness to one or more unambiguously psychic events involving others.

3. Your own experiments for the purpose of investigating psi.

4. Published accounts of spontaneous or experimental psi (regardless of whether studied by you alone or in a group setting). Include here experimental research by others whom you may trust for any special reason as well as the more generally published accounts of spontaneous or experimental psi to whatever degree you believed in them.

5. "Percent of doubt" now remaining as to the reality of ESP.

This question attempts to discover a respondent's impression about the degree and source of his belief in the reality of ESP under the assumption that such belief can be partitioned according to its sources so as to add to 100%. We regard this as a useful assumption, but the question as presented is defective because of missing categories of sources of belief.

The following additional sources of belief were cited by respondents:

1. The opinions or conclusions of others, aside from conveyed knowledge of spontaneous or experimentally observed ESP (6 respondents).

2. Intuitive belief in ESP, aside from any direct experience of it in discrete, recognizable incidents (6 respondents).

3. Reasoning from other beliefs or from empirical facts other than observations of the phenomenon (2 respondents).

It is obvious that all of us are influenced to a degree by factors such as the above. To improve this kind of questionnaire, one might attempt to deal explicitly with this problem by adding two response categories (No. 1 above and Nos. 2 and 3 combined).

In the present circumstances, most respondents ignored such extraneous sources of belief. Where appropriate, we have deleted from data tabulations those who did not.

In simplified form the question we investigated was as follows: On the basis of a complete belief in ESP, how much belief do you have? As a fraction of complete belief how much of your belief did you get from each of several sources; namely, (1) your own spontaneous experiences of psi, (2) the experience of spontaneous psi by persons close to you, (3) your own experiments, and (4) the published literature of psychic research?

The first two sources of belief have in common the idea of immediate experience of psi. We have combined the data from these sources as representing belief having an "experiential" basis. The last two sources, on the other hand, involve the organizing of nature by means of symbols (words) and logic (reasoning), and we have joined them as representing belief having a "rational" basis. To facilitate analysis, those members who reported 50% or more of a total belief in ESP as having come from experiential sources, we have designated as "experientialists," and those who gained 50% or more of a total belief from rational sources, we have labelled "rationalists." (Eight who acquired total belief equally from experiential and rational sources are listed in both categories.) Those who expressed any degree of doubt as to the reality of ESP, we have called "doubters."

Although members were asked to quantify their belief as fractional parts from these several sources so that their data would be manipulatable, the percentage results have been aggregated for presentation in five categories; namely, "none," "weak," "medium," "strong," and "complete," as defined in Table 5.

Thirty-two percent of all responding members had less than complete belief in the reality of ESP. In the responding membership as a whole, the mean belief in ESP was 93%. One-third of this belief

Table 5

PERCENTAGE OF RESPONDING MEMBERS DERIVING VARIOUS
DEGREES OF BELIEF IN ESP FROM VARIOUS SOURCES

Degree of Belief	Sources of Belief in ESP						All Sources Combined (%)
	The Spontaneous Experience of Psi			Rational Sources			
	By self (%)	By close persons (%)	By both combined (%)	Own experiments (%)	Published accounts (%)	Both combined (%)	
Complete (100%)	2	1	4[a]	1	5	15	68[b]
Strong (75-99%)	4	1	9	4	12	25	22
Medium (26-74%)	17	17	36	28	42	43	8
Weak (1-25%)	36	47	28	37	32	13	2
None (0%)	41	34	23	30	9	4	0
Mean belief acquired from respective source(s)[c]	17	15	32	21	40	61	93

Note. All columns total 100% and represent 186 members whose records were complete in this regard.

[a] For example, 2% of the membership acquired complete belief from their own spontaneous psi, 1% from experiences of close persons, and 1% from a combination of these two sources.

[b] 49% (= 68 − 4 − 15) acquired complete belief from some combination of experiential and rational sources.

[c] The mean percent beliefs in this row are exactly the average of the belief scores of all members and approximately the average of the table-stub values of belief, weighted according to the cell entries in the same column. For a statement of the meaning of these calculations, see text.

came from "experiential" sources, dividing equally between spontaneous psi in self and spontaneous psi in persons close enough to be believed. The other two-thirds came from "rational" sources, and of that fraction, twice as much came from the literature of psi as from experiments performed by the members themselves.

Table 6

MEAN DEGREE OF BELIEF IN ESP
FROM ALL SOURCES COMBINED, FOR DIFFERENT MEMBERSHIP GROUPS

	Fraction of Total Membership	Mean Degree of Belief[a]
Total membership	100%	93%
Full members	49	94
Associate members	51	91
Resident in U.S.A.	66	93
Resident elsewhere	34	93
Doctoral training	67	92
Subdoctoral training	33	93
Quantitative training[b]	27	93
Nonquantitative training	73	93
Active members[c]	53	95
Inactive members	47	90
Still members in 1980[d]	76	93
No longer members in 1980	24	91

Note. Sample size = 186.
[a] Calculated in the manner of Table 5.
[b] For the definition of "quantitative training" see Table 1.
[c] For the definition of "active members" see under "Method."
[d] The survey was conducted in 1975.

In Table 6 mean belief in ESP (93% for the sample as a whole) is tabulated for various categories of members. Full Members are found to be slightly more believing (94%) than Associates (91%). Active members are found to be more convinced of ESP (95%) than inactive members (90%). Those whose names are missing from the 1980 membership roll had a belief (91%) only slightly less than those who continued as members (93%). No other differences exceeded 1%. The similarity of distributions of belief in ESP within the Parapsychological Association is remarkable, considering that belief is substantially less than complete.

INDIVIDUAL RESPONSES

The statistical findings speak for themselves, but they leave a great deal unsaid. We take this opportunity to express our gratitude to the many members of the Association who, in addition to answering our questions, shared with us their personal and often intimate experiences. Some of this material has special significance because of the eminence of the member, and all of it will be retained in our files for its historical value. What we present now are anonymous quotations that illuminate the field rather than a person.

Comment on the Questionnaire

Whether or not one agrees substantively with the following criticisms, one cannot fail to be impressed by their tone of aggressive independence. These are not timid souls seeking emotional support from fellow cultists.

From a professor of philosophy whose full acceptance of ESP derives 35% from the experiences of persons close to him and 65% from the literature:

> This is a very poor questionnaire. . . . Why not have someone who has expertise in formulating questionnaires compose one for you?

From an experimenter in parapsychology who has published strikingly positive findings and who listed himself as having 100% disbelief in ESP (we rejected this figure and tabulated the question as blank because it was evident from the accompanying letter that he was protesting the wording of the question):

> The greatest difficulty with parapsychological research today is . . . efforts . . . to frame questions . . . in an almost religious way. This attitude is inherent in . . . your questionnaire. . . . Dogmatic belief or disbelief arising from whatever source has no place in serious scientific inquiry. . . . We are hardly in a position, with our primitive and rudimentary knowledge of the phenomena we study, to affirm or deny any firm statement of the existence of anything which resembles our concepts of ESP at this time.

With regard to this respondent's perception of a "religious" attitude in our formulation of the questions, we can only say that all of the questions we asked have been presented and analyzed under "Statistical Findings." Our own position on the matter of parapsychological terminology is more nearly represented by the following comment from an electrical engineer whose full belief derives equally from his own spontaneous experiences and the literature:

> I think there are valid results being obtained by parapsychologists but that the description of those results in terms of telepathy, clairvoyance, precognition, and PK is questionable.

Criticisms of Parapsychologists as Scientists

The critics of parapsychology are scathing in their denunciation of intellectual sloppiness within the field. So likewise are some parapsychologists, as shown by the following comments. Our own impression is that incompetence is not significantly greater in parapsychology than in other areas of psychology—psychobiology, for example, with which we have some familiarity. Whatever differences there are can be traced to the fact that psychobiologists are better paid.

From a philosophy professor whose belief derives 40% from his own experiments and 50% from the literature, leaving 10% doubt:

> After I started doing research and saw the way data were handled in parapsychology, I started to have some doubts.

From a professor of psychology whose sources of belief were assigned as follows: own spontaneous experiences, 20%; spontaneous experiences in close persons, 15%; own experiments, 10%; literature, 20%; remaining doubt, 35%:

> I am still disturbed by obvious attempts at faking and possible bias in reporting.

From a medical practitioner whose full belief was described as based 40% on his own spontaneous experience of psi and 60% on spontaneous psi in persons close enough to be believed:

> I think that published accounts of experimental ESP cannot overcome skepticism. They are often badly written and contain jargon and concepts incomprehensible to many scientists.

From an electrical engineer who still entertains 40% doubt and who has 45% belief based upon his own spontaneous experience of ESP, 5% based upon his own experiments, and 10% from the literature:

> Quite a number of reports and published articles on ESP are . . . vague and inconclusive [and] have served to weaken rather than strengthen my belief in ESP. . . . It is no surprise if [scientists] see little to get excited about. [My] own spontaneous experiences [are the] best evidence. . . . There should be some form of control on what is written and advertised as authentic scientific material.

Childhood Psi

There are, of course, serious limitations to our forced-choice conceptualizing of parapsychological belief. For example, we inquired as to the "strength of belief" in ESP prior to first familiarity with the literature. For about 10% of the membership this referred to pre-adolescence. As one respondent cogently observed: "Belief/disbelief is not a good way to describe a child's response to psi." The following statements from members who experienced psi in childhood will give some feeling for the problem.

From an associate professor with a PhD in experimental psychology whose full belief in ESP was assigned 80% to his own spontaneous experiences, 10% to his own research, and 10% to the evidence published by others:

> When I was three or four years old, there were two or three occasions when I told my mother very matter-of-factly about things that were soon going to happen. . . . My mother repeated [these] anecdotes to friends and neighbors who would drop in; and this served to change a matter-of-fact occurrence into something rather special. [As a child] I used to amuse myself with a deck of ordinary playing cards, trying to guess whether the next card I would turn over would be light or dark—and almost invariably I would guess [at least] one or two more than half of them correctly.

From a physical scientist whose full belief came 60% from his own spontaneous psychic experiences, 10% from experiences of close, believable persons, 10% from his own experiments, and 20% from the literature:

> I experienced extremely strong paranormal phenomena from age 4 to 7, but learned not to mention them because people accused me of making things up . . . . From age 8 on, my ESP experiences have been relatively minor . . . . I attribute these childhood experiences to the violence of the Blitz in World War II, combined with my parents' divorce.

From an Associate member whose full belief is based upon personal spontaneous experiences:

> As a child I discovered I was "psychic"; so that from my point of view it was always a matter of knowledge rather than belief. [However], it took me some years to resolve skepticism regarding precognition as demonstrated in the laboratory [which] struck me as logically impossible.

On the Resolution of Mental Conflict

Mental conflict reflects concern with contradictions; while belief is the embracing of alternatives. The resolution of conflict is not the same as the acquisition of belief, but for logical minds they tend to go hand in hand. The following comments from some of our respondents throw light on the resolution of mental conflict in the field of parapsychology.

From a well-known experimental parapsychologist who ascribes 75% of his full belief to his own work and 25% to the literature in general, and who admits to a conflict after more than 10 years of research:

> [I] expect [my] conflict to be resolved when we have assured repeatability.

A biological scientist, who assigned his present 98% belief in ESP as coming 10% from his own experiences, 30% from people close to him, 20% from his own experiments, and 38% from the literature, explained that for him the resolution of conflict occurred "in stages," coming 1 year, 5 years, and 24 years after his first exposure to the literature.

The following came from a person who has devoted his life to the advancement of parapsychology and who claims that he has 30% doubt, with 20% belief based upon his own spontaneous experiences, and 50% based on the evidence published by others:

> My sense of conflict still exists to a troublesome degree. I can only express this by saying that at times I "believe" in psi in my "blood and bones" while intellectually rejecting much of the supposed evidence for it as insufficient to carry conviction; then a shift occurs and I find myself viewing the evidence for psi as amply strong enough to demand acceptance, and yet at the same time lacking any "gut feeling" about its reality.

From a physicist whose full belief is 100% based upon the literature but who admits to having had severe conflict for a year after first encountering the phenomenon at age 30-40:

> The only reason I saw this conflict through was that I was involved in a special project with a brilliant student who wanted to replicate some of the results of Helmut Schmidt. I felt obligated to try to understand the background. Naturally, once I changed my life in accordance with the new outlook, I encountered many psychic persons.

Direct Experience as a Factor in Belief

We have already seen from Table 5 that 59% of the responding membership had experienced recognized spontaneous psi in themselves and that another 18% had known of it in close persons whom they believed. Yet only 4% said that such experiences accounted for their full belief in ESP. Table 5 also shows that rational evidence for psi is twice as effective as spontaneous evidence in generating belief. On the other hand, doubters make up 31% of the rationalists but only 9% of the experientialists.

Thus, there would appear to be some question as to the relative efficacy of these two kinds of evidence in affecting belief. To show this, we shall present a spectrum of comments, beginning with members for whom direct experience was the dominating determinant of belief.

From a writer who ascribes 70% of his full belief in ESP to his own spontaneous experiences of psi and 30% to the literature:

> As a teenager I had read Rhine but dismissed this as probable error in the statistics. . . . Later, as a science editor, I felt certain that ESP was a delusion. But when psychic experiences began happening to me . . . I read [Frederic] Myers and became convinced that if ESP were true, then it was the most important aspect of science.
>
> In my opinion, personal experience is far more powerful . . . in changing a person's attitude from disbelief to belief than any statistical proofs. They can be disregarded, but it is difficult to disregard one's own life experiences.

From an active officer in a psychical research society, whose belief in ESP is based 100% on his own spontaneous psychic experiences:

> It is very difficult for me to estimate what has given me my firm belief in ESP. From 1947 I had spontaneous experiences, but I had always doubted the reality of the same. Not until 1949 when I had my first precognition, which was noted beforehand and of which I had made a sketch, did I get 100% belief in ESP. My [spouse] had verified my precognition one week before the event happened.

From an active officer in a psychical research society, fully convinced of ESP by his own experiences:

> I suspect that I indulged in casual ESP all my life but did not know it was ESP [until] I met [the professional medium] Mrs. Leonard and she told me I was psychic . . . . It never occurred to me to doubt its existence any more than I doubt sight or hearing . . . .
>
> More remote experiences, such as apparitions, invisible presences . . . did arouse conflict in me . . . because when I broke away from conventional Christianity and tried to read what the layman can get at about contemporary science, all such things, including survival, were, I learned, impossible . . . . But my evidence for telepathy with the living, at times intentional, I could not reject.

From a social psychologist whose belief was apportioned as follows: to his own spontaneous experiences, 55%; to close person's spontaneous experiences, 5%; to his own experiments, 5%; to the literature, 30%; remaining doubt, 5%:

> It was difficult to accept ESP wholeheartedly until I managed to produce some PK after Madame Kulagina and Felicia Parise.

From a clinical psychologist whose full belief came 10% from his own experiences, and 90% from his own experiments plus the literature:

> I had two or three minor experiences as an undergraduate [and] then nothing personal until I began teaching a course in parapsychology [where I did] group experiments in psychometry . . . . Some of the results were almost too accurate. The superintendent . . . even suggested to the school psychiatrist (for whom I had done a "reading") that I might have been snooping in her purse.

From a college psychology teacher whose full belief in ESP derives 10% from spontaneous personal experiences, 40% from his own experiments, and 50% from the literature. He described his spontaneous psi as in telepathy, clairvoyance, precognition, and PK:

> My own [psychic] experiences have been broad and good. I must comment to you that one conflict which haunts me concerns my own experiences. When they occur, they are vivid and real. Very soon, however, I begin to doubt that these personal experiences really ever happened, and I think most of my real belief in psi rests on the published laboratory material. That I do not doubt.

From a humanities teacher who retains 10% doubt and ascribes his belief as due 35% to personal spontaneous experiences, 10% to the experiences of close persons, 10% to his own research, and 35% to the literature:

> I was not convinced by my own experiences until I saw a body of scientific literature—but I would not have looked at it if not for the experiences.

From a psychologist whose full belief is 90% from the literature and 10% from his own experiments.

> I was certain ESP was all faked until I read the journals and serious books.

Epistemological Diversity

What impressed us most in this investigation was the diversity of approaches to the question of the reality of ESP. Epistemological competence appeared to be little correlated with training. As judged by the responses, the question of belief was perceived in three dimensions.

First, there was diversity as to the meaning of "belief." Our own meaning is essentially probabilistic (McConnell, 1977), but there were those who claimed to have no belief or who disdained the use of the word.

For example, a philosopher, age 40-50, who had first encountered the literature 21 years earlier and who left our fractional-belief question unanswered, claimed: "I have never had either disbelief or belief in ESP." Indefinitely suspended belief is advantageous in that it allows one to examine a question in total comfort—in a leisurely and detached fashion. It is a gamesman's approach to reality.

On the other hand, a well-known experimental parapsychologist, who retains 10% doubt and whose belief is 10% based on his own spontaneous experiences, 40% on his own experiments, and 40% on the literature, remonstrated: "I don't find the construct of belief very useful in the context of science." It may be that he is not familiar with Polanyi's analysis (1958) showing that, even as scientists, we are all creatures of belief.

Second, there was diversity on the substantive issue: belief in ESP. We were surprised to learn how many members had doubt as to the reality of ESP, and also that some differentiated carefully among the various kinds of psi. In formulating our question, "ESP" had been used rather than a narrower or broader term in the hope of avoiding the need for fine logical distinctions. Nevertheless, some respondents explained that they had different degrees of belief for ESP vs. PK, for experimental vs. spontaneous ESP, or for different subcategories of ESP. To a total skeptic it might appear as though they were giving their attention to differences in the species of trees reputedly found growing on the surface of the moon so as to avoid dealing directly with the fact that there were any trees there at all.

Finally, there was diversity in the degree of self-assurance in belief or suspension thereof. Lacking, was evidence of sound criteria for belief—among many of the self-assured and all of the diffident. From other studies we know that lack of criteria for belief about controversial topics is nearly universal among otherwise competent university faculty in the natural sciences. From the present survey we conclude that this intellectual disability extends to parapsychologists as well.

To put the issue bluntly, if parapsychologists cannot agree among themselves as to the reality of ESP, how can the rest of the world have an opinion? Is the evidence truly inconclusive, or is its comprehension merely beyond the capabilities of most scientists—or is doubt sometimes a form of reality denial?

REFERENCES

McConnell, R. A. The resolution of conflicting beliefs about the ESP evidence. *Journal of Parapsychology*, 1977, **41,** 198-214.

McConnell, R. A., & McConnell, T. Occult books sold at the University of Pittsburgh, *Journal of the American Society for Psychical Research*, 1971, **65,** 344-353.

Monod, J. *Chance and necessity.* New York: Alfred Knopf, 1971.

Polanyi, M. *Personal knowledge.* Chicago: University of Chicago Press, 1958.

ANNOTATED SOCIOHISTORICAL
BIBLIOGRAPHY OF PARAPSYCHOLOGY

Compiled by R. A. McCONNELL

The determination of the reality of extrasensory perception and psychokinesis is as much a problem of social judgment as of observational report. Whom or what can one believe? With this question in mind, I have compiled this listing from what might be called the "peripherally illuminating" literature of parapsychology. Included are papers (1) that concern the competence or attitudes of parapsychologists or of widely regarded critics of parapsychology, or (2) that deal explicitly and constructively with the separation of truth and falsity in this field, or (3) that succinctly relate parapsychology to the rest of science.

Beloff, J. Belief and doubt. Pages 189–200 in W. G. Roll, R. L. Morris, & J. D. Morris (Eds.), *Research in Parapsychology, 1972*. Metuchen, New Jersey: Scarecrow Press, 1973. This is the presidential address to the Fifteenth Annual Convention of the Parapsychological Association at the University of Edinburgh. Those exquisitely self-conscious sceptics who are puzzled by their own inability to accept psi phenomena despite much favorable evidence will find their uneasiness enhanced by this tantalizing account of four well known investigators of the past (Brugmans, Dingwall, Besterman, and Riess) who, having obtained and published dramatic, personally convincing evidence of ESP, found belief intolerable and subsequently assumed a noncommittal position.

Condon, E. U. UFOs I have loved and lost. *Bulletin of the Atomic Scientists*, December 1969, *25* (10), 6–8. In this paper an eminent physicist classifies extrasensory perception and psychokinesis with flying saucers and calls for the public horsewhipping of those who teach pseudoscience.

Freud, S. Psychoanalysis and telepathy. Pages 175–193 in J. Strachey (Ed.), *The Complete Psychological Works of Sigmund Freud*, Vol. 18. London: Hogarth Press, 1955. Sigmund Freud saw psychic phenomena as a tremendous and elemental peril to his life work, comparable to the apostasy of his disciples, Alfred Adler and Carl Jung (p. 177). He emphasized his kinship with exact scientists and distinguished sharply between what he described as the mechanistic and materialistic method of psychoanalysis and the wish-fulfilling logic of most of those who believe in psychic phenomena (pp. 178–179). He predicted that the scientific establishment of such phenomena would cause the proponents of occultism to be joyfully hailed as the heroes of a new intellectual populism, and he feared that this could precipitate a collapse of critical thought which it might be impossible for science to prevent (p. 180). As shown by the "case of the seafood death wish" related in this essay (pp. 181–185), Freud reluctantly accepted the reality of thought transference on the basis of his own experiences with patients. He was a Corresponding Member of the Society for Psychical Research from 1911 until his death at the age of 83 in 1939. In 1921, the year in which he composed this essay, he wrote a letter saying that, if he were at the beginning of his scientific career, he would choose psychical research rather than the psychopathology of the unconscious as his field of study. (See: Ernest Jones, *The Life and Work of Sigmund Freud, 3,* 392. New York: Basic Books, 1957.)

Gauld, Alan. *The Founders of Psychical Research.* New York: Schocken Books, 1968. A definitive study, important for flavor and fact.

Honorton, C., Ramsey, M., & Cabibbo, C. Experimenter effects in extrasensory perception. *Journal of the American Society for Psychical Research,* 1975, *69,* 135–149. While this paper was published as a scientific contribution in its own right, it is listed here because it was previously rejected for publication by *Science* and is accompanied by an appendix in which the referees' criticisms and the senior author's correspondence with *Science* are printed verbatim. A source document of importance in the sociological history of parapsychology.

Mackenzie, B., & Mackenzie, S. L. Whence the enchanted boundary?—Sources and significance of the parapsychological tradition. *Journal of Parapsychology,* 1980, *44,* 125–166. A historical treatment of the philosophic implications of psi phenomena by two psychologists from the University of Tasmania. The Mackenzies present what I regard as a brilliant distortion of the relation between parapsychology and orthodox science. It is their position that "Parapsychology is incompatible with the whole course and direction of modern science." After a three-page presentation of G. R. Price's well known misidentification of Western science with naive mechanism (*Science*, 1955, *122*, 359–367), the authors partially dissociate themselves from his point of view by saying: "It makes no difference if the 'invisible intelligent beings' are not the discarnate spirits Price implies but facets of the subject's own mind. . . . The methods of science demand the possibility of detailed, impersonal (mechanistic) explanations. . . . Not only the practice of science, but the very possibility of a scientific understanding of the world therefore demands impersonal explanations and precludes [mind as agency]. . . . Parapsychology therefore constitutes an attack, not merely on present scientific theories, but on the conviction of the accessibility of the world to human reason, and thereby on the potential of reason and science themselves." Beneath this scholarly hyperbole I was delighted to find a general point of view that is congenial with what I have been teaching in my parapsychology course for several years. It appears to me, however, that the apparent antithesis between parapsychology and conventional science can be largely resolved by noting that extrasensory perception and psychokinesis are consciousness phenomena and that, up to now, Western science has been too busy to concern itself with consciousness. When it does, some expansion of its vision will, of course, be needed. The Mackenzie council of despair is good showmanship but out of keeping with the "can do" spirit of the Western scientific tradition.

McConnell, R. A. The structure of scientific revolutions: An epitome. *Journal of the American Society for Psychical Research*, 1968, *62*, 321–327. A comprehensive condensation of Thomas Kuhn's seminal work of the same title. Kuhn's elucidation of "preparadigm science" has brought a new understanding of parapsychology as an emerging field.

McConnell, R. A. ESP and credibility in science. *American Psychologist*, 1969, *24*, 531–538. Topics discussed: Legal vs. scientific proof. Scientific education as a "brainwashing" process. Textbooks as storehouses of knowledge and error. Included is a selection of target pictures and ESP response drawings by the wife of Upton Sinclair.

McConnell, R. A. Parapsychology and the occult. *Journal of the American Society for Psychical Research*, 1973, *67*, 225–243. A brief treatment of occultism as a social movement, spreading beyond the lower classes and masquerading as science. Topics discussed: religious populism today and in the early Christian era; the present-day endorsement of astrology by highly placed public educators; "Mind Control" as syndicated hypnotism-for-profit on an international scale; the reputable approval of medical diagnosis by handwriting analysis and by the noise of rubbing a rubber membrane; extension courses on occult subjects offered by colleges and universities pandering to anti-intellectualism under the guise of serving the needs of the community; and finally, parapsychology as a possible pathway from "alchemy" to understanding.

McConnell, R. A. Parapsychology: Its future organization and support. *Journal of the American Society for Psychical Research*, 1974, *68*, 169–181. With emphasis on the need for professionalism within the field.

McConnell, R. A. Parapsychology in the USSR. *Journal of Parapsychology*, 1975, *39*, 129–134. Analysis of a position paper from the Presidium of the Soviet Association of Psychologists in which the reality of parapsychological phenomena is acknowledged.

McConnell, R. A. The motivations of parapsychologists and other scientists. *Journal of the American Society for Psychical Research*, 1975, *69*, 273–280. Inducements and counterpressures to fraud.

McConnell, R. A. Areas of agreement between the parapsychologist and the sceptic. *Journal of the American Society for Psychical Research*, 1976, *70*, 303–308. A guest lecture given by a parapsychologist in an anti-parapsychological course at the University of Pittsburgh. The physiological psychologist who teaches the course reveals his frame of mind in an exchange of letters in the same journal, 1977, *71*, 223–229.

McConnell, R. A. Foundation interest in parapsychology. *Journal of Parapsychology*, 1976, *40*, 145–150. A survey of 1400 large American foundations, from which it is apparent that, despite "the public image of the foundation . . . as a source of venture capital to start new cultural enterprises in which the possibility of great gain accompanies the certainty of high risk," almost without exception, "foundations are not open to new ideas from the public. Their mechanisms for conducting their normal business affairs will, in nearly all cases, ignore a basically novel idea submitted from an unknown but evidently respectable source."

McConnell, R. A. Parapsychology and physicists. *Journal of Parapsychology*, 1976, *40*, 228–239. Possible relations of psi phenomena to concepts of physics, a summary of the current evidential status of gross psychokinetic phenomena, a comparison of the attitudes of physicists toward parapsychology at the end of the last century and today, and autobiographical comment by the author.

McConnell, R. A. A parapsychological dialogue. *Journal of the American Society for Psychical Research*, 1977, *71*, 429–435. For the educated layman and the sceptical scientist: a brief introduction to the field of parapsychology.

McConnell, R. A. The resolution of conflicting beliefs about the ESP evidence. *Journal of Parapsychology*, 1977, *41*, 198–214. This paper appears as Chapter 16 in this book.

McConnell, R. A. *On the Distinction Between Science and Nonscience in a Pretheoretical Field.* An analytic review of *Future Science*, a 1977 parapsychological fringe work edited by John White and Stanley Krippner in which the separating line between science and pseudoscience has been obliterated. The reviewer sees this book as exemplifying a methodological crisis in parapsychology. Recommended especially for classroom use in university courses on the sociology and method of science. Privately printed in 1978 after rejection as unsuitable in content by the parapsychological journal editor to whose specifications it was prepared. Single copies available without charge.

McConnell, R. A. ESP and the credibility of critics. *Perceptual and Motor Skills*, 1978, *47*, 875–878. A sociological source document consisting almost entirely of the tandem juxtaposition of published statements by two critics of R. A. McConnell's writings and the relevant excerpts from the papers they criticized. Useful for understanding the nature of opposition by psychologists to parapsychology.

McConnell, R. A., & Clark, T. K. Training, belief, and mental conflict within the Parapsychological Association. *Journal of Parapsychology*, 1980, *44*, 245–268. This paper has been reprinted as an appendix to this book.

McConnell, R. A., & McConnell, Tron. Occult books sold at the University of Pittsburgh. *Journal of the American Society for Psychical Research*, 1971, *65*, 344–353. An analysis of the American occult book business, extrapolated from a statistical survey-by-topic at a typical university bookstore. Among the titles encountered: *Practical Candle Burning, More Ghosts in Irish Houses, The Bible and Flying Saucers, Astrology and the Single*

Girl, Lessons in Number Vibrations, Palmistry for Pleasure and Profit.

Rockwell, T., Rockwell, R., & Rockwell, W. T. Irrational rationalists: A critique of *The Humanist*'s crusade against parapsychology. *Journal of the American Society for Psychical Research*, 1978, 72, 23–34. Responsible public questioning of parapsychology as a field of science ceased several decades ago. What do today's critics say? "[Experiments purporting to prove ESP] are the result of scientific research being carried on by closet occultists with PhD's. 'Cult Phuds,' to give them a more convenient name, permit metaphysics to interfere with physics." "So let us do our best to get rid of this ideological garbage, lest it inundate the earth." A counter-commentary by the editor of *The Humanist* and a reply by the Rockwells provide further insight (same journal, 72, 349–364).

NAME INDEX
(Persons and publications)

SUBJECT INDEX

Acceptance. *See* Attitude and belief
American Association for the Advancement of Science, 145, 155, 168, 181
American Institute for Mathematical Statistics, 114
American Psychological Association, 81, 83, 102–117
American Society for Psychical Research, 81, 102
Apparitions, 13, 67, 69, 70
Astrology, 226
Attitude and belief
  affecting psi performance, 87, 98–99, 137
  conflicting beliefs, 156–164, 179, 193–196, 199–222, 223, 224–225, 227
  conflicting motives, 87, 98–99, 106, 115–117
  factors affecting, 41–42, 93–94, 119–120
  of specific individual scientists, 3, 8, 24, 27, 30–31, 46–47, 49–50, 81–82, 132–133, 136–137, 165, 169–170, 177–178, 223–224, *see also* by name
  of grouped physicists, 29–30, 168, 226–227
  of grouped psychologists and psychiatrists, 17, 19, 28–30, 42, 82–83, 102–117
  of parapsychologists, 195, 199–222
  of the public, 14, 18, 29, 33, 57, 116, 165, 194, 224, 225–228
  of Soviet scientists, 44–48, 226
  of undifferentiated scientists, 3, 11–12, 55, 57, 156–164, 165, 181–196, 226
  scientific acceptance of psi, 93–94, 119–120, 181–196, 223–228
  see also Motivation
Automated experiments, 149–152, 171, 184, 188–189
Automatisms, 14
Awareness of psychic event, 54, 96–97

Belief. *See* Attitude and belief
Biofeedback, 147–148, 149, 151, 173
Biological basis of psi, 18, 54–55, *see also* Psychic individuality
Birkbeck College (University of London), 171
Boston Society for Psychic Research, 18n, 32n, 101
Brain. *See* Mind-body, Biological basis of psi
Brain waves. *See* Electroencephalography
British Association for the Advancement of Science, 3, 4

Card guessing, 32, 109–110, *see also* Extrasensory perception
Cartesian world view, 42, 85, *see also* Mind-body dualism
Causality, 121, 126–128
Central Intelligence Agency (U.S.A.), 43
Childhood psi, 216–217
City College of New York, 113, 114, 171
Clairvoyance, 18n, 24n, 111, 137, 169, *see also* Extrasensory perception
Clark University, 102, 107, 109, 114
Cognitive dissonance, 179, 194–195
Columbia University, 113
Conflict. *See* Attitude and belief
Consciousness, 1, 13–15, 18, 198, 225
Control experiments, 152
Cornell University, 106

Decline and other fluctuation effects, 84–85, 87–88, 96, 98–100, 137, 142
Dissociation, 15, 20n, 35–36, 50, 89
Distance, 7, 38, 50, 53, 90, 170
Dreams, 97
Duke University, 27, 83, 96, 101, 109–117, 129, 168, 171

Electroencephalography, 49–50, 153
Electromagnetic radiation, 41, 46–51, 53–54, 174–175
Energy, 49–50, 54, 124–125, 132, 169
Exclusion principle of Pauli, 125
Experimenter/observer, 56–57, 148, 151–152, 224
Extrasensory perception (ESP)
  definition of, 1, 18n
  probable instances (experimental), 6–7, 34, 36, 38, 50–53, 74
  probable instances (spontaneous), 24–26, 67, 73, 77, 79
  see also Psi phenomena

Foundation financing, 226
Fraud, 34–37, 57, 166, 182–184, 187, 189

Genetic influence, 55, 88–89
Ganzfeld. *See* Sensory deprivation
Greece, 197
Groningen University, 106

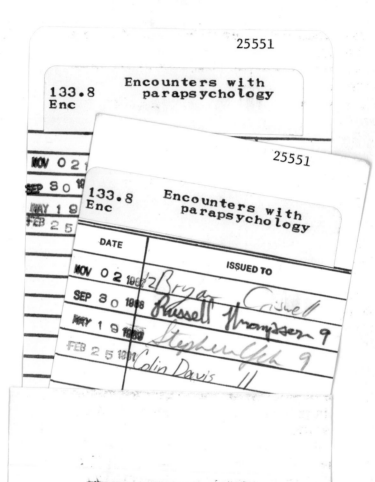

25551

133.8
Enc

Encounters with
parapsychology

25551

133.8
Enc

Encounters with
parapsychology

DATE	ISSUED TO
NOV 0 2 1987	1/2 Bryan Criswell
SEP 3 0 1988	Russell Thompson 9
MAY 1 9 1989	Stephen Yeh 9
FEB 2 5 1991	Colin Davis 11